FROM THE WORD TO THE PLACE:

Essays on the Work of Michael Anania

FROM THE WORD TO THE PLACE:
Essays on the Work of Michael Anania

Edited by Lea Graham

MADHAT PRESS
CHESHIRE, MASSACHUSETTS

MadHat Press
MadHat Incorporated
PO Box 422, Cheshire, MA 01225

The Library of Congress has assigned
this edition a Control Number of
2021951717

ISBN 978-1-952335-37-2 (paperback)

Cover art and design by Marc Vincenz
Book design by MadHat Press
Cover image: *The Fall* by Ed Colker

www.madhat-press.com

First Printing
Printed in the United States of America

For Michael—

These things
astonish me beyond words.

Table of Contents

Foreword

I was a nineteen-year-old junior in college, Michael, a thirty-one-year-old assistant professor, when I first studied with him nearly fifty years ago. I was a strange mix of reserved and petulant, scared and elated, and I was a fledgling poet.

Michael, on the other hand, was comfortable in himself, mind fully formed and ready to guide young people toward a life in poetry. He remembers my first "noticeable" product as an essay on Conrad's novel *The Secret Agent*, in which I quoted Aristotle on the nature of revolutionaries and received an A. I recall the paper but best recall early words with Michael as professor when he told me after reading a poem of mine that I had reinvented modernism, which well took into account my inflection in poetry as well as my naïve status.

Being around Michael even for several ten-week quarters was a life-changing experience in which he introduced advice I still recall:

—Focus on the "real," a concept which included the lushness and scarcity of life as well as the ambient world.

—Examine process, learn how something is made (his example was weaving) and write about it, investigative poetry, as it were.

—Read and read! See poets read!

And it was under the auspices of Michael at the University of Illinois–Chicago that I began hearing poets. W. S. Merwin was the first in a line of visitors. And because it was a late afternoon series on a spare commuter campus, its ubiquitous granite darkened by winter, we were able to see them up close and personal. How gratifying to sit in the room with poets offering their craft: how different from the distance to the literature I was taught in my other classes, where intense study of artifacts such as Arnold's "Scholar-Gypsy" was a lesson in obscurity.

Another aspect of Michael's ministry was his stellar tales of writers and writing, his way with story and language that made a young apprentice understand that there is a veritable atmosphere for poetic activity beyond separate cultures or movements, a way of life. Somehow, as all great storytellers do, he made his topics approachable and filled with warmth, not brags but invitations. This gift of gab also presages his memoiristic, experimental novel *The Red Menace*, a brilliant glimpse of life in Omaha in the nervous and nuclear 1950s. We all have to grow up somewhere: Michael captures his somewhere with perfect pitch.

Over the years I have experienced great pleasure when Michael and I occasionally spoke, and as I continued to receive specialized knowledge from him. When I was staying at the American Academy in Rome and later visiting Florence, his food and art advice was illuminating and gracious. He knew specific churches I should visit to see my beloved Caravaggios or to try a certain pasta dish seasoned with local capers.

Thanks to my son's graduate degree from the University of Texas, which took me on visits to Austin, Michael and I later became close once again, sharing ideas and poetry, family struggles and continuous well-wishes. I dare say my experience of Michael's generosity is shared by many; the marvelous essays in this volume serve as proof. Fifty years of students and poets and critics in the larger world of poetry and prose praise his creation in detail. I won't summarize what the contributors bring to this task; it is best to dig in and experience the depth and expansiveness yourself. Just the variety of contributors and subjects points to Michael's eclecticism and also inventive specializations.

But before I clear the path for your reading to begin, let me quote a recent Michael poem I love, which captures his voice in this *annus horribilis*, aka 2020:

from **Instead of**

> petals spill from Flora's
>   lips like the wishes that close
>   the evening news, Primavera
>
> in her own lock-down,
>   the Arno, Times Square,
>   the Grand Canal, each plaza

everywhere; this is not
  the one world we had hoped
    for, what was photographed

from the Sea of Tranquility
  ands seen whole for the first time,
    the oceans' blue and white,

the dark shapes we live on,
  have names for and call our
    own, and that vast, black space,

the absence of air and its
  accompanying light, of sound
    and substance, of all that gives

us place; *è stato un piacere*
  sentire la tua voce, Maurizio,
    reaching with your son toward us;

victory is in the voice itself,
  the arc of song we ride briefly,
    with you along the ingathering light

Enjoy these essays but more urgently read his beautiful poems, which shine with the grace and complexity of the actual.

—Maxine Chernoff
July 27, 2020

Preface

To read the work of Michael Anania is to feel as though you are in many places at once. It is complex. His poems, novel and essays are a many-roomed complex: the Missouri River; the South Loop, Chicago; dairy barns and roadhouses, Midwestern interstates, inside a Brubeck tune, a solitary moment of domestic space, among and through the words of various writers—Gass, Dickinson, Joyce; hovering just above a specific flower or a Canova sculpture, at a hearth in the hills of Calabria or out on a Nebraska farm at a family picnic.

Anania grew up in the housing projects of Omaha in the 1940s and '50s, moved to Buffalo for graduate school and then went on to Chicago where his teaching career took him first to Northwestern University and then on to the University of Illinois–Chicago. In the 1970s, he spent seven years as editor at Swallow Press. His father was first-generation Calabrese American; his mother, an immigrant from Oldsberg, Germany. He grew up hearing Calabrese, German and Black English. When Robert Archambeau in the opening essay of this book calls him "a synthesizer," he's not joking around.

This book encompasses a half-century of his multiple roles as poet, novelist, essayist, editor, art-collaborator and teacher. In the following essays, you will read about his attention to place and time, the interstices and liminal spaces where thought and sensory experience meet and experience the vast range of his literary knowledge within the work.

Enter these essays that explore an expanse of time and place, the sensual and intellectual. Celebrate this work that has been steady, unrelentingly thoughtful and joy-filled all at once.

—Lea Graham
Florence, Italy,
2021

Modernist Current: Michael Anania's Poetry of the Western River

Robert Archambeau

James Joyce Was Born in Omaha in 1939

James Joyce was born in Omaha in 1939. His first book, *Dubliners*, contained the poem sequence "Stops Along the Western Bank of the Missouri River," which treated his native Nebraska with the intense realism that could only come about under conditions of voluntary exile. Nostalgia and critical distance combined to make the linked-yet-disparate pieces of the sequence so precise that the river could, if necessary, be reconstructed bend by bend from the pages of the poems. A later and much more complex work, *Ulysses*, treated the same Nebraskan territory with equal detail. Its central poetic sequence, though, the ten part "Riversongs of Arion," combined realism with a concern for myth, finding in the quotidian world echoes of a heroic past. The result was a truly modernist synthesis of past and present, the construction of an eternal now along the lines of work being produced by Joyce's modernist peers Pound, Eliot and David Jones.

Okay, you got me, put down your copy of Ellmann's Joyce biography. I know Joyce was born in Ireland. The two points I'd like to make about Michael Anania's river sequences, though, are made most clearly through an analogy with Joyce. I'd like to say that Anania, like

Joyce, is fundamentally a modernist (an *unreconstructed modernist,* one might be tempted to say at this late date, as dusk settles over the ruins of postmodernism); and I'd like to say that the relationship between his two major river sequences, "Stops Along the Western Bank of the Missouri River" and "The Riversongs of Arion" is like the relationship of *Dubliners* to *Ulysses.* The works treat similar material, but the more mature work does so with greater philosophical ambition, a more profound historical sense, and a greater degree of meta-literary self-consciousness.

Omaha as Dublin, Buffalo as Trieste

Leaving Nebraska made it clear that writing about Nebraska was like writing about Rome or Florence—it was tangible, real, nobody knew it, there were concrete things in it for poems and what was absolute familiarity for me was unknown to others.

—Michael Anania (qtd. in Archambeau 4)

Michael Anania left Omaha in 1961, arriving in Buffalo, New York to pursue graduate studies in English. He'd been harboring literary ambitions for years, writing poems, plays and stories and editing the campus literary magazine at the University of Nebraska. But he'd always had some reservations about being a writer: it didn't seem to jibe with where he came from. Growing up in an Omaha housing project, he'd attended schools where, as he put it, "standing up and saying you were a poet would be a little bit like standing up and saying you were a target" (qtd. in Archambeau 4). Literature had felt distant from his impoverished life in a provincial city that seemed antithetical to literature. Enthralled by existential philosophy and the literature of the absurd, he later described himself as "thrilled by anything complicated and remote" (in Archambeau 4). Think of him as a great plains version of Joyce's hero, the young Dedalus of *Portrait* who dreamed of Aquinas and Byron from the horse-piss smelling alleys of a Dublin that had yet to acquire any of its twentieth-century literary glamor. At Buffalo, Anania'd hoped to study Yeats or perhaps Wallace Stevens, both complicated and both remote, with Yeats's universe of gyres and the non-places of Stevens' imaginative pagodas being equidistant from the wrong side of Omaha, Nebraska. Buffalo, though, was the repository of a huge archive of the papers and manuscripts of William Carlos Williams, the then-unfashionable patron saint of "a local pride" in American poetry. Working on Williams was one way for Anania to muster the courage to take on the matter of Nebraska. And like Joyce in Trieste, Anania found the distance between his first provincial place and his new provincial place liberating. What had been stuff too humble to tell in verse became as real and particular as Paris, London, or Paterson, New Jersey.

Nowhere in Anania's first book, *The Color of Dust*, is this more evident than in the series that constitutes one of that book's four sections, "Stops Along the Western Bank of the Missouri River." The tangible realness of Anania's descriptions here reflect his newfound local pride, his sense that Omaha had "concrete things in it for poems" and his growing sense that "what was absolute familiarity" to him could also be the matter of literature. We could just about reconstruct the neighborhood north of Omaha's Clark Street from lines like these, from "A Journey":

> without the regimen of red brick,
> the houses, grey of old wood
> stripped of paint above
> the tilted, broken walks,
> cracked by the roots of the elms
> that hang over the walks,
> break open the retaining walls (3)

A poet like Walt Whitman gets his topography from an atlas; a poet like Anania, following Williams and Joyce, gets his topography from the streets he'd walked.

Along with this sense of the minute details of the local comes a strong sense of the distance between the ideal and the real—a sense we find among a number of provincial literary prodigies, not the least being, of course, Joyce himself. In the poem we've just looked at, for example, Anania notes the ironic distance between the aspirations of a road named "Grace Street" and the actuality of that down-at-the-heels street as it meanders "past a gutted store /with a drawn coonskin / drying on the grey wall" to an old brewery and then "down to the yards, /to the open sewer that /swills into the river" (3). We see something similar in "The Square, Bum's Park," where we read these lines:

> Smells of urine,
> cheap cologne,
> Tiger Rose and sour milk
> hang in the staircase—
> the Chicago Hotel
> the elite of Omaha
> overlooking beautiful
> Jefferson Square. (14)

As in "The Journey," we see the distance between the ideal promised in a world of text and the real embodied in sordid actuality. It is an environment that breeds fascination with "anything complicated and remote."

The distance between language and material reality is explored somewhat differently in "Missouri among the Rivers." Here, we read that "Bluff crests in Fontenelle are quiet, / give no emblem, figured name" (8). The place has only the weakest connection with the kind of language that can charge it with significance and make it known. The place is bereft, lacking the layer of symbolic significance that makes it figuratively, as well as literally, habitable.

In this context, there is a kind of will to create significance for the place, a desire to convert the area's past into a usable and significant history. In "Arbor Lodge," for example, Anania looks at an old block-house and wills it to become a monument and an enduring emblem of the place's history:

> Make it a monument:
> where the highway
> bends past the birches,

the cabin with slotted gunports,
before the shaded gate
fix a new stone marker,
an emblem freely carved. (12)

This will to find and memorialize a significant past for a place that often seems like a debased reality haunted by distant ideals is the strongest strand connecting the nine poems of the sequence. It is present from the very first poem, "A Journey," which concludes with images of the Lewis and Clark expedition. The contemplation of these images leads to a brief moment of epiphany, where ideal and real seem to become one. Addressing the Sacagawea of the expedition as well as the monuments to her, Anania's speaker bursts into the cadences of prayer. Suddenly, we see Sacagawea as the past incarnate in the present, and realize the apparently debased place as a space charged with significance:

We move through intersections
capable of history,
Birdwoman, bronze lady of the river,
figurehead of keelboats,
steel lady of bridges,
we pass in the dead of August. (6)

No sooner does the epiphany come than its moment passes. In the wasteland of the present, history and its associations remain "Afterthoughts. First, // the city in dust."

The sequence ends with a poem meditating on the ironies of provincial cultural inferiority anxieties. "The Park Above All Others Called, Riverview" begins with the image of "A bust of Schiller on a hillside" that "faces east, looking like a Medici" (16). The bust, looking out over the city of dust, is a gesture of civic fealty to a legitimated high culture located long ago and far away. By invoking the Medici, though, Anania reminds us that there was a time when Germany didn't stand for the empire of culture, but looked toward the Italian *quattrocento* as a legitimate elsewhere, a high culture that promised so much more

5

than the seemingly debased here-and-now. The poem rehearses a brief history of such moments of cultural anxiety: "Johannes studied alchemy in Venice," writes Anania, "Monet waited to be French" (16). The poem ends by posing a question—"How does it matter, this view of the park by the river?"—and providing a kind of an answer: "it is the recurrent dream /demanding the voice that speaks through"(17). The place demands its voice, its poetry. And so the young Anania, when he'd packed his bags for Buffalo, went forth to forge in the smithy of his soul the uncreated poems of his place.

The Then That Is Now

> *The man standing beside me is a retired stockyards drover from Sarpy County, Nebraska. The steel-guitar Western twang in his voice is real; so are the stiff curls in his cowboy boots. When he lifts his straw hat, it leaves a deep sweat-band furrow in his hair that no Sunday-morning dose of Wildroot or Brylcreem will erase. The wrinkles at the back of his neck are as sharply cut as cracks in dry soil…. He points across the water to a stand of cottonwoods. That's his camper, an Apache, half-shaded from the midday sun…. We are standing on the Overland Trail. All the pioneers, the Mormons, and the forty-niners who set off from Council Bluffs passed by here early in their long journey west, and it is impossible not to transform his camper and the others circled in the trees into covered wagons. This is the same ground, after all, the same slow, murky river.*
>
> —Michael Anania (*In Plain Sight* 13)

Michael Anania, introducing his prose meditation on the American West with a personal anecdote, may, in the moment, find it "impossible not to" see the present in terms of the legendary past. How could he not? "This is the same ground, after all," he writes, as if the coincidence in space were all it would take to make the significant past incarnate in the here-and-now. The connection between past and present that came only as a fleeting epiphany in "Stops Along the Western Bank of the Missouri River" comes effortlessly here. Such effortlessness, though, is reserved for Anania's prose. When he takes up the matter of past and present in his poetry, it is always more complicated, and the sense of incarnation comes not as an easy breeze of transcendence; it is earned by the sweat of the poet's brow.

Before Anania's next river sequence, "The Riversongs of Arion," (from his 1978 book *Riversongs*) even gets underway, it has posed its central question: what is the relationship between the here-and-now and the there-and-then? It does so in a complicated and roundabout way: through the juxtaposition of these two epigraphs, the first from the seventeenth-century English theologian Thomas Hooker, the second from the journals of Lewis and Clark:

> The Rule is one, like itself accompanied with stability and rest; if once we go astray from that, there is neither end nor quiet in error, but restlessness and emptiness.

> This evening Guthrege Cought a *White* Catfish … tale much like that of a *Dolfin*. (qtd. in *Selected Poems* 56)

The juxtaposition is itself interesting: we have one quote from a faraway *there*, and one quote from the newly explored territories of the poem's western *here*. But there's more afoot here than the placing of English and American texts side by side. Each passage invokes the idea of a present reality lacking the meaning or significance that can only be supplied by appealing to something remote.

The first quote holds out two possibilities: either we find our connection with an eternal rule, a law that governs and unites all things at all times and places; or we are left with nothing but wandering, emptiness, and unquiet; a restlessness bred of a lack of meaning. That is, we either find an eternal truth that redeems time, or we wander in the wastes of error. The second quote gives us explorers who have wandered into new territory, and found new animals. They try to understand the new things by appealing to known things from the faraway world. How do we make sense of this new fish? It is like the dolphins we know from before. Both quotes, then, emphasize the appeal to an *elsewhere* to explain the present world: in the first, there is the elsewhere of eternity; in the second, the elsewhere of the eastern seaboard. Before the first poem in the sequence, then, we find that our matter will be the seeking of connections between a *there-and-then* that supplies meaning for a *here-and-now* bereft of significance. Anania had touched on these matters in "Stops Along the Western Bank of the Missouri River" (in, for example, the meditation on the bust of Schiller). Here these concerns move to the fore—so much in fact, that we see them well developed even before we've read the first poem in the sequence.

If, like me, you're the kind of reader who reads the endnotes before the main text, then you see these concerns developed even further before you turn to the first poem. In Anania's notes to the poem (which, like Eliot's notes to *The Wasteland*, are best read as a part of the poem proper) we find this explanation of the dramatic situation from which the "riversongs" are sung:

> The Arion of this sequence is a contemporary who sets off on a trip down the Missouri River from Omaha and gets stuck just south of the city. On July 22, 1804, Lewis and Clark proceeded north from the mouth of the Platte River about ten miles and pitched a five-day camp, named, for Silas Goodrich's catch of July 24, White Catfish Camp. This Arion's diversions, complaints, and plaintiff anthems while stranded opposite what he supposes is that campsite comprise the sequence. (81)

This Arion, says Anania, is a contemporary. But the Arion of Greek myth and legend (the there-and-then to this Arion's here-and-now) lurks behind him, just as the old artificer and maze-maker lurked not far behind Joyce's Dedalus. The Arion of Greek legend, like this Arion, is a sailor; and like this Arion, he is stuck while sailing. The classical Arion is captured by pirates and about to be executed, but is spared long enough to sing a final song. The song summons dolphins, who carry him away to freedom. A number of questions arise here: if the classical Arion's songs free him from distress, will our contemporary Arion's songs deliver him? If so, from what condition will he be delivered? And what are we to make of the fact that Arion only supposes he sees Lewis and Clark's camp? And why are his songs "plaintiff" rather than "plaintive" (a fact missed by the editors of Anania's *Selected Poems*, who erroneously "correct" the poet's supposed error)? What, one might also wonder, is the deal on those mythic dolphins, given the epigraph from Lewis and Clark that draws a parallel between the white catfish for which the camp was named and the dolphin whose tail resembles that of the catfish? All of these questions are answered (implicitly or explicitly) by the poems of the sequence.

The first poem suggests the nature of the condition from which the contemporary Arion wishes to be set free. The poem shows us Arion's makeshift oil-drum raft in a despoiled modern river, among "slit-bellied watermelons / and castaway chicken heads" as it is caught up "on a rusted snare of dredge cable / with the slow brown water curling / dark foam against barrel heads" (*Selected Poems* 57). The material squalor of the river is reminiscent of similar scenes from a number of other poems, notably Robert Lowell's "The Mouth of the Hudson" with its "unforgivable landscape" and the "Fire Sermon" section of T. S. Eliot's *The Wasteland*. The "slow brown" river, though, points to another Eliot poem, "The Dry Salvages" from *Four Quartets* as a primary allusion. "The Dry Salvages" is the poem where Eliot famously speaks of the river as a "strong brown god." Anania's allusion to the poem is apposite, here, because Eliot's poem poses a problem much like that posed in Anania's epigraphs, the problem of how a bereft *now* relates to a more meaningful *then*. The first stanza of Eliot's poem gives the gist of this:

> I do not know much about gods; but I think that the river
> Is a strong brown god—sullen, untamed and intractable,
> Patient to some degree, at first recognized as a frontier;
> Useful, untrustworthy, as a conveyer of commerce;
> Then only a problem confronting the builder of bridges.
> The problem once solved, the brown god is almost forgotten
> By the dwellers in cities—ever, however, implacable,
> Keeping his seasons and rages, destroyer, reminder
> Of what men choose to forget. Unhonoured, unpropitiated
> By worshippers of the machine, but waiting, watching and waiting.
> His rhythm was present in the nursery bedroom,
> In the rank ailanthus of the April dooryard,

> In the smell of grapes on the autumn table,
> And the evening circle in the winter gaslight.

Does history take us away from the eternal world of gods through a process of modernization to a utilitarian and ever more disenchanted world? For the Eliot of *The Four Quartets* (if not the younger Eliot of *The Wasteland*), the answer is no. The world of gods is still with us, waiting and watching. The *then* that is charged with meaning lurks within the apparently disenchanted now, "waiting, watching and waiting." We only need the poet to find it for us.

Anania, invoking Eliot from within the disenchanted present of his own poem, implies that an Eliotic connection between the significant past and the apparently empty present can be made. The contemporary Arion, then, is stuck not only in a literally desolate river, but in a spiritually desolate present. If the singing of the classical Arion delivers him from a literal captivity, these "riversongs" seek to deliver us from a more metaphysical captivity. Our contemporary Arion is stuck in a world without myth or legend, and his songs, if successful, will deliver him from that disenchanted world.

The second "riversong" offers us our first inkling that such deliverance is possible. Here Arion watches the odd motion of the local catfish as they swim upriver, and is reminded of an old phrase of the men who have worked on the river. "Rivermen," Arion observes, "call this / the catfish dance because / from the banks they seem // stationary" as they bob "up / and down in the dark foam" (Anania, *Selected Poems* 58). This is our first hint that there is more than a squalid material world around us: there is a history of local lore. Just as the dolphins come to rescue the classical Arion, the catfish (compared by Lewis and Clark to "dolfin[s]") come to rescue the contemporary Arion. In fact, the remembered bit of riverman's lore leads Arion to think of other, more significant local lore: "Marquette," for example, "feared the thud // of their bodies against / his canoe" (58–59). The whole history of exploration and settlement opens up, giving the place a significance beyond its soiled, observable surfaces. It is at this point that Arion sees the land nearby as Lewis and Clark's camp:

White Catfish Camp—that stretch

of silt, as good as any, any
song, river, now, like furrowed
loam, dendrite bluffs. They leap. (59)

The imaginative act is willed here: there is no strong evidence for
Arion to believe that what he sees is the site of the explorers' camp, but
it is a place "as good as any" for the imagination to bloom (his willful
use of limited evidence explains the endnote's description of his songs
as "plaintiff" rather than "plaintive"). But the willful act of imagination
(with the catfish as muse) allows Arion to see his river as charged with
history and significance. The complex syntax here allows the phrase "as
good as any" to take on a second valence, one that reveals the liberating
power of the imaginative leap. Now Arion's is a place, and a song, "as
good as any." The desolate here-and-now becomes as fruitful as any
mythic there-and-then.

The third poem continues the movement of re-enchantment that
we've seen developing, but the fourth poem presents a complication.
In the third poem of the sequence Arion remembers the westerns that
he saw in local theaters years before, and sees them as a kind of lore of
the place. The fourth poem begins promisingly, with an invocation of
Sacagawea as a kind of spirit of the place:

Dark-skinned with black hair
drawn tightly back, looking
northward through clay-ribbed
bluffs, she stood, I think,
ahead of the polers
in the keelboat's blunt
wet prow with a Yankee
helmsman facing her back,

and the wind, westerly—
out of my own childhood (63)

She seems to unite past and present, standing in both the legendary past of Lewis and Clark's expedition, and in the wind that blows through Arion's own childhood. But the passage contains a kernel of doubt—that "I think" in the first stanza—that threatens to grow and choke the life out of the living past. Uncertainties about the veracity of his own imaginative drawing of connections between the past and the present haunt Arion, who wonders whether or not the river banks he looks on are "the same shores" seen by Lewis and Clark. "In time," he knows, "the river sidewinds its banks. / Never the same soil" (63). Arion simply knows too much about rivers to believe his own fiction, that the banks he looks on were the same banks where the explorers camped. "All fancy," he laments, as his sense of Sacagawea as a governing spirit of place slips away, "She did not pass here" (64).

If he cannot believe in the literal presence of the Lewis and Clark exploration on the banks he sees, though, Arion can still believe in Sacagawea as the *spiritus locus*. Having used a bit of false history as an imaginative springboard, he can now envision the present city in her image. Instead of a squalid pile of particulars devoid of significance, the city now lives in his mind as her image:

> the city squats above the river, as an Indian woman at her
> day's work might squat—her hands full of the land—
> red corn, dried meats, new skins. (64–65)

Arion may have relinquished his belief in the literal habitation of these banks by Lewis, Clark and Sacagawea, but the afterimage of his imaginative act remains and gives shape to what had seemed a formless and insignificant present. The city is both itself and the image of its legendary past, both *now* and *then*.

This change in the consciousness of place is subtly celebrated in the next—and most Eliotic—section of the sequence. The fifth poem is in the voice of Meriwether Lewis, who, like Arion, tries to find a form or significance in a world of material realities apparently devoid of any shape or significance: "each night I read my Journals / like a novel," says Lewis, "seeking some / inevitability of plot, a hint / of form pointing toward an end" (66). His ruminations are accompanied by the sounds of "the deceptive waterthrush / imitating falling water" and, later, by the actual "far-off / drip of water, thin as birdsong"—an allusion to "What the Thunder Said" in Eliot's *Wasteland*. In Eliot's poem, where dryness is the symbol of a dis-enchanted and therefore sterile modernity, there is no water, only the deceptive sound of the "hermit thrush" that "sings in the pine trees / Drip drop drip drop drop drop drop." In Anania's poem the prognosis for the here-and-now is better than in Eliot's: the "deceptive waterthrush" tells only one side of the story; the water flows, though distantly, and can be heard.

The sixth and seventh poems of the sequence take us through the topography of the region, now seen as the bearer of history: we follow "trails // where Spanish armor rusted into / dark mud" (71). In the eighth section we read that "the present moment trembles within other durations" (73)—a kind of affirmation of the co-existence of the present and the legendary past. The gesture here is profoundly modernist in that it shows (in Hugh Kenner's phrase about time in Pound's poetry) "in transparent overlay, two times have become as one" (*The Pound Era* 29). Time past and time present have (as in Pound) "folded over" letting "*now* lay flat, transparent, upon *not-now*" (30).

The Usual Suspects

Despite the proclamations of a few poets and critics that we have long since entered the post-modern period of American letters, there is little evidence that modernism is dead or even dying. The tradition of Pound, Eliot, Williams, Stevens, and their contemporaries is very much alive and working in nearly all of the poetry being written in America today.

—Michael Anania (*New Poetry Anthology*, 108)

If Anania's transparent overlay of a mythic or legendary past and a quotidian present is reminiscent of Kenner's Pound, it is also reminiscent of other writers who we might include in the line-up of modernism's usual suspects. It is particularly reminiscent of Joyce— especially of Joyce's *Ulysses* as explained by T. S. Eliot. Joyce's use of *The Odyssey* to give a large, mythic significance to what he called the "ineluctable modality of the visible" (*Ulysses* 42) was, according to Eliot, unprecedented. It had "the importance of a scientific discovery. No one else has built a novel upon such a foundation before: it has never before been necessary" (680–81). Such an innovation was the product of a very particular cultural convergence. As Eliot put it:

> Psychology ... ethnology, and *The Golden Bough* have concurred to make possible what was impossible even a few years ago. Instead of a narrative method, we may now use a mythological method. It is, I seriously believe, a step toward making the modern world possible for art. (681)

Although Pound maintained that Joyce's achievement was singular—"*Ulysses* is ... as unrepeatable as *Tristram Shandy*," he wrote in *The Dial*, "I mean you cannot duplicate it; you can't take it as a 'model'" ("Paris Letter" 196)—Eliot disagreed. Writing in the same magazine a few months later, Eliot claimed that Joyce's innovation would launch a fleet of writers along this new route to Parnassus:

> In using myth, in manipulating a continuous parallel between contemporaneity and antiquity, Mr. Joyce is pursuing a method which others must pursue after him. They will not be imitators, any more than the scientist who uses the discoveries of an Einstein in pursuing his own, independent, further investigations. It is simply a way of controlling, of ordering, of giving a shape and a significance to the immense panorama of futility and anarchy which is contemporary history. (680)

The example of Anania's "Riversongs of Arion," with its shaping of local particulars by reference to a legendary past, indicates that this round in the great boxing match of Ole Ez and the fightin' Possum of St. Louis goes to Eliot on points. What Joyce first wrought, others have made anew, and Anania is among them.

Perhaps the most relevant modernist here is David Jones, who, like Anania, found the spatial coincidence of events that happened at different times significant (unlike Joyce, who made his literary echoes through coincidences of incident, character, or style). Anania himself speaks of how important Jones was for him (and for his friend John Matthias), when he says:

> Jones seemed like a pertinent poet to us, pertinent because he took Eliot's modernism in a different direction. For Jones, occasions of historical or mythological or religious or literary replication in space … aren't merely manifestations of the irony proposed by the degradation of the past in the present, as they are in Eliot. Jones is aware of the resonance of place in the significant past, but for Jones this significant past is not the source of an irony about the present: it is part of the synchronistic present. This sense of synchrony is part of Jones' Christianity, in which all time is present in the eyes of God.… For example, when a soldier falls in Jones, and his helmet falls down over his face, Jones associates that with the vision of the visor worn by knights at war over the same ground long ago. ("Talking John Matthias" 4)

For Jones, spatial coincidence provided what Roland Barthes would call the puncta, the point at which different events could be connected. In "The Riversongs of Arion," the coincidence of Lewis and Clark's expedition passing along the riverbank opens up the connection between *now* and *then* that comes to fruition in the vision of Omaha as Sacagawea.

But not so fast, you're thinking. There is no spatial coincidence in "The Riversongs of Arion," only an imagined spatial coincidence. The river is too fluid, too mutable, for any actual coincidence to occur, and Arion knows it. The riverbank is "Never the same soil," says Arion, and Sacagawea "did not pass here" (Anania, *Selected Poems* 63–64). If Anania is using a modernist technique, he does it with a self-consciousness, even a skepticism, that grows stronger in the sequence's final poems.

The New Science: Fictive Certainties

There are, said Pound with his characteristically hubristic confidence, three types of writers. There are, most importantly, "the inventors" who create new techniques (such as Arnaut Daniel's new methods of rhyming) or new ways of perceiving (such as those invented by Cavalcanti). There are also "the masters," who assimilate and synthesize earlier inventions; and "the diluters" who do little with existing forms other than add "some slight personal flavor" (*How to Read* 12–14). Let's put Joyce in the first category, on the ground that he gave us new ways of perceiving the modern person and the modern place through classical myth and legend. If one were feeling uncharitable, one might be tempted to class Anania among the diluters, saying that he does little more than assimilate western local color to the Joycean way of seeing. But this would be unfair, and it would involve ignoring the way that Anania deviates from Joyce. In raising doubts about the modernist process of linking past and present, Anania moves beyond modernism. He assimilates Joycean-Poundian-Jonesian modernism to the experience of his own generation, proving himself to be, in Pound's terms, one of the masters.

Anania's doubts about his own modernist project emerge most clearly in the penultimate poem of "The Riversongs of Arion." Here, the doubts about the permanence of the riverbank, and therefore about the coincidence in place between contemporary and legendary experience, come to the fore:

> The sunlight on the water,
> landfall shadows, treeline
> edging down the slow current.
>
> This is the land I made for you
> by hand, what was touched once
> then misremembered into words,
>
> place where the soil slips out
> from under its trees, where
> stiff weeds fall like rapids,
>
> It is the made emblem of time (75)

Arion acknowledges that the connection in space between past and present in the coincidence of place is fictional. But this deliberate "misremembering" does not make the connection invalid. The place is still the "emblem of time," despite having been "made." The constructed is still real, and the myth of the present as the incarnation of the past lives on as what Robert Duncan would call a "fictive certainty."

Daniel Guillory calls Anania's artistry "self-consciousness" (56), and one can certainly see why. In marking his epiphany of place and time as a construct, Anania distances himself from the modernist ideal of past and present "in transparent overlay," and shows himself as the product of a later generation. This is a generation for whom the affirmations of literature are made in quotation marks. This is the generation that learned from John Barth (who, in turn, learned from Borges) that the *Quixote* is still possible, but only as a quotation. As Barth says of Borges' "Pierre Menard, Author of the Quixote," that Borges' "artistic victory, if you like, is that he confronts an intellectual dead end and employs it against itself to accomplish new human work. If this corresponds to what mystics do—'every moment leaping into the infinite,' Kierkegaard says, 'and every moment surely falling back into the finite'—it's only one more aspect of that old analogy" (qtd. in Barth 69–71). Borges, says Barth, takes an old possibility's current impossibility (being the author of the *Quixote*), and in the act of pointing to that impossibility both cancels and resurrects it. Similarly, Anania's "Riversongs of Arion" point to the impossibility of establishing a modernist connection of the mythic and the real in the coincidence of place—and in doing so outlines what such a connection would be like. This leaves us with a kind of afterimage of what such a connection would be like, an afterimage that endures despite our knowledge that it is a phantasm.

If Joyce (as Eliot maintained) was the Einstein who invented a new way of seeing the universe, Anania is no mere imitator, but a later scientist "pursuing his own, independent, further investigations." The temptation to call Anania an unreconstructed modernist, then, must be resisted. No mere diluter replicating Joyce with new local colors, Anania is a synthesizer, pouring what is most valuable in Joyce into the great postmodern delta.

Like I said, James Joyce wasn't really born in Omaha. As for his nephew Michael Anania, though, that's a different story.

17

Note

Anania's "Afterword" to the *New Poetry Anthology* of 1969 is a fascinating document, not least because what may have looked to some at the time as a rearguard defense of modernism turns out to presage, by a good thirty years, recent observations about modernism by Marjorie Perloff, Pierre Joris and Jerome Rothenberg. Anania notes, for example, the presence of competing versions of modernism, saying that "Most of the quarrelling that created the poetic schools of the fifties and sixties resulted as much from variant readings of the modern tradition as from genuine disagreements of vision and temperament." He also laments the truncation of modernism during this time, which he describes as "the long-lived dominance of certain features of modernist versification" (108). The point is much like that made in Perloff's *The New Modernisms* and the introductions to both volumes of Rothenberg and Joris' *Poems for the Millennium*, in which the variety of modernism, the mid-century truncation of its possibilities, and the currency of its poetics in our own time, are duly noted.

Works Cited

Anania, Michael, ed. *New Poetry Anthology*. Swallow Press, 1969.

———. *In Plain Sight*. Asphodel Press, 1991.

———. *Selected Poems*. Asphodel Press, 1994.

———. "Talking John Matthias." *Samizdat* 9, Spring 2002, pp. 3–5.

Archambeau, Robert. "Michael Anania." In *Dictionary of Literary Biography*, vol. 193. Gale, 1998.

Barth, John. "The Literature of Exhaustion." In *The Friday Book: Essays and Other Nonfiction*. Putnam, 1984, pp. 62–76.

Eliot, T. S. "Myth and Literary Classicism." In *The Modern Tradition*. Edited by Richard Ellman and Charles Feidelson. Oxford UP, 1965, pp. 679–81.

Guillory, Daniel L. "Tradition and Innovation in Twentieth-Century Illinois Poetry." In *Studies in Illinois Poetry*. Edited by John E. Hallwas. Stormline, 1989, pp. 43–60.

Joyce, James. *Ulysses*. Penguin, 1969.

Kenner, Hugh. *The Pound Era*. U of California Press, 1971.

Pound, Ezra. *How to Read*. Desmond Harmsworth, 1931.

———. "Paris Letter." *Pound/Joyce*. Edited by Forrest Read. New Directions, 1965, pp. 194–200.

On Michael Anania's "Eclogue"

Garin Cycholl

Once in conversation, Michael Anania shared that one of his greatest regrets in teaching was that he had not saved his students' workshop poems on Chicago's "El"—the city's series of train lines, both elevated and underground. Riding the El invites odd moments of visual distraction, urban boundary crossing and wordy hiccups. The flickering train cars offer a transient sense of place in the city. Traveling the El regularly brings one face to face with the transparent space of open offices and apartments. Visually itself, the elevated tracks set up a kind of steel forest, particularly along Wabash Avenue downtown, where Kenneth Josephson caught the leafy breaks between track and sky in his black-and-white photographs in the mid-twentieth century. The passing train, an explosion of screech and shade above. Along the El, time can be measured against its recurrent stops, once told in the conductor's garbled human voice. Now though, that time is remeasured in a loop of synthetic announcement.

Grand. Chicago. Division.

Roosevelt. Chinatown. Sox & 35th.

All stops along the insinuated city. The recalled city. The city glimpsed in the approaching train's light as shredded versions of itself in motion—measured and recurrent as a church bell or a morning garbage truck. Passengers giggle when the named stops go out of sync with the city's hard geography below or above them, revealing an inherent tension within "place" itself as occasion. Place, suddenly severed and nonlocal. Place, carried along in voice or as explored in "On the Conditions of Place," where the train's movement reflects

Anania's larger sense of place—"As indistinct as water is in water, places dissolve into places" (143). Caught between what Bachelard calls those unfortunate adverbs "here" and "there," place is glimpsed in the rearview mirror or in a slight perception amidst movement. More or less "here," Anania writes

> Sometimes it seems that more
> has been lost than ever remains,
> that we live in a slow passing
> among indecipherable signs.
> . . . .
> All that we know is consequence—
> . . . .
> names whose sense shapes our memory (*Selected Poems* 143)

This knowing is magnified in urban experience. "Chicago" known as much in light along Lake Michigan as in the skyscraper's glass curtain; a whiff of wild garlic as substantial as a steel skeleton. Anania's Chicago—"occasion" organized along a string of perceptions. Edward Casey recollects place as perhaps proceeding "not merely [from] inert physical body but something organic and ever-changing" (331). Or Charles Olson's "undone business … the sea / stretching out / from my feet" (57). The "False Chicago" inked along Father Marquette's map. The city reflected around Sister Carrie in a department store window. These are Anania's points of transit.

The train itself occupies an interesting notch "here" in and along artistic space. In architectural space, the El crawls along as a thunderous caterpillar, a wrapper that contains Chicago's center. But for Anania, the train's rhythms and movement also narratively marks the city's memory. The El exists both in sight and melopoeically—vision invoked within anticipated sound, punctuated urban experience. The murmur of human voice in a moving car. The sound heard under and along the lines. The ticking and anticipation of a train's approach. For Anania, "words / among words, what is carried along … the probable line of what is seen" (143).

Momentary vision offers this "occasion" for Anania's "Eclogue":

How sudden they seem,
the gradual lives
of flowers, or the faces
you see in the brief
light of a "B" stop
taking, as you always
do, the "A" train. (*In Natural Light* 8)

"Eclogue" is a shambles of sound and light. That light prods the eye; it breaks down between the discrete light of an express train car and the glimpse of other passengers, stuck and waiting along a local platform. The sound, the unspoken roar of the train as it passes that platform into an illusion of acceleration and momentum ahead. Between these things, "you" is insubstantial as that "brief light" or the passed and passing "gradual lives." Chicago becomes stitched in recollection of a common, shared moment along a "B stop"—other travels and waiting, itself never "brief." A well of occasional journeys, the city dissolves along a string of "places."

This poem plays on elements of Ezra Pound's "In a Station of the Metro." Written in Paris during the First World War, Pound speaks of a startling encounter with human faces, experienced as "apparitions" emerging from a crowded subway tunnel. Pound wrote of experiencing these ghostly faces as "splotches of color" in the dark passage, mythically a space of descent. A mythy underworld nests the poem. Pound goes down into the city's underground, a city itself existing just beyond the trenches of World War I. The finality of the phantoms emerging from that world are punctuated by the poem's sounds in its closing: "Petals on a wet, black bough." The poem is an act of urban memory—eye and ear retuned to this underground space. The image as glimpsed, urban experience. Pound described this as a moment where the poem is "trying to record the precise instant when a thing outward and objective transforms itself, or darts into a thing inward and subjective" ("On 'In a Station of the Metro'"). Within this linkage, Pound's poem depends upon its roots in classical myth—an underworld—as much as it inhabits a modern sub-urban space of urban exchange and meaning.

Pound's city maps itself along the underseam of human imagination. It recollects every city disappeared from human memory. The faces hang around in the poem's final, sharply bitten echo: "apparitions" still haunting the poem, reader and city. A departing train. A disappearing city. An "occasional" space planted within and retreating from the poem's speaker.

The train moves along the edges of other artists' imaginations of the twentieth-century city as well. *In The Man with the Golden Arm*, Nelson Algren describes this transitory experience along the El's tracks on Chicago's near Northwest Side. Homebound Sophie "listen[s] to the glistening hum of the tracks, leveling dead-away toward midnight after every El that passed … she could see where the flickering warning lamps burned, along the El's long boundaries, like vigil lamps guarding the constant boundaries of night" (97). The train becomes boundary of individual isolation—outward journey as solitary as journey within— the mythic "lamps" and "constant boundaries of night." Around the same historical moment, photographers from Chicago's Institute of Design were drawn to the lines between the light and darkness strung along the El's raised tracks and underground passages. Photographers like Richard Nickel, Barbara Crane and Harold Allen documented these spaces in Chicago. Their work records the odd inversion of subjectivity and interiority in its visible record, the photograph. Private experience becomes public, transformed into urban narrative. The photographer's eye opens into a wider, recalled vision. Mythically, the American city told as a series of spaces of personal disintegration, flight or transformation.

"Eclogue" reflects a similar mythic track. The poem ultimately recollects Duke Ellington's "Take the A Train," its notes sounding from New York's Harlem to Chicago's Bronzeville. Melopoecially, its syncopation musically narrates the promise of urban journey and the deeper migrations historically and mythologically marking the influx city as well as the wider country. Journeys are taken; place re-sounds. Ellington's tune is initiated along the moment of the train's passing roar. Inside the lighted car, the poem's "you" rides along, destination still in mind, although that "you" is now also stung by the silence left in the train's wake. Along the platform, a face recalled in the blur of a B-stop, a glimpse that reawakens the rider's "place" *here* against a disappearing city. That city is stitched along image and song, as surely as it is laid out along the string of stops. But it is the rail's sound, never actually mentioned in the poem, which provides that stitching between the public city and its private occasions. "Sudden" and "brief," that occasion is sounded through the "you's" stinging memory of other silent platforms. Invoked as such, the screech of rail against wheel rises as the express train moves on. The glass of sparks spray, a moment of urban memory exchanged between the poem and its reader.

Engaging Pound's city, Anania further complicates anything "outward and objective." Place "appears *here*" within one more occasion of a recollected "you" rooted in an experience of anonymity in the disappearing city. "Eclogue" stitches the personal journey along moments that are conscious of the mythic narratives of a distinctly American place that surround them. In the play of light, sound and darkness, the city is vectored between forces of descent, glimpse and memory. By moment, Chicago peers out as American necropolis. The reader descends into the common act of "catching" the train. The platform's props are there again: the long elevator (out of order—again) and the inevitable pigeon caught in the tunnel. The rail rattles with the train's approach, which propels the slight gust of stale air seemingly called straight up out of the earth itself. Glimpsed, the city disappears in a string of visual recollections—partial lives and movement slivered along light and curtained windows. Recollected along a recurrent hum of journeys, the wide bow of city is traveled, there and back again. The "you" seeks a point of connection with passing faces, set in stark relief against the tunnel's "long boundaries." Memory acts *here*—[the] self tuned to time and its rhythms, songs half-recalled and voices swallowed by "brief light." Those boundaries were crossed awhile back, in some other place. The train moves on.

Similarly stitching the city, Anania's "Steal Away" calls Chicago's living and dead into a common space. Working from a flaking image of a Curtis Mayfield advertisement that appears on a building side, the poem explores urban space, "south, you say" (*Heat Lines* 4). The poet recollects a succession of movements and figures now "gone to shadows." Mayfield and Little Walter appear beside the witness of Leon Forrest and Sterling Plumpp—all invoked and then passing in "the moist coil / the song leaves" (5). *Here*, the poem steps fully into the Chicago necropolis, addressing both the living Plumpp and the departed Forrest. The song cries out to a shifting you: "can you see him [Mayfield] ... a dream grown arms, legs"? (3). A restless rhythm roots itself in the litany of names. The poem stirs one glimpse after another, but it is sound that drives the lyric "in the night ear, song; can you see" (6). In this necropolis, the critical sound of descent is anticipated—"the El / screeches out of his name" (5). Memory enters:

> say what it is that's
> rung out track after track,
> the brightness steel work
>
> leaves across steel, names,
> or how too far's edge draws
> us along like a third rail (7)

The embedded, melopoeic *screech* brings the names to "the backs of our eyes" (7). The poet reiterates to the gathered *you's*, "can you see him?" Mayfield as Superfly steps out of a faded poster on the building wall. But it is the returned sound of the El's rail that sings him into being, "coil and rail returning" (8). The city stitched within the next train along the line. *Here*, the "coil" of a rail screeching against wheel returns within the poem without ever being directly re-invoked. The resounded *screech* punctuates the vision. Ever the necropolis, the city steps back into itself. The train disappears (into the steel-stitched city and) into Chicago night.

In his El poems, Anania's work recovers a distinct sense of American place. *Here*, it's no longer a train in the prairied distance, the 1 AM freight passing along the B&O tracks that awakens me, but the anticipated sound of other trains—Chicago's Blue Line returning to its Irving Park platform on its relentless circle to and from O'Hare. The Illinois Central's 63rd Street platform—the last place Emmett Till was seen alive in Chicago. Or more lately, the absence of the Metra's bells along the Electric Line—the late night train from the city cut from its schedule in COVID-time. These incidental musics stitch together the disappearing city in an unstitched America. Anania's lyric recovers these occasions of place along these lines—"names whose sense shapes our memory."

Works Cited

Anania, Michael. "Eclogue." *In Natural Light*. Asphodel Press, 1999, p. 8.

———. "On the Conditions of Place." *Selected Poems*. Asphodel Press, 1994, pp.142–43.

———. "Steal Away." *Heat Lines*. Asphodel Press, 2004, pp. 3–8.

Casey, Edward. *The Fate of Place*. U of California Press, 1998.

Olson, Charles. "Maximus, to Himself." *The Maximus Poems*. U of California Press, 1983, pp. 56–57.

Pound, Ezra. "On 'In a Station of the Metro.'" Poetry Foundation. https://www.poetryfoundation.org/poetrymagazine/poems/12675/in-a-station-of-the-metro.

A Certain Slant of Clear Light: Anania, Dickinson, and the Unfolding Moment

Philip Pardi

Poetry has a unique ability to hold an instant in remarkable clarity.
　—Michael Anania

1.

Maybe it's because I've been ill for months and am just now returning to moments other than my own, or maybe it's because I have recently been immersed in the poetry of Emily Dickinson, or maybe it's because I was walking with Michael Anania's *In Natural Light* in my back pocket earlier today looking for a spot beneath the trees to sit and read when I stubbed my toe on a rock that wasn't there yesterday. Whatever the reason, I find myself returning again and again to poems like this:

October Evening
　for Pat Nelson

West of the near west side,
beyond the ragged line of
watertowers and chimneys

and the tufted nylon rose
upholstery city sunset,
the day is making its way

> with you into the past,
> a slant of clear light
> among the darkening branches
>
> or the Cascades' evening sheen
> the glacier cups into
> a thousand years of snow. (Anania 9)

You could build a lesson on the history of the lyric around this poem.

Or, more precisely, the history of a certain kind of lyric. In the pages that follow, I want to delve into some of that history and in the process explore the power of a poem to create a moment so powerfully present that as readers we are swept up inside it. Far from being told what has already happened or what has already been thought, we find ourselves, each time we bring such poems to life with our own reading, in the presence of thinking as it unfolds. For a brief moment, the poem's present tense becomes ours.

2.

A classic example of what I have in mind appears in "On First Looking into Chapman's Homer," Keats's early and much-studied tribute to the translator who made Homer's texts available to him. After comparing (in the sonnet's octave) a life of reading to a life of travel, and after claiming to have heard of Homer's greatness, Keats famously seeks to render how it felt to experience Homer in Chapman's translation:

> Then felt I like some watcher of the skies
> When a new planet swims into his ken. (64)

The image of the astronomer (possibly Keats has in mind the discovery of Uranus in 1781) renders beautifully a moment of new and sudden perception: reading felt like seeing, like discovery. Where the octave was built on metaphor, the sestet turns to the explicit "like" of simile. As a result, we are perhaps more aware of the act of comparison and, by extension, of the presence of a comparer behind the language, so that not just the world but an experience of the world is in play.

But this simile apparently misses something, because the next line immediately pivots, and the final four lines of the sonnet offer a second attempt at comparison:

> Or like stout Cortez when with eagle eyes
> He star'd at the Pacific—and all his men
> Look'd at each other with a wild surmise—
> Silent, upon a peak in Darien. (64)

With that initial "Or" the thinking takes a turn. The image of the astronomer is discarded in favor of a new and presumably more accurate image: Keats is not simply listing another way that it felt; he has found a better way. For one thing, the octave's metaphor of travel is now resurrected so that the passive stance of the astronomer is replaced by the active role of the explorer. Moreover, in the new simile, we have not only Cortez and his eyes as they behold (in the conceit of the poem, for the first time) the Pacific, but the men who cannot yet see the ocean (we deduce this from the fact that they are wildly surmising) and *can* see Cortez and the impact on him. Seeing and the act of reading for which it stands are rendered as acts that radiate out from person to person in waves of wonder.

Meanwhile, where the astronomer was granted two lines, Cortez and his men get four lines. As the thinking swells so too does the sentence we are reading. First by way of the "Or" and then by way of the more nuanced comparison, we are along for the ride as the mind discovers a new way of thinking its thoughts. If this is a poem about an experience of reading, it is also a poem about finding an adequate language to describe that experience.

3.

Keats, of course, didn't invent this. By bringing to life the moment of the poem's utterance, he taps into a dimension of lyric that is available to any poet. We find examples of such present-tense aspirations in Sappho, who is my placeholder for the beginning of the lyric tradition, and in the work of countless poets writing in the millennia between her and us. Given that vast tradition, we could easily flesh out this idea with any number of poets, but I want to turn next to Dickinson. For one thing, she leans into this aspect of the lyric with great skill, and for another, Dickinson scholars have explored these effects in her work in detail. From her, and from those who have written about her, we learn something about the inheritance that underlies a poem like "October Evening," a poem, after all, that must have Dickinson at least partly in mind when it invokes that "slant of clear light."

An interesting thing about Dickinson's development as a poet is that she seems to grasp early on that the performance of the poem—its existence in the reader's own present tense—is separable from whatever experience is being recounted. A poem copied in 1862 begins

> I was the slightest in the House –
> I took the smallest Room –
> At night, my little Lamp, and Book –
> And one Geranium –
>
> So stationed I could catch the mint
> That never ceased to fall –
> And just my Basket –
> Let me think – I'm sure
> That this was all – (487)

The events of the poem are recounted steadfastly in the past tense, but by slipping into the present tense in line 8, the poem acknowledges the moment of its own telling and introduces a moment of deliberation into the poem's unfolding. "Let me think" bring everything to a standstill, and then—in a moment that lasts the duration of a dash—sufficient reassurance is found to continue. "Yes," the poem says, "I'm sure / That this was all," and the telling continues.[1]

Though she is writing about Dickinson's letters, Erica Scheurer describes the effect perfectly when she observes that Dickinson often "sets up an exploratory mode of discourse—*the mind thinking*, not the mind *having thought*.... The effect of Dickinson's voice is to pull us into the moment, to experience Dickinson at *thought*" (99). Similarly, Robert Weisbuch notes that early in her career, Dickinson "discovered a poetic method which does not dress but illustrates, thus *is*, the pattern of her thought" (*Emily* 12). He adds in a later essay that Dickinson's "poems feel intimate because we see and feel a mind at work; we see thought being thought; we experience ideas as they come into being" ("Prisming" 212). The effect, writes Cristanne Miller, is to create "a sense of performed presence" (97).

A feeling of "let me think" hovers behind many a Dickinson poem, even when there is no explicit pointing. The real wonder is that the creation (what Anania might call the "illusion") of an unfolding present tense is so strong that even a past-tense poem can participate in it. After all, both Dickinson's "I was the slightest in the House" and Keats's sonnet are in the past tense. We know we are reading a poem about something that has already happened; we know the events are fully behind us. But the poems find ways to draw our attention to the telling itself.

What I say here about Dickinson might be said of a great many poems in the lyric tradition. So much so, in fact, that Jonathan Culler identifies this feature as central to any account of what the lyric even is. For Culler, while there is nothing a poem must have or do in order to qualify as lyric, there are a series of qualities (what he calls "parameters") that tend, over countless years of practice by countless lyric poets, to recur. One of these is the status of the lyric poem as a present-tense event, such that even narrated events are "trumped by … the present of lyric enunciation" (36).[2] He argues that a "distinctive feature of lyric seems to be this attempt to create the impression of something happening now, in the present time of discourse" (37) and eventually concludes that the "fundamental characteristic of lyric … is not the description and interpretation of a past event but the iterative and iterable performance of an event in the lyric present, in the special 'now' of lyric articulation" (226).

The implications of such a view cannot be overstated. Among other things, to acknowledge the "now" of the poem's performance sheds light on the lyric's commitment to all manner of poetic and linguistic effects, even when—perhaps especially when—there is no explicit phrase ("let me think") to signal that fact. Consider Dickinson's dashes, for example, or her frequent use of compressed syntax: their contribution to the poem is not simply to tell more accurately what has already happened but to capture and foreground the act of thinking it through.[3] Jed Deppman notes that Dickinson's "poems represent thinking as rapid, uncontrollable, or self-contesting" (50). He has in mind primarily what her poems say about thinking, but his phrase captures precisely the effect in many poems where the poetics themselves capture the contours of thought. Weisbuch similarly notes that there is frequently a "feeling of discovery, of being mid-process, so that things change mid-poem" ("Prisming" 213). The pause-causing dashes, the twists of syntax and the leaps of logic—all these combine to bring to life the feeling of language barely able to keep up, of words being found in the real time of the poem.[4]

We can go further and say (with Culler and others) that a poem's sonic effects—rhythm, rhyme and repetition—point in much the same way to the moment of the poem's articulation (Culler 118).[5] Take Robert Hayden's "Those Winter Sundays":

> Sundays too my father got up early
> and put his clothes on in the blueblack cold,
> then with cracked hands that ached
> from labor in the weekday weather made
> banked fires blaze. No one ever thanked him.
>
> I'd wake and hear the cold splintering, breaking.
> When the rooms were warm, he'd call,
> and slowly I would rise and dress,
> fearing the chronic angers of that house,
>
> Speaking indifferently to him,
> who had driven out the cold
> and polished my good shoes as well.
> What did I know, what did I know
> of love's austere and lonely offices? (41)

The title and first line leave no doubt that we are looking back at a repeated experience from childhood. Every verb in this poem is in the past tense. Yet as you listen, the poem's patterns of sound—e.g. its repeated "k" sounds ("clothes … cold … cracked … ached … thanked" in just the first stanza), its repetitions of words ("cold" appears in each of the three stanzas), and its patterns of assonance ("clothes … cold … No … slowly"), to name just a few—work to foreground the moment of the poem's articulation. Whatever these patterns contribute to the meaning of the poem (for example, by connecting words we might not otherwise connect), it has the deeper effect of making the reading of the poem, its performance, into an event (Culler 14–15). The effect is completed when, in the final two lines, the poem turns to an explicit moment of thinking that stands outside the events being reported. Just as we do when Dickinson asks us to "let" her think and when Keats equivocates with his "or," we follow the mind as it steps from one thing (in this case, recounting the past) to another (reflecting on it). It is looking back that makes the insight possible, and the poem becomes the site for that backward glance, with the repetition of "what did I know" conveying the sense that the words are right now, in our presence, being performed.

4.

To read "October Evening" in this context is to see how effortlessly it participates in and renews a time-honored dimension of the lyric tradition. From the very first line, we know we are in a space where differentiations are being made: "West of … west" and then "beyond" work to locate the scene, and while the exact location remains unclear, what comes through is the attempt to differentiate. If it feels a bit like we are witnessing the poem as it creates the landscape—seemingly right before our eyes—it's because to a certain extent we are. More precisely, though, what we sense is the poem discovering its language as the poem progresses. The feeling is expansive, with the self-contained phrase of line 1 followed by the more complex phrase that take up all of lines 2 through 5.

There is, I want to insist, a kind of joy in getting caught up or carried away in language. As the first stanza yields to the second, we find ourselves in the midst of a drawn-out description: "the tufted nylon rose / upholstery city sunset"—this is language relishing the act of rendering as it swells into another line to complete the image. And there is some magic here, too. Note how, in the gap between the first two stanzas, the meaning of "beyond" stretches, although we are not immediately aware of how much. We don't blink at finding ourselves "beyond the ragged line of / watertowers and chimneys," but before we know it, we are also beyond the sunset. In just five lines, this poem that began "West of the near west side" has left city and earth behind.[6]

Still, the sentence itself remains incomplete, a bit like someone speaking who is finding the words in the process of speaking, warming to the occasion of utterance in the midst of making an utterance. It is only in line 6 that we reach the grammatical subject of the sentence. In fact, the subject and predicate at the heart of this poem straddle its middle precisely: "day is making its way // with you into the past." Everything else is modification, is careful discerning. With its pair of internal rhymes ("day," "making," "way"; "you," "into"), the two lines assert their centrality to the sentence: first subject and verb, then a stanza break that (like all the stanza breaks in this poem) can do nothing to slow the pace and then the rest of the verb phrase and the "you" of poetic address. The thinking no less than the sentence refuses to be stopped.

If what came before the predicate was a rising tide of imagined scenery, what comes after seeks to do justice to this moment of day's passing. With "a slant of clear light / among the darkening branches," with its Dickinsonian "slant" and its yoking together of "clear" light with "darkening" branches, Anania captures beautifully the moment of inbetweenness that is sunset. There is no attempt to reconcile them; the two seeming opposites sit together because, in the moment, that is how they are experienced.

The poem might have ended there; it seems to have brought fully to life the instant of this "October Evening." But there follows one more recalibration, one more instance where our reading overlaps directly with the poem's discovery of what it wants to say. The "or" that begins the tenth line (and the final stanza) leads to a new image. As in Keats's sonnet, language that was found is being recalibrated. And as in so many Dickinson poems, the leaps don't tarry to explain themselves: alongside the "or" there is no extra verbiage to clarify exactly how the lines that follow fit with what's come before, and that is exactly the point.

The breadth of the leap is extraordinary. If we started "West of the near west side" and slowly made our way beyond the "watertowers and chimneys" and the "upholstery city sunset," we are returned, seemingly, to earth, to that same sunlight as it casts a sheen in snow-covered mountains that stand a thousand miles away. And as the current moment is framed by those "thousand years," a new, almost cosmic perspective is brought to bear on this seemingly small and personal experience. If the structural heart of the poem is the sentence split evenly at the very center of these twelve lines, the lyric heart of the poem is that "or," where we feel—indeed, we are left to follow along— the moment when suddenly not only a new and better way of saying something presents itself but also a leap expands the reach of this short lyric in unexpected ways.

Once again, the fabric of the poem registers the experience of a thought as it comes into being. Importantly, and this comes close to the heart of the matter, what becomes clear at such moments is the feeling that the words and thinking contained in the poem didn't exist before it began. Rather, to read the poem is to experience the act of thinking the thoughts and of finding the words, as if for the first time.

5.

Just as there are many ways of thinking, there are many ways a poem might render our thinking:

Somewhat Gray and Graceful
for Reginald Shepherd

Left behind. Consider the frayed
horizon and the likelihood

of birds. Someone in a photograph
glances upward and flight

extrapolates itself as a story
proposed by one thing and then
another, each surface accomplished,
each act a definition, the self

in a prospect of birds, flight
arrived at in the unconsidered
assumption of flight, finches
sprung forward and eased against

the edge of sight, the improbable
reach of this and that, somewhat gray
and graceful, doves in their white rush
like breath anticipating speech. (Anania 13)

This short lyric, which appears just two poems later in *In Natural Light*, does much that will feel familiar after the discussion above. But it demonstrates something of the suppleness of poet's tools and of the poetic and linguistic choices open to us.

Read this poem aloud; read it again; let the moment of its articulation be yours. When voiced, what stands out to me is a kind of sonic circling that reminds me of HD's "Mid-day." There, too, the poem returns to a small fleet of words in an intricate pattern of departure and return.[7] In "Somewhat Gray and Graceful," note how "birds" and "flight" appear in the first stanza only to be repeated ("birds, flight") in line 9 and again ("flight, finches") in line 11. We move from "the likelihood / of birds" to "a prospect of birds" to "finches" and "doves." We move, that is, toward specificity, which is to say, toward ever clearer perception. Once aloft, the sentence hovers, but the hovering is far from still. It's as if the sentence won't finish—cannot be allowed to land—until the thought completes itself.

As in "October Evening," the expansiveness of the sentence captures the way thinking, once started, sometimes takes flight. The story of the sentences is in some ways the story of the poem. Though we might not notice at first, there are just three sentences in this poem: a two-word fragment, an eight-word imperative, and then—draped over fourteen lines of verse—a single sentence that embodies the blossoming of thought. The effect is to mimic how a mind might think something through, tentatively at first, but then with building, budding boldness. The triumphant third line, which constitutes almost the entire poem, is launched almost conjecturally. Just as "Someone in a photograph / glances upward and flight // extrapolates itself," so too this entire poem seems to extrapolate itself from a chance glance and the willingness to pursue "one thing and then / another" until something is brought into focus.

To dip once more into the tradition of lyric, this poem calls to mind O'Hara's poems of walking and pondering. Consider the breathless unfolding of poems such as "The Day Lady Died" or perhaps "Personal Poem," which begins

> Now when I walk around at lunchtime
> I have only two charms in my pocket
> an old Roman coin Mike Kanemitsu gave me
> and a bolt-head that broke off a packing case
> when I was in Madrid the others never
> brought me too much luck though they did
> help keep me in New York against coercion
> but now I'm happy for a time and interested (32)[8]

If the pace and tone of thinking are different, the effect of making our reading a present-tense experience of thought as it takes flight is consistent. I'm reminded also of Milton's early lyric "At a Solemn Music," which reverses the order to create a dizzying effect. Using semi-colons to keep sentence and thought afloat, Milton's two-sentence poem begins with a sentence that spans twenty-four lines, after which (following the period) there is a four-line apostrophe to the muses (82–83). What unites these otherwise different poems is that our reading experience is in large part the meaning of the poem: this, these poems declare, is how it feels to think this through.

6.

To yoke together HD, O'Hara and Milton and to set them alongside Anania, Dickinson, Hayden and Keats, all this goes a long way toward indicating just how diverse are the ends to which the present-tense aspirations of the lyric might be put.[9] Before ending, I want to touch on a third poem, "Apples," which is all that sits between "October Evening" and "Somewhat Gray and Graceful" on the pages of *In Natural Light*. Like those two poems, "Apples" reveals (and invites *us* into) a moment of unfolding thought, but it does so in a way we have yet to fully explore.

The poem is too long to quote in its entirety, but the effect I have in mind can be found in the first two stanzas:

> The news—precious little
> to hold onto—cuts and burns.
> In Buffalo, six taxi drivers,
> murdered, their hearts
> cut out and carried away.
> Lebanese shards. All across
> the country victims sprawl.
> Terrorists in New York.
>
> In Indiana, just south of the dunes,
> brown cider is put out in Dixie cups,
> apples cinched up in plastic bags
> along the floor—Jonathans, Red
> and Golden Delicious, Winesaps,
> frost-skinned Cortlands, Romes—
> shelves of amber, home-strained
> honey, prize-winning gourds. (Anania 10)

The opening stanza offers snatches of images; the thinking moves forward in steps, like a pawn from square to square. By contrast, the unfurling of the second stanza is steady, more like the sweep of a bishop from one end of the chessboard to another. It could stop at any point along the way, but it doesn't, finding instead, at each potential break, more details to add, more of the world to depict. The stanzas feel different because of the way syntax metes out and measures the progression of thought. Stop and start, on the one hand; this and then this, on the other.

There is, in short, something of a leap between stanzas: in the gap in between, something happens.[10] The effect is captured delightfully by Mark Doty, who writes of Whitman's "Song of Myself" that in the "white space of silence between stanzas the poet seems to be gathering himself, feeling his way toward his next assertion. The mind pauses, dwells, prepares to speak" (58).[11] What Keats achieves with "or" and what Dickinson achieves implicitly with dashes or explicitly with "let me think," Whitman achieves by letting one thought end and then, simply, pausing. In the gap between one stanza and the next, Doty adds, "it seems as if the speaker waits, as we do, for the next idea" so that "we pause and watch thought loom up out of silence" (59).

To return one last time to Keats, I can't think of a better example than the final two stanzas of "Ode to a Nightingale." Keats writes of the bird's song that it is

> The same that oft-times hath
> Charm'd magic casements, opening on the foam
> Of perilous seas, in faery lands forlorn. (371)[12]

This brings to an end Keats's meditation on the history of the nightingale and its song, as well as the penultimate stanza of the poem. There follows the blank space of the stanza break and then the final stanza, which begins

> Forlorn! the very word is like a bell
> To toll me back from thee to my sole self!

That first word might as well be in quotation marks because what the line registers is the use of the word at the conclusion of stanza 7: the poem essentially asks, "Did I just say 'forlorn'?" To Doty's suggestion that the gaps between stanzas offer a moment of pausing, waiting, and preparing to speak, we might add that they offer an opportunity for self-hearing. And because we, as readers, experience this same pause, we too experience, as the poem waits and then proceeds, the way thought "looms up out of silence."

In "Apples," the gambit of the first stanza is to take the broad view of news from "across the country," from Buffalo and from New York. The language proceeds haltingly, stopped five times by periods, at which point the stanza ends. In retrospect, we can see that the stanza break is haunted by the notion that there is "precious little / to hold onto," as well as by those place names because when the second stanza begins, it takes its cue from the first: we leap from New York to Indiana and, as the stanza continues, the poem succeeds in finding something "to hold onto," namely the scene that will take up the next five stanzas. The second stanza not only follows the first, it responds to it. In the gap between stanzas, the poem finds precisely what it had earlier despaired of not finding. Now, having found something "to hold onto," the language warms to the task, and the second stanza unfolds in a single, thought-filled offering.

7.

With its passing mention of "slant," Anania's "October Evening" cannot help but gesture, however gently, toward Dickinson. She uses variations of the word in six poems, most famously when she advises us to "Tell all the truth but tell it slant" (1089), using the word as an adverb to delineate a poetic strategy of indirection. Only once, though, does she use the word as a noun,[13] and it is this occurrence that comes to mind when I think of the "slant of clear light" that cuts through Anania's evening:

> There's a certain Slant of light
> Winter Afternoons –
> That oppresses, like the Heft
> Of Cathedral Tunes – (338)

In Dickinson's poem, the "Slant" (capitalized for emphasis, perhaps) has an outsized effect: it "oppresses," and the poem as a whole will trace how it does so. Dickinson's use of "it" is a subject unto itself, but in this poem each occurrence can be read in reference to the "Slant" of the first line.

Having discovered the metaphor of religion in the last line of stanza 1, the poem continues with it in stanza 2:

> Heavenly Hurt, it gives us –
> We can find no scar,
> But internal difference –
> Where the Meanings, are –

The step here is reminiscent of the step in "Apples" and the effect described by Doty. The poem could go anywhere after that first stanza, but in that brief space, the decision is made to stick with the religious simile. As we proceed, there is no "like" or "as," so that, as metaphor, we sink still deeper into the imagery of faith. And deep we go. Part of the wonder of the poem lies in how quickly the thinking progresses: in eight lines we have gone from a stray ray of winter sunlight to the spot within us where "Meanings" are located.

As the poem continues, it spells out, with increasing detail and resonance, the feeling of "imperial affliction" that is triggered by this seemingly brief moment. And then, in the fourth and final stanza, the full impact of this "Slant of light" becomes apparent:

> When it comes, the Landscape listens –
> Shadows – hold their breath –
> When it goes, 'tis like the Distance
> On the look of Death –

Written in the present tense, with regular rhymes (in lines 2 and 4 of each stanza) to shore up its structure, the poem unfolds easily, reminding us that there is no contradiction between precise poetic structure/form and the act of thinking something through as if in our presence. But what stays with me when I set this poem down, more than anything, is the journey of that "Slant," the way it launches the poem and, as the poem develops, assumes an awesome presence in our world. By the end of the poem, it has the power to silence the landscape and to leave us face to face with our own mortality.

In "October Evening," the effect is radically different:

the day is making its way

with you into the past,
a slant of clear light
among the darkening branches (9)

As both "day" and "you" move into the past, the poem likens the slant's experience to ours, so that where Dickinson's slant oppresses us, Anania's share our fate. Implicit, though, is the understanding that this spot of clear light must soon succumb to the darkening: the two can coexist but for only so long. And it seems to me that it is precisely this realization—the insight that the "slant of clear light" exists alongside a "darkening" that it cannot hope to overcome—that provokes the remarkable final stanza:

or the Cascade's evening sheen
the glacier cups into
a thousand years of snow. (9)

First with "or" and then with this newly discovered image, the poem finds something larger on which to pin this moment of evening. As in so many of the poems above, we are present for that turn, a turn that is in some ways the result of self-hearing: crucially, in the gap between stanzas, what becomes clear is that ending with this moment of clear light and darkening branches would fall short of the fullness of the moment. Something more is needed, and the slant is set aside. Where Dickinson's "Slant" (even in absence) dominates our experience, Anania's slant cedes to a broader image, moves with us into the past and yields to a deeper sense of time and world.

8.

It would take a broader study to set these lyrics into the greater context of Anania's poetry. Like Keats, like Dickinson, like pretty much any formidable poet I can think of, Anania writes various kinds of poems.

(Culler might say that such is lyric: the present tense ebbs and flows, available when needed but certainly not always the primary concern.) But when a poet leans into this dimension of the lyric, I happily surrender. Anania might say this aspect of the lyric resembles another art form he loves: "Music," he says, "seems always to be in its own present" (Graham). Comparisons between music and poetry are easy to make, but in this they align: the commanding power of the present-tense performance to draw us in.

I'm reminded of a comment by Peggy O'Brien: "There is no poet," she writes, "who lives more on the edge of every single second than Emily Dickinson" (469). O'Brien's words might well be said of Anania or of any poet who brings this dimension of lyric to life. Such poems, whatever else they are "about," are at the same time performances that are restaged each time we read them. In such poems, even if at one level we know we are reading a poem that has already been written, we feel the thinking taking shape in language as we proceed. If there is some sleight of hand here, so be it. "Poetry," as Anania observes, "has a unique ability to hold an instant in remarkable clarity." He adds, "In my poems, that clarity is both essential and steeped in illusion" (Graham). That illusion, in part, is of a moment created so powerfully that, however briefly, its moment becomes ours. We might be reading "October Evening" far from Chicago, in a distinct moment of history, in the most distant of landscapes, under a tree about to bloom, but the poem works to join, however briefly, its present tense to ours.

Notes

1. For a still earlier appearance of "let me think," see "What would I give to see his face?" (Dickinson 285).

2. Elsewhere, Culler describes the characteristics of lyric as "a system of possibilities" (6).

3. See, for example, line 2 of Dickinson's "What would I give to see his face?" (quoted above), where the dashes introduce a moment of hesitation into the thinking as it unfolds.

4. Such textual moments (e.g., Dickinson's dashes or her "let me think," Keats's use of "or" to usher in a better way of saying something) should not be taken as holdovers

from the composition process. Whether they appear in a first draft of a poem is irrelevant. If Keats were intent only on finding the best analogy, after all, he could have deleted the two lines about the astronomer and devoted the entire sestet to Cortez. Similarly, Dickinson—after stopping to think—could have added the thoughts that came to her in that pause and deleted the signposting. The essential point is this: by including such moments, a poet chooses to foreground not just the result of thinking but the very *process* of thinking. These are poems that honor the effort of language-finding.

5. Culler builds here on the work of Robert von Hallberg, who argues that a central contribution of musicality relates to poetic authority: "Poetry and music collaborate deeply and darkly. Sounds warrant what poets say by giving words palpable form: one hears the orders, senses the achievement, and extends credence." Robert von Hallberg, *Lyric Powers*. U of Chicago Press, 2008, p. 228.

6. We are also beyond the literal "line" of "watertowers and chimneys" because Anania has made a poetic line of those three words. Which is to say that, while my argument is that the poem mirrors certain aspects of thinking, there is still ample room for complex textual effects. Poems of this kind are not to be mistaken for spontaneous effusions that haven't given thought to deeper structural or textual dimensions. The appearance of spontaneity is almost always the product of work. Think, for example, of haiku: it is made to seem spontaneous, but the syllable counting is precise.

7. In "Mid-day" the word "seed" occurs five times while ten other words appear at least twice.

8. O'Hara eschews periods, but "The Day Lady Died" is essentially a three-sentence poem, and "Personal Poem" is, depending on how you parse it, either two or three sentences. The effect in both cases is of building momentum and real-time unfolding.

9. Culler grounds his theory of lyric in the work of a wide array of poets including Sappho, Ovid, Baudelaire, Goethe and William Carlos Williams, among others. He would doubtless point to another similarity between these two Anania poems. Both are, to some extent, acts of apostrophe (one by virtue of the "you"; the other by virtue of the imperative "Consider …"). Apostrophe, in turn, is inherently linked to the present tense: an address necessarily invokes a moment of shared time between addresser and addressee. See Chapter Five of *Theory of the Lyric*.

10. Palpable shifts between stanzas are common in poetry. My guess is that they are rooted in lyric's affinity with (and pre-history as) song, where the gaps between stanzas (verses) are more than brief and are often separated by a refrain or chorus. Poets have been mining the possibilities of such gaps for as long as we have been writing poems without music. Dickinson, for example, generally respects the stanzaic unit, which opens up the prospect of movement between stanzas; Robert Hayden often achieves remarkable effects by doing first one thing then another. Both "Those Winter Sundays" and "Dogwood Trees," for example, employ end-stopped first

stanzas followed by second stanzas that flow into the third, creating important textual effects. Similarly, in O'Hara's poetry, it is not uncommon for a poem to begin with stanzas that are end-stopped but to end with one stanza flowing right into the next as happens in both "The Day Lady Died" and "Personal Poem."

11. Doty goes on to write that Whitman's use of stanzas "suggest that the poet is coming to knowledge *as the poem is being spoken,* not simply offering an orderly recitation of an insight already attained" so that the "poems seem to come into being before our eyes" (59). This sounds exactly right, although I would add that Whitman—like Dickinson, Keats and all the others—is far from unique in finding his way to this crucial dimension of what a poem can do.

12. For ease of quoting, I omit the indentations of certain lines in Stillinger's edition.

13. In the other five poems, it functions twice as an adjective and three times as a verb.

Works Cited

Anania, Michael. *In Natural Light.* Asphodel Press, 1999.

Culler, Jonathan. *Theory of the Lyric.* Harvard UP, 2015.

Deppman, Jed. *Trying to Think with Emily Dickinson.* U of Massachusetts Press, 2008.

Dickinson, Emily. *The Poems of Emily Dickinson: Variorum Edition* (3 vols). Edited by Ralph Franklin. Harvard UP, 1998.

Doty, Mark. *What Is the Grass: Walt Whitman in My Life.* Norton, 2020.

Graham, Lea. "A Range of Experience: Conversations in Place with Michael Anania." *Paper Streets,* Spring 2006.

Hayden, Robert. *Collected Poems.* Edited by Frederick Glaysher. Liveright Publishing, 2013.

Keats, John. *The Poems of John Keats.* Edited by Jack Stillinger. Harvard UP, 1978.

Miller, Cristanne. *Reading in Time: Emily Dickinson in the Nineteenth Century.* U of Massachusetts Press, 2012.

Milton, John. *Complete Poems and Major Prose of John Milton.* Edited by Merritt Y. Hughes,.Hackett Publishing, 1957.

O'Brien, Peggy. "Telling the Time with Emily Dickinson." *Massachusetts Review* vol. 55, no. 3, 2014, pp. 468–79.

O'Hara, Frank. *Lunch Poems.* City Lights Books, 1964.

Scheurer, Erika. "'Near, but remote': Emily Dickinson's Epistolary Voice." *The Emily Dickinson Journal* vol. 4, no. 1, Spring 1995, pp. 86–107. https://muse.jhu.edu/article/245289.

Weisbuch, Robert. *Emily Dickinson's Poetry.* U of Chicago Press, 1975.

———. "Prisming Dickinson; or, Gathering Paradise by Letting Go." *The Emily Dickinson Handbook.* Edited by Gudrun Grabher, Roland Hagenbüchle and Cristanne Miller. U of Massachusetts Press, 1998, pp. 197–223.

Michael Anania's Meta-Poetical Riff: "This Cup," These Rings, This Spiral

Celia Bland

"This Cup" opens with the equivalent of a long tracking shot: a sentence that runs effortlessly for fourteen five-line stanzas.

"This Cup" engages texts by Wallace Stevens, William Gass and *The New York Times* in a kind of interactive poetics. "This Cup" encourages us, Anania's readers, to participate in his practice and process of close-reading by providing in-line citations for these texts.

"This Cup," a poem from Michael Anania's 2017 collection *Continuous Showings*, opens with a visual link to Gass's novel *Willie Masters' Lonesome Wife*. That metafictional experiment, told primarily in the voice of the titular wife Babs, draws playful parallels between her body as a vessel for amorous advances and as a text for the reader's imaginative displacement. In *The Metafictional Muse*, scholar Larry McCaffery describes the process by which:

> The lonesome lady of the book's title, who is gradually revealed to be lady language herself, creates an elaborate series of devices which she hopes will draw attention to her slighted charms [and] force the reader to confront what she literally is: a physically exciting literary text. (172)

In other words, this novel, like "This Cup," "embod[ies] dimensions of reflexivity and formal uncertainty" (Waugh 2). This novel is, in the first edition that Anania cites as "*Tri-Quarterly*, 1968," a project of kerning fonts, multi-colored paper stocks, nudie photos, footnotes, and wandering narratives. "This Cup" is a playful tribute to Gass's novella and Gass's project; Anania, in fellowship, in remembrance, in celebration, will reveal the poetic armature by which he writes—and penetrates—a work of art. As Gass wrote: "poetry, like love is, in and out, a physical caress" (219).

If we were to map "This Cup" as a series of storyboards, Hitchcock-style, we would begin with the poet, his coffee cup, and a newspaper open to a review of Jhumpa Lahiri's short-story collection *Unaccustomed Earth*, illustrated with a photo of the author.

Action! The poet sips his coffee and places his cup on the newspaper, staining Lahiri's pixelated photo with a brown ring. Contemplating Lahiri's

> bright eyes,
> her modest round earring
> and stern but endearing
> refusal to smile (59)

encircled by a coffee stain that excerpts her "sweater set," the poet is reminded of the typographies of *Willie Masters' Lonesome Wife*, and the way "random" placement of coffee rings eventually "impose[d] an order of their own" upon its fractured storylines.

In "This Cup," Anania parallels Gass's imposition of order on a foundational substrata of texts. Anania accomplishes a Coleridgean hat trick—that is, he creates in one poem an elegy, paean and critique—prompting the reader to compose their own thoughts about the poem even as the poet marshals and builds his ideas.

"This Cup" defines a poetics even as it enacts one. It complicates the reader's experience in the way that a meta-fictional novel creates sub-plots that comment on the novel's action, characterization and "message" (scare quote *de rigeur*) even as the plot unfolds. The poet's cup, or more specifically, the coffee rings it casts, initiates a jar-equivalent: "This Cup" as commentary.

The first lines of "This Cup" echo Wallace Stevens' "Anecdote of a Jar." In Stevens' poem, an anomalous man-made jar, inviolate in its empty usefulness, tames Mother Nature. Randomly placed, it nevertheless becomes the center of the frame, the focus of the eye. Nature's chaotic feminine is dominated by a man-made object:

> I placed a jar in Tennessee,
> And round it was, upon a hill.
> It made the slovenly wilderness
> Surround that hill. (820)

Compare this to Anania's opening stanza:

> I placed a coffee cup
> on Jhumpa Lahiri's
> sweater set (*NY Times*
> *Book Review*, 4/6/08)
> and round it was, the stain
> of it, that is, and dark (59)

The poet's cup, or more specifically, the stain the cup leaves behind, encloses the beautiful novelist's chest within a tongue-in-cheek captioning, an editorial accident. Just as a coffee ring annotates the photo, a jar can alter the landscape's context. The shape of the ring is a jar's mouth, an eye open in surprise or terror. Anania's imagination, like Stevens' "slovenly wilderness," spirals in analogic "muddy ring[s]." His chromatic Ananian "take" on Stevens, Gass and photo creates a poetics of collaboration with the reader, with modernism by contextualizing "This Cup" as a chance operation. The rings are careless in both senses of the word:

> as though some
> careless reader had put
> his cup down here or there
> willy nilly, though the text
> begins to gather itself into
> the rings and eventually
> comments on them, so it's
> the writer not the reader
> or the writer as reader

> who was careless or perhaps
> deliberate and careless
> or deliberately careless
> with his cup (59–60)

As the epic first sentence finds its end in stanza fourteen, Anania maps new meaning-intersections of language and time, reminding the reader

> that there

> was a time of composition
> that preceded the book,
> its duration different
> in so many ways from the duration
> of reading, though each, reading

> and writing, can be put aside,
> each ringed by its own
> neglected cup,

> the circles
> left there imposing an order
> of their own, ungrammatical

> and asyntactic

The poet's recognition of Gass's coffee rings as a means toward artistic and textual self-awareness prompts readers to grapple with rings as thought-bubbles, as

> something
> the text seems to rise up toward
> the urgent way that messages
> rise through the inky black of
> an eight ball to tell us the future (61)

Words emerge in the eight ball's "small dark window" as if Fate were playing a part in the poem's composition, mimicking the way that words rise to the screen of the poet's mind. What is the significance of the circle/window that features nullities and validations: "*Most likely*" and "*Reply hazy, try again*"? Here is a coffee ring as a wheel of fortune, as Saturn's rings, as an instrument of divination.

These circles within circles may push the reader to reconsider Yeats's gyres, or another experiment with circles within circles, Robert Smithson's land art installation *Spiral Jetty*. Anomalous, immense, *Spiral Jetty* is a basalt fiddlehead projecting 1,500 feet into Utah's Great Salt Lake. It, like Stevens' jar, offers "a gallant attempt to teach Nature her proper place"—Oscar Wilde's definition of art.

Its rings-within-rings, to appropriate Anania's words, "impos[e] an order/of their own," by focusing the way viewers "read" the landscape. Spectators inevitably become a part of the work, perceiving it and being perceived in relation to it.

In its useless grandiosity, its domination of the desert landscape and its domination by weather, water tables and time, we see what Anania calls a "tangle of causes at once/intended and accidental" (Crump). *Spiral Jetty* can only truly be seen from the air—a requirement for his art, according to Smithson, necessitated by the bombings of Cambodia in 1969–70. "Land art," writes *Brooklyn Rail* critic Jason Rosenfeld, "treats the earth as an object, as a surface to be changed and manipulated" (Rosenfield). *Spiral Jetty* was never intended to be finished; sea levels and weather affect our experience of it. It is submerged under water for years at a time. Currently all 6000 tons of its rock structure are visible, but, fifty years later, it has become eroded and discolored by salt.

Which brings us into the undertones of 1960s experimentation and radicalism submerged in the references for "This Cup." *The Lonesome Wife*, published in 1968 at the height of civil unrest in the United States, flaunts conventions of the genre of fiction. *Spiral Jetty*, completed in 1970, confounds expectations for art's materials, its scale and installation. Both works question the "use" of art, its relationship to its reader/viewer. Gass uses *double entendres*, asterisks, puns and non-linear narratives to prick readers' assumptions and relay a flashpoint temporality. Art is empty as that jar, awaiting the participation of nature and human, imagination and flesh. On the last page of his novel

In the Heart of the Heart of the Country, Gass asserts the need for a

> diction which contains the quaint, the rare, the technical, the obsolete, the old, the lent, the nonce, the local slang and argot of the street, in neighborly confinement. Our tone should suit our time: uncommon quiet dashed with common thunder. (62)

His work—like our examples by Anania and Smithson—practice the tenets of self-conscious meta-fiction (a term Gass invented in 1970). One might even posit that the subtext of "This Cup" elegizes the loss of an art radicalized by energy, of a time that valued such experiments. This poem elegizes an anarchic approach to art's conception and execution—lost in this jaded, ironic age.

In its final stanzas, "This Cup" returns to the coffee ring "blistering" Lahiri's "stern" photo. Unlike the fictional Babs, the very real Lahiri only plays the muse; as a successful author she resists the poet's attempt to create his own "physically exciting literary text" (McCaffery 172) with the reader's knowledge of her own mastery of fictive consciousness and versatile syntax. The poet's meditations on her photo—"at once fictive and tangible"—move to the two "mother-of-pearl or plastic" buttons of Lahiri's sweater. Here, in describing Lahiri's buttons, Anania provides a near-quotation from earlier in the poem. His quotation of Gass's "this is / the moon of daylight" becomes in Anania's own words "twin / crescent moons in their own daylight." The poet links these moons to "the last coffee stain" of *The Lonesome Wife*—the one encircling Bab's navel.

The reader may be forgiven for considering this eight-ball of a navel in a Babsian light; do these ocular coffee-moons cast Lahiri's button moons as models of mammary circles?

Should we reconsider the author photo, that stained and blistered artifact, in the light of Gass's salacious classic? Who is to say that these two moons aren't Lahiri's breasts illuminating Anania's poetic exertions? ("Mother" of pearl, indeed!) Struggle as she may against fulfilling Bab's traditional role as "lady language" penetrated by male poets, she has certainly been blistered by his virtuosity. His chance-muse has produced a very real artifact of thought—"This Cup"—and revealed the multi-layered apparatus of writing—and "nailing" (to use Babs' word)—a work of art.

Certainly, the poet's meta-poetic melding of *Tristram Shandy*-style hypertextuality with a beautifully composed and yet informal poetic voice—has moved the poem, in Lockean terms, from sense to impression to perception to concept. The thought-experiment of "This Cup" exposes the apparatus of reading—and writing—a work of art. Further, the reader's textured experience of this poem and this project models a chance operation of composition and revision: "*Signs point to yes.*"

The poet's own awareness—like the reader's—is heightened by a thoughtful movement from poem process of thought, to poem as artifact of thought, stained but shining. At its conclusion, "This Cup," chalice-like, holds the potentiality of poetic imagination. The reader has been invited into an amplified comprehension of how

> words [are]
> pressed against the ball's small,
> dark window so briefly
> it is often hard to be sure
>
> what you read there (62)

Thusly, this poem illuminates the ways human lives—so brief!—are pressed against the ball of the earth, lit by the ball of the moon. But sometimes—"*Signs point to yes*"—they catch some ambient light and create, for a moment, their own daylight.

Works Cited

Anania, Michael. *Continuous Showings*. MadHat Press, 2017.

Bioy Casares, Adolfo. *The Invention of Morel*. NYRB Classics, 2013.

Crump, James (director). *Troublemakers: The Story of Land Art*. First Run Features, 2015.

Gass, William. *In the Heart of the Heart of the Country*. NYRB Classics, 2015.

———. *Willie Masters' Lonesome Wife*. Dalkey Archive Press, 1989.

Gorgoni, Gianfranco. "Fifty Years of *Spiral Jetty*/Simthson and Gorgoni." From the Portfolio *Smithson's Spiral Jetty Photographs, 1970–2014*. Utah Museum of Fine Arts, 15 November 2020, https://umfa.utah.edu/50-years-of-spiral-jetty.

Hicks, Tyler. Photograph: "Jhumpa Larihi." *New York Times*. April 6, 2008. https://www.nytimes.com/2008/04/06/books/review/Schillinger3-t.html.

McCaffery, Larry. *The Metafictional Muse: The Works of Robert Coover, Donald Barthelme, and William H. Gass*. U of Pittsburgh Press, 1982.

Rosenfeld, Jason. 2017. "Walter De Maria and The Lightning Field at Forty: Art as Symbiosis." *The Brooklyn Rail*. 17 December 2017. https://brooklynrail.org/2017/12/artseen/Walter-De-Maria-and-The-Lightning-Field.

Waugh, Patricia. *Metafiction: The Theory and Practice of Self-Conscious Fiction*. Routledge, 1984.

Michael Anania: "Some Other Spring"

Paul Hoover

When I was his student at University of Illinois Chicago in the early 1970s, Michael was one of the professors in the newly founded Creative Writing emphasis of the English Department. The other poets were Paul Carroll, who had edited *Big Table*, which had helped to establish the Beats, and John Frederick Nims who had once edited *Poetry* and was formalist in his poetics. Michael had been a student of Charles Olson at SUNY Buffalo and that influence was apparent in his poetry and reading interests. There was a delicacy and precision in his work and a keen sense of the poetic line, but you would not think *Black Mountain* when you read it.

Anania's editing of Swallow Press was important, and he had a strong following on campus. An entertaining lecturer, he knew much about poetry, the breadth of which impresses me even more today. He was a fluent conversationalist, quick-witted and honest. I have never had a conversation with him in which I did not learn something. He is good company.

I would like to focus on what I will call living realism in Michael's *In Natural Light*, for instance in his poem "Some Other Spring (for Teddy Wilson)":

> "You know how it goes,"
>   he said—the quick shift
>   of light and dark, the day

>   itself like music,
>   playing, an instance
>   of balance, presumed,
>
>   like the moment,
>   entirely imagined,
>   then seen, when the ball
>
>   hesitates, spinning, against
>   blue sky, bright day, its
>   first green dawn along
>
>   dark branches, the arc
>   of so much to account
>   for in time, time in his
>
>   left hand's intermittent
>   certainties, the right
>   airborne, at play, playing. (27–28)

It is a portrait of a great pianist playing, especially that moment of stop-time inherent in jazz. Stop-time is the moment of understanding, gravity and the actual. It is what poetry searches for when its mode is realism, not the mythic or historical (which bears its own myths), the speculative or the fictive. It is life itself action, as seen by one who knows and marvels. Teddy Wilson is studiously and actively *at play*. However, the poem's tone is not one of playfulness. Its focus is on lightness as weight, in the Italo Calvino sense: "Lightness for me goes with precision and determination, not with vagueness and the haphazard. Paul Valéry said, 'One should be like a bird, and not like a feather'" (qtd. in Calvino 16).

In the poem's cinema, stop-time occurs

>   like the moment
>   entirely imagined
>   then seen, when the ball

hesitates, spinning against
blue sky, bright day (27)

Our point of view is just beneath the apex of a spinning ball tossed. It is "entirely imagined" but we love the moment for its lasting reality. It is that quality with its undeniable clarity that can serve as a moral model: *claritas, gravitas* and *levitas*. The real is also established by the book's title, *In Natural Light.* It is not theatrical, metaphysical or philosophical. It is the light you see when you open your door to a field. It is also common sense and world embodiment for which readers are grateful. The poem's realism consists of a moment of balance, the hand suspended above the keys. Silence is experiencing "intermittent certainties."

When I was his student, Michael once referred to the "fictive" quality of my poems. I had not conceived of my work that way, but his comment was insightful. Raised in a German idealist religion and by nature Platonist, I was creating philosophical fictions. The English metaphysical poets have always been high on my list. The poem "Some Other Spring" is philosophical in another way. It presents rather than represents, which is admirable. It invites us to join in a moment that we immediately recognize as graceful and truthful. Imagine a glass of water on a table in a Harold Pinter play.

Popular American movies are often based on heroic fantasy, featuring gods and cartoon demons. Marvel comics is the source of such Nietzschean cinema. It is entertaining, but its philosophy is dystopic. It asks us to join in capitalist, expansionist and imperialist values. To find the fringe in American movies, you have to go to low-budget productions about real life, for example *Silver Linings Playbook.* Michael's poem asks us instead to imagine a blue ball reaching its apex, backwards spinning. The drama lies in the real, in semblance. When it is over, there are no severed heads on the landscape, and the New York cops still wear soft blue hats.

Different as they were in style, Williams and Stevens both valued common objects like red wheelbarrows and blackbirds. Stevens wrote that poetry is "that which suffices" (qtd. in Hoover). Its charm lies in being just enough. Something necessary happened one evening when the listening was bright, and the player's hand was paused above the keys. In perfect stop-time, it is just what we needed.

Works Cited

Anania, Michal. "Some Other Spring". *In Natural Light*. Asphodel Press, 1999.

Calvino, Italo. *Six Memos for the Next Millennium*. Translated by Patrick Creagh. Harvard UP, 1988.

Hoover, Paul. Interview by Melissa Hohl. *Colorado Review*, 10 April 2014, https://coloradoreview.colostate.edu/2014/04/paul-hoover-interview-for-the-colorado-review/.

Another Cowboy in the Boat of Ra

Sterling Plumpp

I have known Michael Anania for over forty years. While we were, in fact, colleagues for three decades or more, I came to know him in a variety of roles. During our time and in our engagement at the University of Illinois–Chicago, he supported me in many ways. For the sake of confidentiality, I cannot comment on all of them. At the same time, I can say with great certainty that he has been responsible for numerous events that enhanced my career: readings, publications and awards.

Anania is diversity. He grew up in Omaha, Nebraska, where athletic greats such as Bob Gibson, Bob Boozer and Gale Sayers were born. Educated in the East, Anania possesses the linguistic acumen of a New Yorker. Knowing region, recognizing difference and measuring distance, he, literality, bobs and weaves through the language. In this display of mastery as a poet—tracing the nuances of diverse languages and musical idioms—he is able to suggest the skill of a jazz trumpeter with his sudden (slick) line breaks, what I call riffs. A big band virtuoso.

Michael laid the foundation for excellence in the Creative Writing program at UIC through the remarkable reading series he organized. Chairing this series, which brought a number of notable writers to campus, including Nobel laureates V. S. Naipaul, Derek Wolcott and Toni Morrison, he pushed the program and extended its boundaries, inspiring his colleagues and our students.

I was hired into the UIC English Department in 1971. Almost immediately, Dean D. B. Doner asked me to transfer into African

American Studies. This provided me with an opportunity to work with Grace Holt, assembling a curriculum and attracting faculty members for a fledgling program in an emerging field. Michael proved to be a staunch supporter of African American Studies as it evolved from a program to a department. Always totally honest, his support, along with that of Professor LaVonne Ruoff, was vital to the growth and success of African American Studies at UIC. As senior faculty within disciplinary departments, Michael had a say in African American Studies hires, due to it being an interdisciplinary curriculum. Never easy, these negotiations required a quick mind and a broad smile. Michael met the criteria.

Anania is an oddity: a cowboy in New York wardrobe, which is to say he is unique. Someone writing poetry that reflects intellect and excellent training. With his art and scholarship he has continued to navigate minds over diverse landscapes.

A Tribute to the Collaborative Spirit of Michael Anania

Simone Muench & Jackie K. White

Since the two of us first met as students of Michael Anania at the University of Illinois, Chicago in the early 2000s, he has had a profound influence on our work—first, as individual poets, and more recently, as we've been writing collaborative poems—mainly through his encouragement to take risks, frequently quoting the Frank O'Hara anecdote, "You just go on your nerve. If someone's chasing you down the street with a knife you just run, you don't turn around and shout, 'Give it up! I was a track star for Mineola Prep'" (875).

In fact, we would argue that Michael's pedagogy and its continued influence on his students can best be summed up by the word "encouragement," with its sense of advocacy, but highlighting more its intent "to make brave." In the classroom, Michael embodied the following assertion by Kenneth Koch: "You make yourself happy by saying 'infinitesimal.' If you say 'the infinitesimal sun,' it's wonderful. It's not any good, but it's not to be disdained. To disdain it is like going around cutting down the first little green shoots in the garden: you never get any flowers" (155). His encouragement, like his overall teaching style and his approach to the reading of his students' poems, was also challenging, as it centered on finding— and teaching the student-poet to find—the crux of the poem and the structure and language which the poem itself demanded. To do so, he would ask us to fulfill those demands with a freshness of diction, a tightening of syntax, and especially, a sharpness of form and voice—the poet's authentic voice and vision, free of self-absorption and faux sentiment.

Both Michael's lectures and workshops constantly emphasized language, not ego; repeating the phrase "poetry is about language, not feelings." In many ways, the process of collaboration addresses his concept beautifully because collaborative writing constantly sidelines individual ego and thereby calls for recentering language. Not surprisingly then, Michael also placed emphasis on the joy of collaboration, as he would frequently speak of the pleasures and insights found in his own collaborative endeavors with artist Ed Colker and others.

Michael, in an endorsement of the book *Disappearing Address,* wrote that successful collaborative work "feels entirely seamless, as though it were not a collaboration at all but the work of a single, virtuoso poet with a very broad range of imagery and a finely tuned sense of how diction can coalesce varied materials." Since we began writing collaboratively, we have striven for that sense of seamlessness, that third-voice that is neither of ours. And, because Michael repeatedly stressed risk-taking, in developing the following poem as homage to him, we decided to add a new third voice to our collaborative efforts: Michael's. Influenced also by his teachings on Gaston Bachelard and the resonance of *Poetics of Space* within Michael's poetry, we drew from his poems both as an ignition device and as a source for our scaffold of images with special attention to what he would call "the resonant particular." In that way, we hope our poem illustrates Bachelard's blend of "the space of intimacy and world space" (203), such that, as Michael once noted [in a PhD exam], "the poem is an element of spontaneous myth, engages more than its elements, has a hyper-reality, and offers a threshold that invites participation." If that is so, our poem, in its blending of cento-like Michael lines with our two intermingled voices, features a very Ananiaian method for tribute: wave and breath, sentences and ceremony becoming a three-forked river that all leads to the sea. A fusing of our three voices as "Midwest travelers."

Works Cited

Anania, Michael. Blurb for *Disappearing Address*.

Bachelard, Gaston. *The Poetics of Space.* Translated by Maria Jolas. Beacon, 1994, p. 203.

Jenks, Philip and Simone Muench. *Disappearing Address.* BlazeVox, 2010.

Koch, Kenneth. *The Art of Poetry: Poems, Parodies, Interviews, Essays, and Other Work.* U of Michigan Press, 1996, p. 155.

O'Hara, Frank. "Personism: A Manifesto." *Postmodern American Poetry,* 2nd ed. Edited by Paul Hoover. Norton, 2013, pp. 875–76.

Midwest Traveler

for Michael Anania

I have traveled this river south,
he said, midwest traveler, rowing the words
in our ears: *Here. Hold this. Feel this—*
the breath of things quickening.

From hazelnut to bridge, highway to leaf,
something is certain to carry
shadows of boats that appear flickering,
dreams fluttering like pages—

they are nodding, *yes, yes,* palms pressed
as if to oar or pen or lover's palms,
scattering the thousand prisms of self,
one more loose sentence to puzzle over.

Ceremony is, after all,
the pulse within all bodies;
the impulse in each one of us
"to find a pathway in a field of doubt."

We are a multiplying sigh
between breath and breath, restless,
altering what we see with what we sing,
its swirling sentences like fire in motion.

This is, I suppose, how we hold the sun's
luminous text, in bright lines there,
and visible as waves, the river's wavelets,
and just as fleeting and timeless.

Be Like Mike

Jeffery Renard Allen

One of the great things about poets is that they know a lot of stuff. I recall Michael imparting this piece of wisdom in a workshop almost thirty years ago. Of course the statement was first of all true about himself. He knew a lot of stuff about a lot of things. At the time, I was a student in the graduate Creative Writing program at the University of Illinois at Chicago. I was primarily a fiction writer, but UIC allowed us to take workshops in both fiction and poetry. I was in my mid-twenties and struggling to figure out much about the world and myself. I thought that by engaging with poetry as a poet myself I could, if nothing else, unlock some of the secrets of language. But poetry was mostly a puzzle for me.

Michael seemed to be at once erudite and casual, with plenty of anecdotes and examples at hand. And he was often humorous. Once he said to the class, "When I told my mother that I was going to be a poet, she started crying." Of course we all laughed. But it would take me years to recognize the lesson in that joke.

Michael was the embodiment of style in the way that he dressed, on the one hand far more formal than most writers, and on the other, put together with an elegance that few professors achieved. A tallish man, you always saw him outfitted in a snazzy blazer complemented by slacks that were just the right color, his collared and buttoned shirt complimented by just the right silk tie, then the socks with creases and patterns, and fine leather shoes, always freshly polished. A precise dresser.

Michael often talked about precision in poetry, perhaps a quality he valued more than anything else. His poems are clean and linear, and perfectly voiced, and as a teacher he had much to say about such matters in the work of some of the poets he admired most: Frank O'Hara, Robert Duncan, Robert Creeley, James Wright, Denise Levertov, Kenneth Koch, John Ashbery and C. S. Giscombe, among others. Since many of these writers were friends, you were always lucky when Michael passed on some choice detail in that pre-Internet age. John Ashbery calls himself a girl. But speaking about the writer was always a way of speaking about the aesthetics that informed a poem. For this reason, casual moments with Michael—at dinner, or at a bar, at a reading—were also opportunities to learn. He had the generosity of a great editor, which he in fact was at Swallow Press and for a number of periodicals.

I recall standing with Michael once in the poetry section of the bookstore, where a Michael Ondaatje volume was on display.

"Do you like his work?" I asked.

Michael took the book off the shelf and turned to a page. "Look how quickly that moves," he said. He followed the lines with a finger. When he read poems aloud, both his own poems and the work of others, he had the habit of raising one hand then pointing with his index and tracing the rhythms of the poem on the air. So, speed and lightness, these were important qualities. Michael was a formalist in this way, holding little regard for narrative poetry; and he had an intense dislike for confessional verse, an aesthetic that he found self-indulgent, outdated, and simply boring.

Michael was unlike many poets in that he read widely in fiction, and was an accomplished fiction writer himself. In my time at UIC, I had the privilege of meeting a number of world-class fiction writers that Michael brought to campus, including John Edgar Wideman, Ishmael Reed, Gilbert Sorrentino (whose poetry Michael admired for its precision), and Toni Morrison, who had tears in her eyes after she read a section from *Song of Solomon*.

Michael was my mentor in so many ways, but he was also a friend. I could fill up pages recounting the times when I did something boneheaded and Michael came to my rescue. He never chastised me or judged me.

I recall him saying, "You think that the problems are all outside in the world, when in actuality the true problems are inside." At the time, I had no idea what he was talking about, blinded as I was then by my hodgepodge belief in a kind of Marxist humanism mixed with some good old-fashioned, pseudo-African mysticism.

Michael always seemed to maintain his cool, even in awkward public moments. For example, at the oral defense for my dissertation, another professor was talking (favorably) about my short stories in a way that Michael clearly found ridiculous. He simply said, "These stories are in the Gothic tradition of Nathaniel Hawthorne."

The other professor, an African American like myself, did not take kindly to the comparison. Said, "You certainly seem to know a lot about it."

"Yes I do," Michael said. And that was that.

In my final semester at UIC I found myself in a happy conundrum, as I had two job offers, one at a university in Kentucky, the other at a university in New York. For Michael, it was a no-brainer. "You're competitive," he said. "You should go to New York."

I had never thought of myself that way.

Just one of the many things I learned from Michael back then. But our friendship has continued to this day.

I have so much to say about how Michael supported the publications of my books, and how he has supported me professionally in many other ways over these past thirty years. Truth to tell, because he knows things, he will always be a mentor. Indeed, I often turn to him for advice about one thing or another. Who are you reading these days? What painters interest you? Did you hear the new album by ___? What do you think about ___? What is your favorite restaurant in Rome? Did you catch that Lakers game the other night?

Last fall, I suffered through a disheartening experience where I was outvoted by my fellow judges on a jury board for a highly prestigious award, the book most deserving of the award losing out to a far less-accomplished book. For weeks after, I found myself in a bad space, completely disillusioned with the literary world. I told Michael about it.

"These things are always political," he said.

Of course.

But my relationship with Michael for the last thirty years has always been that way: of course.

Now I value the rare times when Michael and I are able to see each other at a book festival or a reading, or when he can visit with my students—rare occasions in Chicago, or Austin, or New York, or Charlottesville, times where we can slip away from writers and the life and enjoy a good meal. Ever the conversationalist, Michael has many stories. And he knows things.

Introduction to *"Gratia, Poeta!"* in Glorious Past-O-Vision!

Frank Rogeczewski

Day four of my PhD exams: Poetics. I've pretty well aced the first three and this one should be a proverbial stroll in the park. Five or ten minutes of mulling over the prompts and I boldly begin this final exam with what I consider an O'Hara-esque sendup/tribute to the history of poetics. No ideas but in *thinks*. However, after a page or so I begin to worry that perhaps some part of my committee will perceive this supposed-to-be serious examination essay a bit too much like one of my prose poems and by way of *argumentum a simili* downgrade or diss this last of my final exams. As my *alma mater* is the University of Illinois–Chicago, what then is Michael Anania but "my brudder from anudder mudder"? But also, my mentor and at times my proverbial model.

Anania warns a Modern Poetry class that Ezra Pound was not just fooling around with fascism; he informs a workshop student who's written a quasi-surreal garden poem that she really shouldn't title it "Strange Fruit." [During discussion of] one of my lefty poems in a graduate workshop, he likens the radicalism of Percy Shelley to the Communist Party, William Blake's to the Trotskyites. He suggests I might somehow get into the poem the look or feel of the woodcuts that appeared in *New Masses* or *Rebel Poet*. Michael Anania knows where a poem wants to go.

David Ray Vance and Catherine Kasper will fall in love in these workshops. I will try to take Anania up on the woodcuts idea. I will write an essay on the raging debate: is LANGUAGE poetry a revolutionary disruption of the commodification of language or is it pretentious moving wallpaper? Mike Barrett and I will have a beer upon arriving at the UIC Writing Program's student and faculty readings at the campus lounge one evening. Michael Anania will read the silence and music of his lines.

Coming from a working-class background—as did many of us—Anania reacted to the university with the proper amounts of respect for intelligence and creativity and irritation with academic applesauce (it's not made from real apples). He handled the academic milieu with confidence and he built with us a camaraderie poetical ever after. He dedicated the poem "Considerations in Time" in *Heat Lines* to David and Catherine. Anania argues the LANGUAGE poets are postmodern surrealists. In workshop he tells the story of Carl Sandburg at an event for the Brotherhood of Sleeping Car Porters. Sandburg is up on the stage repeating the union's name again and again to hear the music, the beauty of the name and what it stands for. *The Brotherhood. Of Sleeping Car. Porters. The Brother. Hood of Sleep. Ing Car Porters.* "It's something a poet would do," Anania explains, "but it didn't go over well with the whole audience."

This is the fate of my final essay as well. One [doctoral committee] party pooper misconstrues my serial sketches as moving wallpaper. Then there's the clatter and clamor of my heart in my brain as I get nervous at the first of the oral exams. But years later when Michael Anania retires, I take up the *argumentum a simili* as sword and shield—or maybe crucifix and wooden stake—and do us both proud.

Gratia, Poeta!

Well, that settles it. I looked up her website and there's not one
mention of Charisma Carpenter, who plays the role of Cordelia
on the TV show *Angel*, being the daughter of John Carpenter
(director of *Vampires, Ghosts of Mars, Prince of Darkness*, the
original *Halloween*, and the remake of *The Thing*). This means the
greatest father/daughter horror team of all time existed only in
my *imagination*, a word for a concept that has pretty much always
been with us poets, albeit in a somewhat ambiguous relationship
with *fancy*, that being an abbreviation of *fantasy*, from the Latin
phantasia, itself a transliteration from the Greek, making all these
terms more or less kissing-cousins, but I don't want to get all
ancient aesthetically philosophical or etymologically medieval
on you, so I'll skip right to the part where Michael Anania used
to mention in workshops that getting into and out of the poem
were two of the most difficult tricks for a poet. Also, he made it
clear that you have to earn your O's. In the postmodern world
of today the time's long past when the poet can get away with
exclaiming all over the poem, let alone apostrophizing this, that,
and the other Muse. People just can't suspend disbelief in your
transmogrification of an abstraction. When I first signed on as
an undergrad, I was like, "Yeats, Yeats, Yeats." I sounded more
like a poodle than a poet. Michael Anania and Ralph Mills were
kind enough to bring me over to America and plant me a bit
more firmly in the 20th century—William Carlos Williams, Ezra
Pound, Frank O'Hara, Susan Howe. It's a good thing too. I stopped
dreaming of ascending in the ranks of The Hermetic Order of
the Golden Dawn—from novice to cloak-holder, I'd fancy—and
started thinking more seriously about poetics in the late 20th/
early 21st century, which, of course, reminds us that *Angel* is a
spin-off from the TV version of *Buffy the Vampire Slayer*, which
stars Sarah Michelle Gellar and apparently is going off the air this
spring. The character Angel, played by David Boreanaz on the

71

eponymous TV show, is a vampire cursed with a soul so that he
suffers remorse over the evil he has committed and now wants to
fight for justice—and also for truth and beauty, I like to think, you
know, being a poet and all. In his role as professor of literature, if
Michael found you reading *Nova* in class, instead of, "That doesn't
go here," it'd be, "You read Chip Delany?" He wouldn't express
the same enthusiasm for, say, Stephen King. I'm on my own there.
Michael doesn't read anything more graveyard than the graveyard
poets, who were a meditative and melancholy bunch, and guess
what was their favorite setting for those meditations—meaning I'm
grateful that a poet who could see exactly where any poem wanted
to go spent time on my poetry, which always wants to go places
like Frankenstein's laboratory, Dracula's crypt, Freddy Krueger's
boiler room, It's sewer main, the Dead's shopping mall outside of
Pittsburgh, and the Bates Motel. Named after an Avon perfume,
Charisma Carpenter began playing the role of Cordelia, a high-
school friend of the vampire slayer, on *Buffy* and then graduated
to *Angel* with that show's premiere. And though Charisma had
only a handful of commercials and a guest appearance on *Baywatch*
on her resume, and though Sarah Michelle Gellar has starred in
Scooby-Doo, won a Blockbuster Award for Best Supporting Actress
for her role in *I Know What You Did Last Summer*, and has become
a spokesperson for Maybelline, I've always thought Charisma
the more interesting actress. Sexier too, especially now that she's
impregnated with a demon fetus and positively evil herself. (You
would think people would be *negatively* evil, but it never works out
that way—some situations simply cry out for an oxymoron.) I guess
you could say that for me Sarah Michelle Gellar is like the fancy
and Charisma Carpenter the imagination. In the Romantic sense
of the terms. You know, where Blake's like, "Imagination is spiritual
sensation" and Coleridge is like, "It dissolves ... in order to recreate
or ... to idealize and to unify," comparing the imagination (in a
more or less roundabout way) to "the eternal act of creation in the
infinite I AM." Where fancy "is no other than a mode of memory
emancipated from the order of time and space." Now you can see

why John Carpenter should be her father. With his fine sense of
the horror film ad her presence and acting skill, why, we'd return
to a new heyday of horror, one recalling sublime partnerings of
previous eras—Elsa Lanchester and James Whale, Janet Leigh and
Alfred Hitchcock, Jamie Lee Curtis and John Carpenter. Not that
I'm in any way putting down Sarah Michelle Gellar. Even though
William Carolos Williams says, "Yes, the imagination, drunk with
prohibitions, has destroyed and recreated everything afresh in the
likeness of that which it was," the fancy is no slouch either. It may
even be—since *imagination* came to be used by the Romans as a
substitute for *phantasia*—that fancy and imagination are cousins
that've been doing more than kissing. Or they are Siamese Twins.
And if I were still a member of the Hermetic Order of the Golden
Dawn, I'd have to wonder whether there wasn't some cosmic
conspiracy at work when *Buffy the Vampire Slayer* goes off the air
at the same time Michael Anania retires. Well, there probably is. I
mean, how do you thank someone for sharing his knowledge of
poets and poetry, his way with line breaks and pentameter? Those
of us who've learned from Michael Anania consider ourselves
spin-offs from a more critically acclaimed, popular, and longer
running TV show. Coleridge's secondary imagination related to
the primary imagination, so to speak. Whoa! All these imaginations
and fancies in my head! They're making me dizzy and I didn't
even take my antihistamine today. And did you ever notice how
the pharmaceuticals these days sound like something from the old
Flash Gordon series? With his pals, Dr. Zyrtek and Dale Allegra,
Flash faces the Emperor Ming and the evil Princess Viagra. By
the way, I thought I saw Michael Anania on TV, standing next to
Mayor Daley at a celebration of Chicago's one hundred and sixty-
fifth year, and I thought, "Wouldn't that be something if Michael
retired into a whole other career: his own TV show—if not on the
WB, perhaps on UPN, in the time slot *Buffy*'s left unfilled?" It's not
unheard of—a poet on TV. Somebody told me he'd seen Charles
Bernstein reading a phone book with Jon Lovitz on a Yellow Pages
Commercial. Can you imagine? Longinus sees in the imagination

the source of the sublime when "moved by enthusiasm and passion you seem to see things whereof you speak and place them before the eyes of your hearers." Anyway, it's certainly a show I'd watch, whether Michael played a vampire slayer or a poet/professor. And O! Charisma Carpenter! If you would co-star with him, that would be marvelous!

Michael in the '80s

Vainis Aleksa

Michael once began a graduate poetry workshop by reading a poem about Donatello's statue of young David. We got riled up, outdoing each other with interpretations of the poem's rich resonance. "Who's it by, Michael?" It was by one of the sophomores in his undergraduate workshop. We were hushed. Michael said, "Poetry is not always a matter of experience, vocation, or sometimes even will. It can happen at any point of a writer's life, even in the beginning and even only once." This wasn't meant to humiliate. At the moment, the poem seemed better than anything he wrote as well. Eventually we got it. Poetry is bigger than any individual author. Poems are less created than surrendered to. Doing poetry included letting go of our own poems, ourselves.

Michael loved the story of how his friend Charles Boer stood up in the middle of a poetry conference and said, "Guys, it's just poetry." It was "just poetry" for Michael, too. What he meant was that poetry was not an end in itself. He didn't like self-referential poems. Poetry had to pay homage to experience. In the end, this was no simple matter, as it did not diminish any of Michael's love of language or conviction that lyricism had power to make us see and hear what matters most. Poetry was, as it was for Williams, a "wedge" into experience, a way of opening experience up so that the world could see itself naked and full of wonder.

What Michael himself found after cracking open experience was something that was in plain sight all along. Michael talked of H.D.'s father, an astronomer, who used to spend his nights looking through a telescope. Michael saw that this influenced H.D.'s own powers of observation. In a sense, poems like H.D.'s about the seaside were the result of scientific meticulousness and careful looking. For Michael, who was quoting a lot from *Scientific American* in those days, poetry was as good as science in arguing for what is really there. For Michael, of course, poetry built on such foundations could not help but take science a step further, towards what?

Good observation was both sensual and metaphysical. Michael felt he had to teach us that. Our assumptions were by and large what he called "post religious." A kind of positivism seemed to dominate our perspective, making it hard to capture the part of the poem that exceeded the concrete. "Twenty thousand years of humanity had it wrong. In the last century we got it figured out. No spirit, no after life." Michael's sarcasm didn't stem from religiosity or mysticism, but Duncan's poems about "she that is under the hill" were always on his mind. The best way to understand Michael's sense of spirit was his democratic understanding of archaeology. "Dig down *anywhere*, and you'll find something." For Michael, it is important that the land we stand on is impregnated with pieces of the past. Whether we let it or not, those things are attached to the forces that shape us, pull us back into the land. That's what his *Riversongs* is about. The poet cannot trace the steps of Louis and Clark, not because the factories along the river stand in the way, but because the river is too populated with the spirit of the past. The poet learns that he can make contact by simply standing still and looking hard. In plain sight are the same kinds of trees, the same bluffs, the same moon, the same current, the same words. They refract time for the poet, who extends himself into the penumbra of experience, retrieving a full, though often plain-looking, life.

Michael talked. Conversations were not bound by the classroom. Often, talk began in an elevator and continued after class in the hallway by his office. It was expansive talk, determined, opinionated, concentrated, piercing, deep and joyful. The conversation did not count unless someone was quoting and counter-quoting. But finally, the goal of almost any conversation was to get inside a poem. Not to figure it out, not to judge or classify it, but to stay suspended in it—doing the opposite of the so called "unpacking" of literature—this was its packing. Talking was about creating another expanded version of the poem in a parallel universe. It was the best kind of schooling for a young poet, always leaving you with dozens of fresh ideas for new poems.

Michael's work at the university was characterized by sociability. Michael was always at school, always with visitors in his office. People hung out, sprawled in the hallway by his office door. The vicinity became an occasion for poetry. You didn't have to be directly talking to him When he read aloud, it would be loud enough for us to hear in the hall. He read better than anybody. I learned Pound, not through scholarship, but through the inflections in Michael's voice, making Pound seem as straightforward as the evening news.

They weren't easy times. The writing program was still trying to catch up; where were the women poet professors? Why was everyone so doggone European? So straight? Michael was at the center, taking the hits as well as giving them out. Comments in workshops were easily overdetermined. Some people sat through the classes smoldering. Michael kept it all from spinning out by focusing on the poem. Even the most disgruntled poets recognized what a powerful reader he was, articulating the premise of a poem, and then using its own rules to dictate what belongs where. Poets who worked with Michael continue to include him in their imaginary audience—what would Michael find tiring? Simply clever? Not musical? Sometimes he would pull you aside and say, "This one is really good." But never in the public eye of the workshop. You scored when he didn't say all that much, but kept rereading the poem, performing it for you. No matter how inexperienced a poet was, it seemed that at least once during a semester the stars would come together, and a poem worked and was read by Michael.

Michael's favorite Frank O'Hara story: a thief holds up O'Hara in a stairwell as O'Hara is heading home. The thief asks for money. O'Hara says, "I ain't got time for that kind of crap" and keeps going, *only* to get shot in the ass. Michael didn't waste time either. He couldn't—there was too much to know, too much life to appreciate. I still remember the range of topics on some days: Heidegger, the red shift of starlight, the balance of Mozart's triplets, Keats, sailing—handled as if he had been researching and reflecting on each topic for years. I learned about Derrida in a poetry workshop a full year before I heard any other professor mention him. Michael was so many different things to so many different people. Like Pound, Michael could outtalk anyone, but unlike Pound, he was good-humored and knew how to pull just about anyone into an energizing and positive take on life.

Out of Ordinary:
The Extraordinary Collaboration
of Michael Anania and Ed Colker

Lea Graham

Art is, in many cases, about ordinary people doing extraordinary things and extraordinary people working with and out of the ordinary. It is, of course, difficult to think of Michael Anania as an ordinary person in his ability to imbue the ordinary with significance and grace. In knowing his work, we are led, as readers and writers, into awe before our own experience. As Vainis Aleksa noted in his essay "Michael in the '80s": "Poetry for Anania, as it was for Williams, [is] a 'wedge' into experience, a way of opening experience up so that the world [can] see itself naked and full of wonder" (81). Anania has maintained an allegiance to this "wedge" in his poems, novel and essays; his enduring interest in other artistic forms and, notably, with the *ordinary* production of art.

Anania's interest in artistic production includes a knowledge of typography and the production of journals which came through his work in the 1960s and 1970s as editor of Swallow Press. The press was housed in an old warehouse at 1139 South Wabash Avenue in Chicago. According to the poet Charles Boer, "You had to go up to the office floor on an open freight lift loaded with crates and supplies. It made you feel that the poetry you were producing was an actual tangible product, more like a pipe than a pipe dream" (9). Anania's immersion in production, the everyday handling of paper and poems comes across on his own page, his own poems time and again. He has an affinity for the tactile or to connect with one of his early and enduring influences, Williams' "made thing." As the critic Leslie Fiedler stated, Anania "manages to remain faithful to the homeliness of colloquial American speech and yet somehow rescues it from banality, endows it with elegance and grace" (7). This faithfulness to the ordinary, the turn towards elegance and knowledge of made things, neither elitist nor exclusionary, intersects with the work of the print and bookmaker Ed Colker. Each of the artists share a commitment to the ordinary and extraordinary, the traditional and improvisational.

An appreciation for the tactile object is central to what Anania and Colker share. Paper and typography are a meeting place for these two artists—figuratively and literally. During the Great Depression, Colker's father was a paper merchant in Philadelphia and, as he tells it, there were three important components in his household during childhood: paper, books and Judaism. He remembers "Fresh clean paper was nice to feel" and reminiscent of fresh, new clothes or linens which were not common during those times. The house was also full of books, and as a boy he read his way into other worlds through Jules Verne and Flaubert. It was also a Jewish household, and so these influences intersected with the idea he was raised with in being part of "the people of the book, the Torah" (Colker, Interview).

Colker's career began at the Pennsylvania Museum School of Industrial Art. According to David Acton in *The Stamp of Impulse: Abstract Expressionist Prints*, after serving in the U.S. Army in World War II, "he returned to the Philadelphia Museum School as a GI Bill student, studying intaglio printmaking with Ezio Martinelli, who introduced him to Stanley William Hayter's prints, Gorky's paintings and the work of other Abstract-Expressionists." In 1949, Colker graduated, joining the school's faculty and developing its typography lab. During these early years he "continued to be inspired by the energy and spirit of Abstract-Expressionism … [and] was acutely aware of the relationships between automatist delineation and musical improvisation." These years laid a foundation for his exploration of what lay beyond conscious control, and his interest in and enduring commitment to the tradition of his craft.

The exhibition *The Artist and the Book 1860–1960* at the Museum of Fine Arts in Boston "was another recognizable source of inspiration for Colker, an epiphany." He began to think about his combined interests of painting, typography and his love of poetry. In 1961, he won a Guggenheim Fellowship and traveled in Europe where he continued to be influenced by his examination of some of the finest *livres d'artistes*. There he visited Georges Le Blanc, "who printed at Atelier 17, the Parisian studio of Roger Lacouriere, who printed for Matisse, Joan Miró, and Yves Tanguy." When Colker returned to New York, he continued his studies at New York University and began producing "folios of his own prints, melding select typography, engaging design, beautiful papers, and meticulous printing" (202). The exposure to both French book making (a tradition that weds the poet and the painter) and to the improvisation of jazz and abstract expressionism helped him find his medium.

The confluence of a traditional sense of art, the influence of jazz, abstract expressionism and the New York School of poets is another shared space between Colker and Anania. While more than ten years apart in chronological age, they share an artistic time period, the sons of post-war artistic inspiration and opportunity. According to Acton, this post-WWII period was characterized by the rapid spread of "the ideas and imagery of abstract axpressionism...." National magazines and traveling artists helped to disseminate its forms, but its underlying concepts of personal introspection and improvisation were in the air, passing naturally like teenage slang to permeate all American creative endeavor (11). This period reflected the tension between tradition and "making it new," the very American use of ordinary objects to provoke or create the extraordinary—that which delineates the work of Colker and Anania, and is the heft and spring of their collaboration.

In describing Colker's work in *Five Decades in Print*, Peter Bermingham quotes the reaction of the poet Stanley Kunitz to "a poem about a monkey accompanied by an artist's drawing of—what else?—a monkey. 'What a bore!' proclaimed Kunitz. Ed Colker, you will discover, does not do monkeys" (5). While the abstract image of his prints highlight movement, possibility and evocation, one can discover, according to Anania, the "coincidental" image, the bird, for example, which "trembles toward both flight and abstraction" (6). The prints and poems on which they've worked together, or in response to each other, serve as amplications rather than illustrations. They are "illuminations," according to Colker, creating a new awareness for the other in their movement, the quotidian and the imaginative. Each medium then becomes a voice metamorphosing the other.

In rereading the texts of Anania's poems and revisiting Colker's prints, I am always struck by their strangeness—a strange beauty that draws me towards the work—to read again or to look closer, more deeply; then outward, turning me towards possibility and my own imaginative associations. My surprise at the continual delight to their work is an echo of theirs to each other. Anania writes that "Ed Colker's work as a printmaker always catches me with the same sense of surprise: the prints so often seem to exceed the likely possibilities of prints" (qtd. in Colker, *Five Decades* 6). Colker mirrors those words: "I'm always surprised in going back to Michael's work at his eye; the way in which his images provoke [my own] ... the way they fall into my expressionist mystery" (Interview).

If their shared artistic space is that of post-war inspiration and their consistent ability to evoke and surprise the other, then meeting was a coincidence of geography. The two artists met in the early 1970s when Colker served as both the director of the school of Art and Design and research professor of art at the University of Illinois–Chicago. Anania was an assistant professor in the English Department at the same institution and an editor at Swallow Press. Colker had been in Chicago since 1972, beginning the collaboration with Anania in full when he received a grant from the Graduate College that afforded him the opportunity in 1977 to produce two books, *From South Dakota* with the poet Kathleen Norris and *The Fall* with Anania. Thus began the collaboration that has spanned a period of more than twenty-five years and has included *The Fall*, *Esthétique du Râle*, *Two Poems*, *Four Poets/Poems*, *Sounds/Snow*, *Pochades* and *What Are Islands to Me Now*. When asked about their working friendship, Colker has said that it is shared through their common interests, fed "by anecdotes … [which] adds to an inventory … like two young historians talking on Andrew Jackson" (Interview).

Anania's and Colker's texts metamorphose ordinary occasions, into flight or expansion. *Esthétique du Râle* was the second and most "genuine[ly] ordinary" of the conversations between these two artists early on. Their concerns focused on the dramatic—what they perceived as the destructiveness of the art world during that time period. "The conceptual art, installation art, earthworks and body art" that were being produced at the time and in which the Museum of Contemporary Art in Chicago was involved became a central part of this conversation (Colker, *Five Decades* 7). The conceptual performance pieces (namely "Shoot" by Chris Burden in 1971, which involved a friend of the artist shooting him in the arm) was a point of particular contention for Anania. According to Colker, Anania was revolted by body art, perceiving it as "excesses of mutilation" and an undignified "maiming of each other" (Colker, Interview). Anania's answer to this was the poem "Esthétique du Râle"—the death rattle of the art world.

The poem begins as a proposal: "What we are confused by / is hardly less relevant / than what we know" (Anania, *Selected Poems* 128). These are hopeful lines in the midst of a perceived artistic exhaustion. Moments into movement or speech and perception are explored: "a single leaf defines a field of light / and light curls at the leaf's edge" (128). The poem moves tenderly among its images and abstractions:

> Amused fingers amid amorous conversation
> how the tree veins itself to the touch
> It all goes on like an afternoon
> something past into which we propose
> these other occasions, habitual landscape. (128–129)

Yet, the poem moves out of these slowed, reflective moments and addresses the futility that the poet sees the art community headed toward:

> They have taken to heaping dirt
> in abandoned places, firing kitchen

> matches, Buck Rogers fashion, at
> their wives. Perhaps it was too much
> to ask them to resolve our difficulties (130)

The poem begins in a contemplative state providing us with slowly unfolding images, picking up speed as the critique intensifies:

> Even the paint—how elegant it is!—
> seems to want to fall away with each
>
> passing semi-trailer truck. We know
> how the day went, the guest list
> of the party down the road, the Cadillac's
> fish-tail and impact, have seen the lunge
>
> slow-motion, chest pushed forward,
> arms out, the head's brief hesitation (130)

Even as the poem speeds toward its end, the images are simultaneously held in "slow-motion." We are watching the "fish-tail" of Jackson Pollock's Cadillac, his representative body at final impact, a world speeding towards its own end, as we hear *"le dernier cri"*—its final cry (131).

Colker's accompanying prints in the book *Esthétique du Râle* are done on silver paper with a grid overlay. They incorporate found images of the human body, the "internal landscapes" of epidermis, teeth, ear, arms and a backbone angling phallus-like from the musculature of legs. In contrast, the more painterly images include a vine black cloaking the legs' "upper body" (or what is imagined of it). In another figure, the black creates a landscape between a small sun and the single miniature conifer at the bottom of the print. "In keeping with the sense of currency [they] wanted, the portfolio was printed offset. Then as a kind of reprise for the conventional object ... a frontispiece etching ... was added," a four-handed etching that they did together (Colker, *Five Decades* 7–8). The etching, done in silver against vermilion, seems both regal and hopeful—a contrast to what they saw happening in the art world, and a connection to and reminder of earlier enthusiasms:

Larry Rivers and Frank O'Hara's collaboration for Tatyana Grosman twenty years before "passing the crayon back and forth between them as they drew on the printing surfaces, using a mirror to write the text in reverse" (Acton 16).

There is a story about the old Hollywood producers no longer working that Ed Colker likes to tell. Guys sitting around playing cards. When one of them asks another what he wants, the reply comes, "I just want to be interested in something" (interview). Colker himself believes the desire to be provoked or roused to be central to his work. This desire has very obviously been fed on the part of both artists. Years later in his poem "What Are Islands to Me Now," Anania commemorates the etching done together for *Esthétique du Râle* in Colker's Chicago studio:

> carved wood, bronzes, tracings ice
> crystals leave on the windowpane:
> coat it with paraffin, then scratch
> whatever you like into the wax,
> the design can be quite delicate;
> an acid bath—careful, the least
> splash will burn your flesh away (*In Natural Light* 59)

The poem sparely presents the various possible images suggested by the etchings and then moves into the immediacy of the remembered work: "coat it with paraffin, then scratch / whatever you like into the wax / ... —careful." The lines here capture the fascination with images, process, and a "careful" respect for the collaborative relationship.

In another turn, Colker is roused by the poem, responding with the print "Untitled," which was reproduced in the *Bluesky Review*'s 2003 tribute to Anania (103). The print neither resembles the original etching done in the '70s nor does it illustrate the more recent poem. Rather, it seems to bridge the past and present. It is a refraction of the etching in *Esthétique du Râle,* a gesture towards the quasi-amoebic figures done in vermilion and silver over twenty years earlier. Likewise, the browns, blues and yellow ochre in the more recent print suggest "the long dark slope / of the land" (Anania, *In Natural Light* 59)—and just as easily the more abstract "things left out in plain sight" that comes in the next section of the poem (60). This bridge between the early and later work is itself an extension and furthering of their collaboration. The result, grown from a critique of an art world in its death throes, has been a generative process stretching over the last part of this century. This "sustained engagement"—especially in the face of what they've created against, is what Norris calls "a modern miracle" (qtd. in Colker, *Five Decades* 43).

"Gin Music" was a collaboration done in 1999 as a commemoration of the work they had done over the years together. Colker asked that three poems be provided from Anania's early, middle and later work. These became part of the book *sounds/snow.* "Gin Music," an offset lithograph, was the representative poem of Anania's "middle" work. The poem is accompanied by a print of grays, blacks, greens and purples against white and suggests the smoky "joint" that "you got off to." We can intuitively feel the rise and fall of Bill Evans' music through the image and memory's companionate desire.

> How she waited just for a second for the words
> to fall out the way they had to and how you
> waited, your mouth already shaped into what
> you were about to say, and here it is back again,
> the ache of it.
> . . . .
> So you put the record on
> or you hum through it or you go off to some joint
> just in case it comes out right, but mostly
> you want to play it yourself, just once
> so that your fingers would be the ones
> settling down on the keys, and it would be
> your shoulders hunching, then pulling back (*Selected Poems* 197)

The poem is an ordinary occasion of desire in many ways: a moment between lovers (or "almost" lovers), a desire to play music and recapture a moment. It gives us sound, the "breath … expelled," "words" that "fall out the way they [have] to," juxtaposed with what's about to be said, "something you need to say." Sophisticated yet casual, vulnerable and adept, these words are spoken half to a self and half to anyone who might listen. This play pulls us in as if a whisper: "listen … listen" as the feeling attached to the music and moment is recaptured or reshaped.

The poem also works as a set of possibilities, what is partially happening or is at the edge of happening. That partiality or those edges capture what the "facts" cannot. It suggests a periphery in its "half-listen[ing]" and Evans's hesitation "as thought the keys are pressed part way down" (196). The desire to play "just once" then becomes the imagined act of playing: "the flat of the keyboard soften[ing] / in your hands," "the music … pull[ing] you along" (197). The poem weaves tense, capturing the effect that the music has on the speaker, a gradual effect in which "You listen for a long time" (196). We move among the present, future and past, not surprisingly ending in the subjunctive—the possibility:

And the smoke would curl its faded indigo
over the black lacquer of the piano,
and the ice would clink clink in the dark,

and faces would half turn and turn back,
and the song would ease its way out into
the room like a root extending itself
into damp soil and take leaf and flower. (198)

The last line moves out from the subjunctive "would" and its imaginative possibilities and extends into becoming with its "leaf and flower."

Colker illuminates both the specifics and the mystery of the poem through his print. It provides for the centrifugal movement of the music and curling smoke; and the centripetal sense of the moment within the speaker's head, the pianist bent to his instrument. It draws us back to the center, the image's coincidental stigma, even as its grayish-greenish petals loll outwardly. The center's purple moves outward and into smudging the greens and grays that rise and pool at the periphery, a near-ethereal black that seems to float on the surface of the other colors, buoyed up (*sounds/snow*).

The print's color queries the experience of music to the ear. The colors intensify in different places—specifically, the purples at the heart of the work, recede and drift. It is a subtlety that, like Anania's conversation, pulls us in for closer inspection. A closer look suggests the figure hunched over a piano, the music like smoke rising, filling a room; and the curve of earth with what appears to be a leaf or flower opening. The intensity of color attracts us and then recedes like smoke. In the recessive sage, lilac and soft black we see or hear the private moments—those between the speaker and "her," those between speaker and self, thereby reflecting the artist's sense of the way music moves around us, within us, its residual impact.

The external landscape that Colker proposes is land in which we see what is beneath the ground and the horizon above. It is also the landscape of a single flower or that of the gin joint that the speaker possibly goes off to: the smoke curling, the black lacquer of the piano, the pooling of the music itself. Through color and the various landscapes, we hear Evans—the hesitation at the keys, the sigh. The exchange between what seems to be lovers is felt in the lightest of sage and lilac. The black that floats above the green and purple, also suggest the geography of a water stain—what might have been written on a cocktail napkin, a name bled, smudging the edges. What is simultaneously ephemeral and enduring: that night, this part of the song, a flower—dissolved through and etched into memory.

It's this enthusiasm for what feels to be impossibly rendered that is Anania's gift and what he has seen mirrored (although as much refracted as reflected) in the word of Colker. The collaboration between Anania and Colker has produced, besides beautiful art, a reach out of the artistic tradition into untraditional subject matters. I marvel each time I look through *Esthétique du Râle* at its brashness in combining the very physical found images of a medical journal (after all, Colker did spend time early in his career as a designer of medical journals) with the more traditional abstract etching and the elegant font of the poem. Indeed, we see the combination of the untraditional with the traditional throughout Anania's work: the "firing of kitchen matches Buck Rogers fashion"(*Selected Poems* 130), the immediacy of collaboration, various moments that hover at the edge of consciousness, a flower. His ability to maintain the tension between the tradition of poetry and unlikely materials is itself generative.

The word "conversation" has its roots in the Latin *convertere* which means "turn round, transform." Its later histories through the Old French include the contexts of "dwelling" and "social life." It is only in the late sixteenth century that the specific modern sense of "talk" comes into play (Ayto 135). The conversation between Colker and Anania inhabits all of these meanings. Their talk has become a shared space. Their enthusiasm and admiration for the other's work is apparent, carried through tones of voice and color. Their dialogue has produced "turns" and "transformations." A poem turns out a print; from a print a poem arises not as pictorial or illustrative but as a progression of thought or feeling. We are amazed in the continuity of conversation, the progression of the work. Voice, paper, word, stone, ink. These two artists have sustained an artistic conversation for over a quarter of a century. Their conversation keeps hitting a note with the other, evoking, surprising them and us—out of the ordinary occasion and familiar things.

Works Cited

Acton, David. *The Stamp of Impulse: Abstract Expressionist Prints.* Worcester Art Museum, 2001.

Aleksa, Vainis. "Michael in the 80s." *Bluesky Review* II, 2003, pp. 81-83.

Anania, Michael and Ed Colker. *Esthétique du Râle.* Exhibition at the University of Illinois, 1986.

———. *In Natural Light.* Asphodel Press, 1999.

———. *Selected Poems.* Asphodel Press, 1969.

Ayto, John. *Word Origins.* A&C Black Business Information and Development, 2005.

Boer, Charles. "Preface 'To an Old Philosopher in Rome.'" *Bluesky Review* II, 2003, p. 9.

Colker, Ed. *Five Decades in Print.* Haybarn Press, 1998.

———. Personal interview. 16 May 2002.

Fiedler, Leslie. Introduction. *In Plain Sight: Obsessions, Morals and Domestic Laughter.* By Michael Anania. Asphodel Press, 1991, pp. 7–9.

Michael Anania and Ed Colker Collaborations (Haybarn Press/Editions du Grenier)

Esthétique du Râle, 1977.

The Fall, 1977.

Two Poems, 1985.

"Pochades" in *Four Poets/Poems: Anania, Hawks, Shapiro, Swann,* 1993.

Once again, flowered, 2000.

sounds/snow, 2002.

In Adami: Four Poems, 2004.

The Petrarchan Folio (42r) for Center of the Book Arts, New York City, 2005.

Keepsake for Poets House Exhibition, New York City, 2002.

Keepsake for Century Exhibition, New York City, 2004.

Stopping Time in *The Red Menace*

Kevin Clouther

I met Michael Anania on a fall day in Omaha so sunny and reasonable people could do little but stare into the sky in mute disbelief. Indeed, the colleague who introduced me to Michael did precisely that while Michael summarily dismissed a poet of some notoriety whom we both knew. I prodded at his objection: was this poet too clever, too coy?

Trivial was his verdict. I knew we would get along. We made plans to get together a few months later when we'd be in San Antonio for a conference.

Coronavirus prevented that meeting. This was the week before everything shut down. From my hotel, I got Michael on the phone. For seventy-five minutes, we talked about Omaha, where I live and he grew up. The Omaha he described was both recognizable and not. I suppose that's always the case when someone describes a place as it existed seventy years ago.

He would describe a street corner, and I would think of it as it exists presently, but then he would note some element—a nightclub, a streetcar—and I would remember that we were moving through different worlds. Michael Anania grew up in a housing project in a neighborhood that was—and remains—mostly Black. His mother was German and his father Italian. Anania spoke those languages, as well as English, in the home. My family is Irish, and my wife's family is Cuban. Our kids go to a neighborhood park where half of the kids are Asian. Omaha is a more diverse place than many non-Nebraskans realize; it has been for a long time.

When Anania left Omaha to pursue his graduate studies, he increasingly saw the place as both strange and familiar. He'd surrounded himself with writers who felt that way about Europe. He realized he could write about Omaha the way others were writing about Rome. Plus, he'd seen things. He went to school with Gale Sayers and Bob Gibson. "Bob would pitch," Michael told me, "and you could hear it." For the uninitiated: Bob Gibson was better at pitching a baseball than almost anyone who has ever lived. Gale Sayers was among the most gifted people to carry a football on planet earth. "If you look at a place," Michael told me, "its mythology emerges."

After we spoke, it was his novel, *The Red Menace*, that called to me. Maybe that's because I'm a fiction writer and always a little in awe of poets who write novels (think Ocean Vuong, Anne Carson or Michael Ondaatje). *The Red Menace*, published in 1984, is interested, from the first chapter, in the movement of time, forward and backward:

> We turned onto Cummings Street and entered the ordinary school traffic, so we could pass by the malt shop, a vestige of the school's failing link with the middle class. Eventually the building itself would be pushed over by highway improvements. In the afternoon it was packed with customers for malts and sodas; mornings, it was a place for serious coffee drinkers, high school seniors mostly, working at being adults. It was an artifact of another world, another class, a passing era. Cheerleaders in furry sweaters preened over danish pastries; their boyfriends in earnest cardigans and sport shirts buttoned to the neck practiced looking like men with irreversible morning habits. (Anania 18)

The first sentence is set firmly in 1950s Omaha, but by the second sentence, the protagonist is thinking ahead to the pernicious effects of "highway improvements," perhaps the segregation that followed the construction of Highway 75. When he returns to the 1950s, he is in "another world," a "passing era," with sartorial details rooted in the moment: "furry sweaters," "earnest cardigans," and most evocative of all, "sport shirts buttoned to the neck" that signify "men with irreversible morning habits." Such temporal elasticity is reminiscent of Muriel Spark or even Marcel Proust. Various Omahas exist in the character's—and, by extension, reader's—mind simultaneously.

If *The Red Menace* were published today, it would be classified as autofiction. It is an intensely personal novel. Unsurprisingly, the death of Anania's father holds particular resonance. After suggesting that "fathers who die young are all thus shrouded in odd intensity by their sons," Anania produced this remarkable sentence:

> I alone have, then, these islands of clarity, like the evening of the day after the fight where every detail is completely available, the drawer in the oak cabinet from which Old Man Merritt counted out those five cigarettes, for example, or the way my sister stared at the chocolate on my hand as though in addition to stealing him away for nearly an hour I had also managed to steal something precious and irreplaceable from her ice cream cone, the fresh marks of the scoop along the edge and more dear, even, those rills and furrows the chill holds on the surface so briefly. (54–55)

What is autofiction but "islands of clarity," tastefully cultivated? How does one account for the memory where "every detail is completely available" when the vast majority of experience is lost forever—why this and not that?

Here *The Red Menace* puts itself in the company of Frank Conroy's *Stop-Time*, another story of mid-twentieth-century American adolescence that distinguishes itself through its precision of detail, that isn't sure if it's a novel or memoir. Anania was stopping time when he kept his father for himself, a time that stretches out of proportion in memory. Nothing is more ephemeral than a son's time with a father who dies early, not even the "rills and furrows the chill holds" on a melting ice cream cone.

The Red Menace is not always so personal. Sometimes the protagonist disappears, so as to make room for other characters—mostly young men—who travel North 24th Street. Often, these men are portrayed not only as they existed then but also for who they would become. Consider Alvin, a not atypical case, for whom "high school and his carefully bordered delinquency provided a pastoral interlude before the weight of lower-middle American life"; at the end of one chapter, he's "rocking around the clock, with all the dedication and sense of limitation that implies" (105). Is Alvin aware of his fate? It seems so. In refusing to divorce present Alvin from future Alvin, the protagonist presents the character as a continuum.

Not much happens in *The Red Menace*. A lesser poet would compensate in the novel with action; Anania felt no such pressure, choosing his spots judiciously and giving them space. Here is another remarkable sentence, this time from the last chapter:

> Arnie swings back into the right lane just as he crosses a small bridge, the kind your tires thump over quickly, almost unnoticed, and the Oldsmobile Rocket 98 jumps up like a clown from a jack-in-the-box, skidding sideways briefly on two wheels, then nosing forward into an end-over-end front flip, chrome accessories, headlights, Arnie, Linda, Darlene, and Meatball lifted up into the fog as well, arms and legs spread wildly, swimmers just for that instant, and you recall the chill that snatched at your legs as you kicked through the quarry's skim of sunlit warm water, the terrifying cold that grappled at you all day long from the farthest corners of the cut stone below. (145)

The shift to second person happens quietly—"almost unnoticed"—and so surreal is the accident that Anania jumped from simile to metaphor: the car is a "clown from a jack-in-the-box," its inhabitants "swimmers just for that instant." So awful is the carnage that Anania again stopped time to leave the accident and meditate on a very different memory, one of cold, deep terror.

Eleven years later Tobias Wolff would publish a famous story in *The New Yorker*, "Bullet in the Brain," which travels just as abruptly from tragedy to memory. As a bullet plows through a bank patron's brain, the character considers a day from childhood when he found himself mesmerized by another child's diction (206). From tragedy to memory: there is something instinctively human in that journey.

In the midst of the coronavirus shutdown, I drove the length of North 24th Street, the setting for much of *The Red Menace*. The housing project where Michael Anania grew up is gone, as are almost all of the schools and businesses detailed in the novel, but the street remains important, particularly to Omaha's African American communities. Among the recent successes is the Union for Contemporary Art, which moved to North 24th Street in 2017 and was founded on the premise that "years of disinvestment and the stigma of race and poverty had drawn an obvious line between North Omaha residents and the rest of the city" ("North Omaha").

On this day, the street was abandoned. Sidewalks were empty, and buildings had their lights off. I looked from blank window to blank window, wondering who would be the next artist to imagine this world into existence.

Works Cited

Anania, Michael. *The Red Menace: A Fiction*. Thunder's Mouth Press, 1984.

"North Omaha." The Union for Contemporary Art. https://www.u-ca.org/.

Wolff, Tobias. *The Night in Question*. Vintage Books, 1996.

Michael Anania's *The Red Menace:* A Study in Self-Production

David Ray Vance

Although marketed as a novel and specifically touted as a *fiction* (by way of its subtitle), to most readers today Michael Anania's *The Red Menace* is apt to read something more like a cross between nonfiction memoir and what we now call cultural criticism. Non-linear and largely non-narrative, Anania's account of growing up poor in 1950s heartland America lacks the sort of plot and character development generally associated with a coming-of-age story. Instead of chronicling the narrator's maturation by way of some series of conflicts and epiphanic resolutions, Anania provides a number of analytical sketches by which he recounts personal experience and integrates it into a larger, historical/cultural perspective. If there is an organizing principle by which these sketches are ordered, it is certainly not chronological, nor does their common mooring in experience—i.e., the fact that each takes as its starting point some facet of the narrator's childhood or adolescent experience—prove adequate to the task. Instead, what makes the parts cohere is the narrator's mature, erudite analyses of the forces that shaped the culture of his adolescence. That is to say that the narrator's mature mind imbues the experiences he chooses to recount with meaning more so than the experiences can be said to explain or elucidate the maturation of his mind.

For readers expecting a more linear, conflict-driven narrative focused on self-discovery, *The Red Menace* is likely to prove dissatisfying.

To read this text as something other than a novel (and a fiction), however, is to undervalue the way in which its resistance against generic expectation serves to reinforce the text's central notions about identity, specifically the limited/limiting means by which selves are constructed in a capitalist, mass-market, consumer society. Anania's first-person account suggests that identity is less a product of discovery than a process of decision-making whereby the individual chooses whether or not to "identify" with various ideas, practices or products. One's options in this respect depend a great deal upon socio-economic and cultural factors beyond one's personal control, yet Anania implies that all can be rejected to one degree or another, even if they cannot be rendered irrelevant, and that it is perhaps imagination, more than anything else, which determines the range of possibilities with which one can potentially identify. Ultimately, Anania emphasizes self-determination while still acknowledging the limits of self-production imposed by these socio-economic and cultural factors. The text's overtly non-linear form then signals the dynamic nature of the decision-making process, treating self-production not as linear process but rather as recursive, simultaneous and on-going, identity by its very nature being continuously created or staked out via adoption or refusal of dominant (and/or recessive) cultural values.

Anania's dynamic notion of self-production closely parallels Bourdieu's account of "cultural production" as delineated in the "The Field of Cultural Production." In this essay, Bourdieu builds on Foucault's notion of the "field of strategic possibilities," suggesting the "field of discourse" must also be considered, that we must "relate works ... to their social conditions of production" (33). Bourdieu's relational thinking is primarily naturalistic in so far as it suggests that culture is the product of human choices themselves largely determined by conditions/conditioning beyond our control, but it has existential leanings insofar as it acknowledges that the "field of possibles" is extraordinarily complex and that choice (and the responsibility which comes with making choices) renders the outcome something other than predetermined. Most importantly, Bourdieu emphasizes that the forces at play exert influence simultaneously and in fact influence one another as well, so that the range of "possibles" has multiple and shifting determinants. In *The Red Menace*, Anania anticipates and enacts Bourdieu's relational thinking particularly in the way he characterizes the role of personal choice in self-construction. In keeping with Bourdieu's reasoning, Anania acknowledges that self-construction is primarily motivated by a desire for power, but unlike Bourdieu, he invites us to consider whether the motivation to power might not itself be culturally derived—i.e., insofar as our valuation of power largely ignores the responsibility inherent in having and exercising power.[1]

In "Good Morning to You, We're All in Our Places," the first chapter of *The Red Menace*, Anania adeptly sketches the cultural field in which his adolescent subjects exist by orienting his readers to the various spheres of influence (and/or signification) which delineate the range of possibles available to them in terms of self-production. Specifically, Anania establishes 1) Economic and Social Class, 2) Family/Ethnicity (& Race), 3) Political Ideology, 4) Sexuality/Gender and 5) Market Capitalism (including Popular Media) as locations for self-production and/or signification and as forces that influence self-production.[2]

Interestingly, it is not until the second chapter that our narrator actually refers to himself (and/or his younger self) as a character in the text, and when he does so it is to recount adult experience and to describe an adult self remembering childhood. As a result, the subject of the text becomes primarily the "we" of childhood (the community of adolescent peers), and insofar as the "I" functions as a subject, it is the adult "I" which predominates. While the speaker does refer to his adolescent self in the first person in later chapters, he does so only after establishing that there is a distinction to be made between these selves. How or why the narrator comes to make this distinction is not the primary focus of the novel. Rather, the focus is expressly on making sense of that adolescent period for which the speaker has such vivid recollections.

Adolescence is, of course, a particularly formative period marked by intense self-absorption and self-speculation, in other words a period of self-discovery, but Anania's characters are from the start engaged in complex forms of signification. Discovery and performance are thus conflated, and the emphasis is placed on asserting and otherwise performing identifications with specific attitudes and beliefs (whether normative or otherwise). We see this particularly in the ways the boys play with (and against) already established cultural motifs and expectations, not least in the ways they mimic patriarchal language that objectifies women. It is clear, in this sense, that Anania's characters are products of cultural forces even as they are in the process of producing themselves—i.e., choosing how they wish to be perceived or understood in respect to these various forces.

I will not presume here to catalogue the means by which Anania introduces the various spheres of influence or how he begins to set them in relation (suffice to say they are almost all acknowledged by the end of the third page), but a brief look at the way that the television set functions in this first chapter should offer some idea as to the complex interrelationships he establishes in this regard. In order of appearance, what the adolescent characters view and respond to on the television screen is first a dancing chimpanzee, then a nuclear bomb test, then a puppet show displaying African bushmen puppets dancing to a mainstreamed (read "white") version of an otherwise highly sexual and arguably "anti-social" African American song. Immediately, we have insinuated all manner of concerns about ethnicity, race and racism, gender and sexism, political ideology and national identity (as understood at the height of the Cold War), not to mention issues of class (the boys being gathered around this one television because only Richard's family has been able to afford one) and distinctions between highbrow and lowbrow entertainment. And, of course, we see here as well the ways in which market forces in the form of commercial television serve not only to locate these issues but to establish the dominant culture's values, specifically its privileging of hegemonic global power (via nuclear arms), male sexual dominance, and the myth of white supremacy.

These values directly inform the attitudes these boys perform, and especially the value they place on both physical power (including dominance over women) and the power to influence others by way of language and ideas (jiving). We see their influence particularly in the

100

final scene of the first chapter, where Anania's characters tap into the primary social-cultural conflict of the period. Having just watched the nuclear bomb test, the four boys are lumbering their way toward school when they begin singing what our narrator describes as "a cartoon cat version of Cab Calloway—Is you or is you ain't a Commie? *You is! You is!*" They sing this song even as they pass the malt shop full of teenagers, and in fact, they mug up to the window and clown for the onlookers, who in turn respond with a mixture of confusion and anger. This performance represents an overt challenge to these other teens, a verbal defiance. The narrator and his cohorts are outsiders in that their poverty and their cultural/ethnic diversity as a group sets them apart from the relatively affluent, predominately white culture represented by the "malt shop teens." The window glass that separates them is as symbolic as it is real, and their clowning serves to confront this boundary and the hierarchy it represents.

As Bourdieu explains "newcomers [outsiders] 'get beyond' the dominant mode of thought and expression not by explicitly denouncing it but by repeating and reproducing it in a sociologically non-congruent context, which has the effect of rendering it incongruous or even absurd, simply by making it perceptible as the arbitrary convention that it is" (31). That these boys ape Senator McCarthy's famous question "Are you now or have you ever been a member of the Communist party?" serves both to call into question their own loyalty and the loyalty of the teens to whom they pose the question. More importantly, this mocking calls into question the communist/capitalist binary which dominates thinking in this period.

At the same time they challenge this hierarchy, these boys essentially engage in the same brinksmanship which marked American foreign policy of the period. A violent and catastrophic response is a real possibility for our protagonists. In fact it is almost surprising when the boys continue on their way unmolested and the chapter draws to a close. We expect such antagonism to give rise to violence in part because violent conflict is so much a part of the convention of the coming of age stories of this period (*Rebel Without a Cause, Blackboard Jungle*) and even more so because the question our protagonists so flippantly pose to the "malt shop teens" amounts to a serious accusation. In the America in which these boys are living, to treat communism as something less than serious is to transgress the normative bounds set by the dominant culture and to invite reprisal. Indeed, the message of the atomic bomb test the boys had just witnessed was that communism posed such a serious threat to American style democracy that it had to be opposed with utmost violence. To announce yourself as a communist in this era was to invite your own destruction. To accuse someone else of being a communist was to threaten their destruction and, in turn, to invite violent reprisal.

Political ideology predominates this novel's treatment of self-production not simply because the debate between communism and capitalism was so characteristic of the historic period in which Anania locates his characters, but because this debate is expressly about deciding how to balance the needs of the individual (self) with the needs of the society as a whole. Anania's central interest is identity, how it is we construct it, what it means to be self-made. The argument against communism/socialism is that they value the collective state over the individual, essentially limiting the choices individuals have to a select few determined by a centralized government. But, of course, the argument against capitalism is that it privileges the elite and leaves the vast majority of people with only the illusion of choice and/or opportunity. The irony of the fifties being that in the fight to defeat communism and defend individual rights, anticommunist leaders called for rigid conformity, ultimately emphasizing national needs over those of individuals. Their message was that democratic capitalism (the better system because it values individual choice) must be defended at all costs, even if the only way to do so is to sacrifice or otherwise limit individual freedoms.

The nation's obsession with political ideology informs not only the obsessive attention Anania's characters give to the bomb (a major tool and symbol of the cold war) but also their obsessive attention to automobiles. Indeed, the conflict between communism and capitalism, between individual and society, is exemplified by way of the role the automobile plays the protagonist's self-construction.

It is not coincidence, of course, that the automobile figures so heavily in Anania's analysis of 1950s American culture. Historically speaking, the 1950s saw a dramatic rise in car ownership as military production shifted to the private sector. In this period, the automobile came to symbolize middle-class status, and as more models were introduced, the car became a significant marker for personal identity. Why the car? In part because cars are such public objects. Television viewing skyrocketed during the '50s much as car sales, but there was far less sense that one's television served to convey one's identity. What one watched might be significant, but that could be kept private, and it mattered very little finally what model or brand of television one owned. Cars, on the other hand, were public objects, and so value was attached to not only having a car, but having a car that bespoke your social status and/or ambitions. For those with middle-class aspirations, the appeal was all the greater. Not only was car ownership more attainable than home ownership. but it offered a way for those who hadn't quite arrived to give the appearance that they had. Cars, in other words, offered an opportunity to fictionalize the middle-class status that one hadn't legitimately attained to play the part.

Anania makes the link between the automobile and political ideology quite explicit in the first chapter, and at the same time alludes to the fictionalizing function:

> The bomb had special properties for us. It was as though it belonged to us by right of attentive devotion, the same devotion that gave each of us a girl, girls hardly spoken to, sometimes fearfully taken as partners in class, but attended to, watched carefully, offered the role of leading lady in the movies in our heads. It is a form of possession or right of first possession, this faithful, diligent kind of fantasy. It was like the way in which we dealt with cars.... At twelve and thirteen, we had independently invented one of the central premises of American advertising—that a product is made valuable by the amount of attention it is given and the precise detail, however fraudulent, used in presenting it. We shaped ourselves by our loyalties to various products in ways the advertisers could never have dreamed. (12–13)

It is important to note that Anania suggests that our "loyalties" shape us as much as we shape them, that the relationship is not unidirectional. Still, even more important is the fact that the identification these boys have with power by way of the bomb and the automobile is essentially an illusion. The fact is that they have very little power. They represent, in truth, the least powerful in the culture: poor children. (Although, poor female children would arguably be even less empowered than our male protagonists.) In this sense, their aspiration to power involves a certain amount of self-negation.

That said, cars in this text exemplify the manner in which Americans signal identity through product loyalty. As well, they serve to point out the problem inherent in asserting individuality in a mass-production, capitalist economy, the problem again being that the options available to the average consumer represent an illusion of choice more than actual choices. In the chapter titled "A Real Bomb," the narrator describes buying his own first used car and in the process catalogues the many ways a car would be modified by teenagers of the period. What we recognize, of course, is that our speaker's choices are quite limited indeed. Most cars are simply out of his price range, and of those he can afford only a few offer much in the way of potential social capital, and then only if properly modified. These modifications, however, do not function to individuate the automobile. Rather, they are themselves products of cultural predetermination and represent a limited range of options in the marketplace of ideas. "Decking" a car and amplifying its exhaust system, in other words, did little more than signal the owner's membership in a subgroup loyal to this aesthetic, an aesthetic that happened to emphasize the car as machine and which was itself born out of the technological revolutions and preoccupations of the age. In this sense, such modification represents mere fashion, an expression of the collective imagination rather than an individual one, a fact that Anania's mature narrator acknowledges forthrightly.

Although the opportunities for individuation would seem to be quite limited so far as the car is concerned, the attitude persists, and ultimately the car comes to represent in this novel the particular brand of American individualism that became fashionable in the 1950s, which is to say the sort of individualism that locates rebellion against the status quo in leather jackets and hot rod cars instead of in intellectual dissent or artistic creation. This link between cars and individualism is made explicit in the second chapter of the text, titled "I Am Not Now, Nor Have I Ever Been." Here, the speaker describes a visit he makes to a poet friend in Upstate New York. This friend is described as having been a hard-line communist, one that didn't back down from his views even during the worst of McCarthy's blacklisting days. The speaker takes the train out to his friend's place, and while crossing through Grand Central Station, he sees on display a brand-new red Mustang positioned on a green carpet with spotlights shining down upon it.

Of course, it is tempting to read this red Mustang as representing another sort of "Red Menace," a threat to American individualism on par with the threat communism was made out to be. But before we can formulate this reading, we must recognize the fact that in the course of their visit, the speaker and the poet friend have a disagreement about communism. This disagreement is located specifically in the speaker's refusal to refer to childhood friends by nicknames in a poem he has written. His argument that in "mixed" neighborhoods this was simply not done conflicts with the friend's views which presume a certain informality amongst the proletariat. The narrator's point is finally that the lower classes which communists hoped to convert (and who otherwise had the most immediately to gain from bringing about revolution) were fiercely attached to notions of personal superiority even as they resisted dominant notions about social superiority.

The speaker ponders this disagreement when he takes a walk in the woods while his poet friend takes a nap.

> Communism ... somehow always misunderstood the peculiar aggressiveness of the American proletariat—the serious use of full names among the children supported by the ADC in a Nebraska housing project ... never once assuming social equality but inevitably asserting personal superiority.... It made sense that the New Left had been composed primarily of middle-class and upper-middle-class students. They were the only groups for whom the disguise of proletarianism was a sufficiently interesting lie; for them it could be,

as it never could be for a worker on the line or a housing project castoff, an aggression rather than an identification, style rather than class. (22–23)

As he explains later in this same chapter, for himself and his real life proletariat friends, communism was appealing only insofar as it was deemed outrageous and because "any scheme that would take away property and divide it evenly would put all of us ahead, since none of us had any property" (27). Otherwise, it held only moderate appeal, and so far as we take the speaker's experience as representative, the survival skills one needed at the bottom of the socio-economic ladder didn't lend themselves to charging the barricades once the revolution arrived. Consider how Anania describes avoiding direct confrontations with the police during the protests that characterized the 1968 Democratic Convention in Chicago. Of his poet friend, the speaker concludes, "I admired him, but I could not think about him without thinking that it had all been a waste. It was a judgment that came, I think, from my continued dislike of extreme positions and that had its roots in a deeper, pre-intellectual duplicity." Clearly, at least in this moment, the narrator is torn in his loyalties, at once admiring his friend's idealism, but at the same time viewing communism as a lost cause insofar as it fails to appeal to the very people it is meant to save from oppression.

It is at this point that the speaker leaves the friend and returns to Grand Central Station where he is again confronted by the spotlighted, red Mustang. He concludes

Back in Grand Central Station only the advertisements that circled the great hall were bright. Centered in the dingy station, the Mustang gleamed, haloed by its circle of floodlights, the figure of the conquering deity presiding over one of the last surviving temples of the locomotive. In alcoves off the terminal's knave, rows of high-backed, uncomfortable benches faced their various clocks, like pews in the chapels of a great cathedral—remnants of an earlier contract with the machine, a symmetrical fancy involving the timepiece, the far-flung system of rails, the corporation, and the polity that now seems slightly comic. The Mustang, by virtue of its name and the wild horse embossed in its chrome door, its dash of sports-car individualism and its mass production egalitarianism, had no need to diagram its preeminence. Parked there on a platform of plush green carpeting, it was a reminder that each commuter line ends in a parking lot, that the collective journey had become merely a brief concession to the city's snarl, and that out there in the middle distance waited an anarchy of Mustangs, Cougars, Barracudas, and Darts. It was as if I had spent my day jostled between two pasts, my own and my friend's, one almost irreconcilable with the other although for a time they had shared the same calendar.... What persisted in my mind as I headed for my hotel was the flashy arrogance of that red Mustang in the train station. (33)

But what are we to make of all this? Clearly the "flashy arrogance of that red Mustang" signals an indictment of the dominant culture, the one that emphasizes the communist threat to individualism over the threat posed by capitalism. Read in relation to the speaker's previous indictment of his friend's communism, specifically the assertion that it had been a waste of time, there is a sense that the battle has been fought, that capitalism has vanquished communism. This arrogance attributed to the red Mustang is then arguably well-earned. Yet, and in keeping with his aversion for "extreme" positions, the narrator doesn't finally side with either communism or capitalism in this ideological debate. Insofar as the car is demonized and equated with ferocious, animalistic self-absorption—by way of its association with "Mustangs, Cougars and Barracudas" and with weaponry by way of its association with "Darts"—it must also be understood as a symbol of the often overlooked threat that capitalism poses to individuality and self-expression. But again, this criticism is not totalizing. Repeatedly we see evidence of the speaker's (Anania's?) own infatuation with (and appreciation for) the automobile, an infatuation that may grow out of "pre-intellectual duplicity," but which he never rejects altogether. This seems particularly the case when we consider the important role the car plays in the narrator's own coming of age. I do not mean simply his own adolescent infatuation with his first car and all the freedom (especially sexual) that it seems to promise, but the gift the car makes possible when his father is able to borrow one to drive his son around town and show him the places where he worked, the fruits of his "menial" labor. The criticism Anania levels at the car is then the same criticism to be leveled generally at any system that privileges mass production (be it capitalistic or communistic), which is that it substitutes the purchase of an object for the making of one, it equates getting with doing, acquisition with production. Anania does not suggest the world would be better off without cars, but that in locating self-worth/identity in mass-produced objects, we risk cheapening the human spirit.

Of course, this argument depends upon our reading the last chapter of the book, titled "Autoclysms," as primarily symbolic in the way it depicts automobiles as destructive. In this chapter, our speaker describes the various driver's-education films students were made to watch in hopes of frightening them into respecting the awesome responsibility that comes with driving a car. As well, he describes various accidents to which he has been party, either as a participant or as a witness. He tells us, "There is something irresistible about crashing and a certain invulnerability that goes with having just once totaled a car. Even the slang gave it a special authority. 'Anania totaled his car!' Among all those active verbs … that one held sway. *Totaled*" (149). The specific emphasis placed on active verbs hearkens to the notion that action might afford more genuine opportunity to create identity, but here again Anania refuses to totalize. Instead, what we see is that action can be just as catastrophic. In one instance he describes losing control of his car while taking a lunch break between college entrance exams. Education, we understand, intellectual prowess, are no defense against the temptations of raw power, even when such power threatens our own destruction. In this sense, the red Mustang (the car) is irresistible, not because of the social capital it represents, but because of the genuine physical power it possesses. Our training may lead us to avoid trouble, to only backtalk the cops once they're out of hearing distance, but it cannot train us to forego asserting power altogether, either as a way of taking control of our lives or giving it up.

The Red Menace ends with a brief dialogue in which the speaker tells a friend about seeing a car full of fellow teenagers crash, describing in grim detail the four bodies flying into the air and finally the violence done to them, the resulting deaths. The friend acts as inquisitor and in the course of making seven inquiries, twice asks whether the car was totaled. This repetition is disturbing because it shows his interest is in the car as much as in the four teens who have died. Given the larger context of the book, one cannot help but register this as yet another criticism of capitalist consumerism. Implied is that by trafficking in products as means for self-identification, we risk losing our identities to the object. Indeed, we risk becoming mere objects ourselves, mere body parts. Metaphorically and literally, we risk losing our heads, but then it would seem we lose our heads first, that it is our lack of respect for the power and responsibility that comes with exercising choice that represents the real menace from within and which genuinely threatens our continued existence both as persons and as a nation of persons.

Notes

1. In addition, *The Red Menace* as a text (as an act/artifact) can be understood as a purposeful resistance against the social/cultural expectations which predominate coming of age stories specifically in terms of its organizing principles. For the purposes of this essay, however, I will be analyzing only how Bourdieu's relational principles are exemplified in Anania's text.

2. When I speak of a sphere of influence, I mean to intimate both a position (a site of conflict) and the social forces/pressures associated with that position. Again, these spheres are not distinct from one another entirely, but rather they overlap and influence/limit one another to varying degrees.

Works Cited

Anania, Michael. *The Red Menace: A Fiction.* Thunder's Mouth Press, 1984.

Bourdieu, Pierre. *The Field of Cultural Production.* Columbia UP, 1993.

From "Two Kinds of Autobiography: II. *The Red Menace*"

John Matthias

Michael Anania's *The Red Menace*—"a fiction," he calls it; I call it an oral autobiography which he has dictated to himself—begins with the image of an atomic test on a television screen over the cereal bowls and milk bottles of countless American homes in the 1950s. I remember these tests well. The images certainly provided a bizarre focus for our scarcely conscious minds as, groggy and irritable, we stared uncomprehendingly at the black-and-white flickerings of those primitive TVs. For Anania, the images became a fundamental element in what he thinks of as "the snarl of things we call awareness." This is what we all were looking at and what it is that Anania's characters (his friends and/or antagonists) go off to school talking about.

> The screen was instantly blank, not bright, just blank, then slowly from its edges, as though seeping back, the gray of the sky circled in around a light at the center, which in turn began to grow outward against the recovered sky. The circle of light grew to the size of a baseball, darkening at the edges, rising on a column of smoke that ridged and fluted itself as it supported the ball, the ball itself grown smoky, flattening as it moved upward. The horizon was plain again, and to the right of the burgeoning cloud there were three thin streamers of smoke that rippled as they extended off the top of the screen. The wooden shed was gone. The screen belonged to the cloud,

which stood still, or seemed still except for the constant pumping of smoke into the crown from the column below. The announcer droned on about height, times, size, and the picture changed (9).

"Jee-zus," one of the boys says, while the others rise "as though responding to a benediction." "Shee-it" "Fuckin' A" ... "Damn Straight" the rest incant in their turn, reacting to various outrageous claims— "you know you could carry one of them things in a suitcase?" (10)— made by one or another of them about the bomb. The jive is part of the snarl of things which Anania says we call awareness and which, in his own case, we might just as well call memory. Anania is a great rememberer. My own method of dealing with the particular madness of the 1950s was simple: the cultivation of total amnesia. I hated and feared both the strange intensities and stultifying inertias of the decade, from its music, cars, movies, heroes and politics to its style of sexual swagger or sexual innocence. As soon as it was possible to forget—at about the time, I suppose, of Kennedy's inauguration—I forgot. But Anania forces memory upon me. To some extent, his experiences were also mine, which was not the case, of course, with what Jiri Wyatt remembers from his childhood in Slovakia. But 1950s America is another county, too, and many of its characteristic or defining images are as simultaneously familiar and alien, once held up in their own authentically garish light, as a half-remembered room in an eastern European village is to a returning exile.

The snarl of things ... awareness and the memory of awareness and the awareness of memory. Anania grew up in Omaha, Nebraska, and lived in a housing project named for Logan Fontenelle, the last chief of the Omahas. German on his mother's side, he got his "bits and pieces" of a Bremen pastoral mainly from his grandmother, who returned to Germany as an old woman after the war. His mother's immigrant experiences "foreclosed all but a few images of an earlier, green life in another world" (37). Anania's father, whose southern Italian background made him something of a *don* both in his own mind and in the Calabrian community, died young after a life in which tuberculosis made steady work impossible. He shined shoes, sold papers, dealt cards, helped build a water wall for the WPA, and ended up on welfare living "not so much by his wits as his sense of style" (56).

Outside Omaha was the Macy reservation where some of Anania's friends, none of whom seems actually to live there, visit older relatives on weekends. Russell, the Omaha, in Anania's high school who has a plan to steal the bomb, has the classic profile of the figure on a buffalo nickel and drives a Pontiac with its Indian hood ornament "jutting into the traffic" (72). (Anania, importantly enough at the end of the book, drives a Plymouth with the *Mayflower* on its hood.) High-school friends and acquaintances include a range of ghetto Blacks, ethnic working-class Whites, inaccessible upper-middle-class girls [called] "Cottonwood fluff" (111) and some truly violent delinquents for whom high school provided a kind of pastoral interlude "before the weight of lower-middle American life settled in" on them (105).

All the boys brooded on the bomb—made it their own "by right of attentive devotion"—while brooding with an analogous intensity on particular girls "attended to, watched carefully, offered the role of leading lady in the movies in our heads," and particular cars which were "nosed" and "decked' with "an almost Bauhaus purity" to the point that they resembled bombs or bullets. The music accompanying all of this was either Black rhythm and blues (aggressively defiant and kept off the radio and out of downtown record stores) or early white rock 'n' roll. Movies in the mind were based on movies in the movie theaters; dangerously suggestive films like *Blackboard Jungle* on the one hand, and studies in the conflict between masculine honor and domesticity like *Shane, High Noon* and *Rebel Without a Cause* on the other. South of town was Offutt Air Force Base which, as headquarters of the Strategic Air Command, would make Omaha a certain target for a Soviet nuclear attack. Lewis and Clark stopped on their journey west to hunt on the river bluffs into which the SAC administrative building, a kind of inverted skyscraper, was sunk down to its lowest subterranean level where Curtis LeMay sat before the NORAD communications system dreaming of Grands Prix and his Ferrari, like a high school student before a blackboard dreaming of the dragstrip and his Olds or Merc.

Anania early on establishes a connection between the bomb and sex, and between both of these and the souped-up cars that looked like bombs in which sexual desire could be relieved in the backseat or, more often, compensated for by tearing down a country road at ninety miles an hour. The "Red Menace" of the title is simultaneously the threat of the bomb in enemy hands; a name given to Russell, the Omaha, by one of his classmates; the swollen phallus of the sexually famished but frightened teenage male; and any of several bright, fast, dangerous, and desirable cars. While Anania's book begins with an atomic test assuring us again of the actual possibility of the much imagined cataclysm of nuclear holocaust, it ends, after episodes in which the dilemma of sexual power, like that of political power, is seen to be powerlessness and defeat, with an emblem for the cataclysm in what he calls an "autoclysm"—an orgasmic crash, described in nearly pornographic detail, in which the car is "totalled" and everyone is killed (144, 149).

If the autoclysm is the most memorable emblem in *The Red Menace*, it may be that "The Real McCoy" is the most important. Readers of Anania's poetry will remember the real McCoy, a revolver which Anania's father kept in a green steel box wrapped in a handkerchief, from an early poem in *The Color of Dust* called "The Temper." There as here, it represents something solid, authentic, and durable in the threatened and unstable atmosphere of Anania's world. This is the passage from "The Temper":

> It is something to covet—
> what my father said of the real McCoy,
> the gesture and all of
> holding the revolver in his hand,
> tapping the butt on the table,
> saying, that is solid,
> more than this table, solid,
> tempered blue sheen thunk
> reflected on the table top,
> snubnosed, hammerless real McCoy. (55)

In *The Red Menace*, the real McCoy surfaces in the fourth chapter, in which Anania's father successfully organizes a funeral for a woman who suddenly dies in the housing project and then breaks up a neighborhood fight that develops in an afternoon of drinking when the group of pallbearers returns home. Anania's memories of his father constitute remarkable "islands of clarity" (54), as he calls them, retrievable moments and images very like those presented in the early pages of *Against Capitulation*. Remembering his father's pleasure in breaking up the fight, Anania also remembers the day he sat him down at the kitchen table and showed him the gun which the young boy thought he might also have shown to the men in the fight in order to stop it. The gun "was a lesson in the weight and hardness of real things" (55). Anania's father traces the crosshatch of the grip, turns it in the light to show off the bluing on the trigger guard and muzzle, and then, as in the poem, "holding it just above the table, he let the butt fall, thunk, and the whole kitchen seemed to shake" (155).

Anania thinks his father was obsessed by "the spectacular reality presented by the surfaces of finely accomplished things—his gold watch, the case work on our Zenith radio, the leather box he kept loose tobacco in" (56). He hankered, Anania thinks, "after a hard lustre in things, the deep burnish of the real in metal, the weight of leather, the flex in a hat brim of Italian felt" (56). Well, the father's aesthetic, one feels certain, is also the son's, and the distance from the real McCoy to the cars customized with a Bauhaus purity to the textures of Anania's verse and prose is not very great. Anania admires energy, even deadly energy, held in elegant control, and the powerful sports car which he covets today is only the child of James Dean's customized 1949 Mercury in *Rebel Without a Cause*.

Even when the energy is not held in control, elegantly or otherwise, Anania draws aesthetic implications and establishes implicit analogies. In the concluding "Autoclysms" chapter, it is as if the real McCoy were no longer simply admired for its workmanship, but fired point blank into somebody's face. Along with the final and appalling car crash in which four of his high-school classmates are killed, Anania describes several others—including two close shaves of his own—and also the "corpse of a Studebaker Golden Hawk" that had been "front-ended," resting in a towing company garage. The Studebaker's windshield is fractured in such a way that the passenger's headprint is discernible and a cigarette, with a faint trace of lipstick on the filter tip, is embedded in the rubbery film of safety glass to which a few strands of blond hair are still attached. "The mangled front end, impacted bumper and grillwork, fenders closed like concertinas, all of it radiates from that collision in the glass, as though the whole wreckage were a crystal whose center was perfect and which grew amorphous only at its most extreme edges." He says that it verges on the sublime, and calls it "a geode … revealing in its deadly amethyst the impeccable record of the moment of impact." "'Verges?'" he asks. "It's hard to imagine anything more awesome, more eloquent in its obedience to natural law" (146). And when he describes an accident in which he himself is involved as three cars and a boat being towed behind one of them "angled off into various ditches like billiard balls in a trick shot," he talks about "another kind of time" when "all the clocks changed," something that had to do "with the sudden perception of cause … as well as with increased adrenaline and focused attention, an instantaneous etiology that alters the perception of time" (147). These are essentially aesthetic responses: that of the connoisseur (to the geode of the smashed Golden Hawk), and that of the artist himself tangled in the processes which he has unleashed but over which he loses control. Does aesthetic experience at its most intense require violence or danger? Must the real McCoy resonate with either suicidal or homicidal implications? Does the arsenal of nuclear weapons exist, as Armageddon may always have existed, "to intensify life?"

Another kind of violence entirely results in what one might call the book's alternate ending—violence done to Anania's system and perceptions by an experiment in sacred mushroom eating at the Macy reservation. After Whisky-Nose Louie—about whom more will be said in a moment—Russell, who is in fact the great-grandson of Logan Fontenelle, is my favorite among Anania's acquaintances in the book. Russell doesn't say very much, but he represents a great deal. And he is the one who is responsible for Anania's hallucinatory or visionary experience.

Russell is contrasted early on with a mixed Otto, Ponca and Pawnee named John who wants to become a nuclear physicist and, as it were, acquire the bomb, which really means becoming a kind of Indian

Oppenheimer who would build someone else's bomb and be someone else's scientist. Russell, who would steal the bomb rather than build it, "had never given up the essential secrets of himself as an Indian. Tough as he was, his real strength was in mystery. Remembering that early, his deep antagonisms to the society were crucial to that bomb-stealing vision of his" (79–80). When Russell claimed that the Indians had taken the bomb off the testing tower in the desert and hidden it in a mountain cave at the end of an Apache trail that no one but an Apache could follow, what he understood

> was what all the rhetoricians of apocalypse have always understood— that the signal points of our real fears are lying all about us and that turning them to any purpose is a poetic act of cultural alignments, a fine tuning, conducted through language, of what is already in scrambled view. Finally, the bomb is no more real than the stereotypical movie Apache, the painted desert no more tangible than the hulking Russian agent. There is no measured ontology to the stuff of this culture; there are only levels of energy. In one way or another everything in America is an icon (75).

When Russell and his cousin and uncle out at the Macy reservation share their hallucinatory mushroom with Anania so that they might "all dream together," Anania, thinking he's been poisoned, jumps in his Plymouth and heads for home. On his way, he notices "a second highway brightly lit that veered to the right and upward, as though following the face of a steep hill that was not there" (141). He tries to blink away the vision, but it persists; the car seems to be pulled by some kind of force toward this second road which "lifted and furled, banking as it turned westward, a finely worked contrail spiraling against the pure lapis of the summer sky" (142). If this is the road not taken by the culture—and it clearly is—it's a road no longer takeable as well. Anania's car jolts to a halt in the loose earth of the first road's shoulder, "weed crowns splitting across the bowsprit of the *Mayflower* at the point of the Plymouth's hood" (141). After falling asleep in his car, he wakes to a final, fleeting vision: Russell and his cousin lifting the remains of the firebird which the cousin had earlier described to him, and placing it on its tail where "it looked more like a mushroom than a bird" (141). In the form of a firebird, Russell and his cousin have the bomb. The visionary writing in these paragraphs of *The Red Menace* is exceptionally beautiful and a good contrast to something like Hugh Brody's very plain account of the trail to heaven in *Maps and Dreams*. But the road Anania sees cannot be taken in his Plymouth. "We have come back to the Indian now for his secrets and his blessings," he says. "If he is smart, he will give us neither" (80).

For the rest, there is a great deal of *talk* in this book—talk as when one says colloquially "*just* talk," the voluble bluster of verbal bravado—and much of it is hilariously funny. The best of the talkers is Whisky-Nose Louie, an alcoholic dishwasher at the grease joint where Anania works whose nonstop monologues make the jive of even the most advanced talkers at Tech High School sound amateurish by comparison. "He could go on ... for eight hours, rasping out sexual advice, insult, salvation, and could curse longer without repeating himself than anyone I ever knew" (82). One of his favorite subjects is communism, and one set piece in a scene taking place in the grease joint is worth the price of the book:

> "You ever see the women that go around with Communists?" Louie asks. "Ugly and fat, every damned one of them, big fat arms, legs like pool tables. That's cause they hate good-lookin' women, just hate 'em." "Louie," someone says, "that doesn't make any sense." "Course it doesn't. If they make any sense, they wouldn't be Communists. You meet a Communist, you ask 'em what he thinks about good-looking women, then look out, cause you're gonna get a two-hour speech about capitalism and jewelry and widows with nine kids hitched up to plows and bankers and how a poor woman suffers for every jewel a fancy woman wears. All the while, he's got some quarter section a beef in a brown dress sittin' in the corner bitin' her fingernails. Never trust a man who's got a smart reason for havin' somethin' he don't want.... I was in Portland one night, in a freightyard, not botherin' nobody, drinkin' Seattle wine with this here gandy-dancer. And up come this Communist. Spends half-a-minute talkin' 'bout the weather, then gets goin' on the capitalists and how they put us all

outa work, and I says to him, 'Where's your fat girlfriend?' And he says he ain't got a fat girlfriend, and I tells him that the Communists fucked him straight cause he's entitled to a fat girlfriend. Then me and that gandy-dancer bust a gut laughin.' And he asks what's so funny, and I says, 'They're s'posed to give you a fat girlfriend. It goes with bein' a Communist.' And he says he ain't no Communist, he's a socialist worker. And I says, long as you're gonna be somethin' dumb, might as well be a Communist, cause a fat, ugly woman is better than no woman at all" (86).

All this, needless to say, is *talk*, not conversation, and the book is electric with it in a variety of idioms. In the end, however, it is sad rather than funny. For *The Red Menace* ends with talk exactly like the talk that began it—the simultaneously aggressive and self-protective teenage jive which has an analogue in the gossip of adults. After the final autoclysm that kills Linda, Arnie and Meatball and decapitates Darlene on a telephone-pole guidewire, the talk echoes off into silence. "No shit, you could see 'em flying off in every direction.... Arms and legs out, towels, bathing suits, everything in the car" (150). Anania has written a poem called "*Esthétique du Râle*" which is as intimately related to the conclusion of *The Red Menace* as "The Temper" is to the episode at the housing project when his father takes out the real McCoy. It has to do in part with the degenerative history of modern art—from imagism and cubism to the work of minimalists and conceptualists and the "body art" of someone like Jack Broden—and with the deaths of modern artists, whether a James Dean, a Jackson Pollock or an Albert Camus, in the autoclysms of the 1950s.

"Something is ending," Anania writes in the poem "*Esthétique du Râle*," and, "Perhaps it was too much/to ask them to resolve our difficulties" (*Selected Poems* 129, 130). If artistic style, as Denis Donoghue maintains, is a compensation for the loss of conversation's true communion, then gossip, *talk*, a voyeuristic (and indeed a journalistic) focusing of attention on an artist's life and death, is certainly our compensation and a very poor one too, for the loss of art. "We know / how the day went, the guest list / of the party down the road, the Cadillac's fishtail and impact" (130), Anania writes in his poem. And in the final lines of it a field of flowers as inauspicious as the jive about Darlene and Meatball waits, as talk, to receive the wreckage of one Red Menace among others:

> It is only in isolate flecks, swift
> and mutable, light finds its shape,
> all that the form fails to exclude,
>
> the almost unbearable clamor, every
> gesture ambled among traffic; this day
> or any other, talk settling in with the
> portioned words, meant, I think, to be
>
> a flower, a field of flowers, where
> the wreckage seems oddly comfortable,
> a seaside morning dew over bent metal
> and blue Quaker ladies, *le dernier cri* (131).

Works Cited

Anania, Michael. *Selected Poems.* Asphodel Press, 1994.

———. *The Color of Dust.* Swallow Press, 1970.

———. *The Red Menace: A Fiction.* Thunder's Mouth Press, 1984.

A Survey of Michael Anania's Poetry

Mike Barrett

1. Geomatics

The opening poem in Michael Anania's first collection, *The Color of Dust*, begins with an epigraph from Pablo Neruda:

> When this problem has been thoroughly explored,
> I am going to school myself so well in things
> that, when I try to explain my problems,
> I shall speak, not of self, but of geography. (2)

Anania's career demonstrates what such schooling looks like. Following form that evolves out of the modernist image, Anania's poetry maps consciousness in the scale of language.

Wallace Stevens, in an essay on William Carlos Williams, writes, "Imagism is an ancient phase of poetry. It is something permanent" (244). An image brings the outside (blue, green or sung by the sea) *inside*. The image is a speaking picture of the world that Pound called "phanopoeia." Phanopoeia throws "the object (fixed or moving) on to the visual imagination" (38). Images are visual components of consciousness—pictures on a screen, projections of the outside on the inside. The projector that throws the visual image onto the poem's screen is, of course, language. Take a city street scene, for example. We see it as intersecting relations among precepts which are delivered by words:

Just north of Clark Street
Grace Street, disheveled,
without the regimen of red brick,
the houses, gray of old wood
stripped of paint above
the tilted, broken walks,
cracked by the root of elms
that hang over the walks,
break open retaining walls,
that spread green over the gray
light green after the torn husks
sift into the broken walls
and down to the earth
beneath the canted, cracked sidewalks. (*Selected Poems* 2)

The opening phrase, "Just north of Clark Street," orients us. We observe the houses and sidewalks, the trees growing through concreted neglect; we learn how they relate to each other: "above," "hang over," "break open," "spread," "sift," "beneath." Like projective geometry, tree roots and time transform the scene; they make walls crumble, crack and twist the sidewalks. Anania's syntactical control arranges this extended visual image in a single sentence.

When images are located geographically, they are also social: "we move through intersections /capable of history" (5). The disheveled wooden buildings are compared to the "regimen" of red brick homes in some other neighborhood. The images move downstream from "Grace Street" and end as human waste, "down to the yards, / to the open sewer / that swills into the river" (3). The landscape is drawn according to a perspective that includes class relations and urban infrastructure.

"Stops Along the Western Bank of the Missouri River" and "Riversongs" (from the eponymous collection) clearly show Anania's relationship to Charles Olson. The poetic meets the geomatic in Gloucester, as it does on the Missouri River:

Locust Street viaduct behind
him,

. . . .
the drive-in movie
angling east; beam crane dead
ahead; windward (*Selected Poems* 60)

The poet navigates through image "drive-in movie / angling east," surveying the seen, "beam crane dead ahead." You can also hear George Oppen (a sailor as well) in this poetry—cityscapes rendered with the same intensity the pasture conventionally inspires.

Visual art is an aestheticization of geomatics. Painting, for example, measures the world in line, form and color:

morning sunlight
caught by crystals
that grow from
the edges of the glass
like plaited leaves,
so garlanded, chill blue (109–110)

The poem contains line ("edges of the glass"), form ("caught by crystals") and color ("chill blue"). Color adds depth and light adds value to the two-dimensional grayscale of the printed page:

trees, nearly bare,
a network of bruised limbs
that resurface this dark sky-
glaze and texture of Bosch-
with occasional bright red
red of maple and sumac,
opening sinfully where
wet with morning, the branches cross (31)

The subject trees are only one part of the poem's arrangement; there is glazed texture and color for emphasis. Color also opens the dimension of pathos—Bosch paints the fall of man and sin follows the fall with red. As Kandinsky argues, color produces an effect that corresponds to a spiritual vibration in the spectator. It changes the mood like a key change in music.

Anania intends a painterly poem. He states this explicitly in "A Hanging Screen":

> I wanted to make this poem
> of silk, stretched tight
> and polished, an ink wash
> drifting ambiguous mountains,
>
> words gathered like momentary
> details, instances of wind
> and water among loose foliage,
> painting *au plein air*; that is
>
> alive and painting a surface
> of perpetual change (119)

In the open air, the poet composes images in such a way that the experience of the outside, its details, its flux and dynamic purpose, are inscribed onto the surface of the poem, textured and textual. However applying paint arrests the "perpetual change" the painter seeks to paint on.

Anania's painterly sensibility is one lineament that connects him to the New York School. Another is that visual art and visual artists function as poetic subjects:

> Albers
> spin any of them
> at the center and
> the colors whiten
> away, an early
> lesson, one color
> only and its varied
> absences (*Riversongs* 56)

For Josef Albers the study of color was practical—not what you know about color, but how you see it, "What counts here—first and last—is not so-called knowledge / of so-called facts, but vision— seeing" (2). Stevens notes that Williams is "a writer to whom writing is the grinding of a glass, the polishing of a lens by means of which he hopes to see clearly ... they are the rubbings of reality" (244). The poem is a way to see clearly and thus know clarity.

But the conscientious sight of the seer can't see all of reality, only what the body and mind allow it to. As Albers notes, "In visual perception a color is almost never seen as it really is / —as it physically is" (1). The world visualized is not the visualized world. In geomatics, fundamental errors affect the accuracy of surveying:

1. No observation is exact;
2. Every observation contains errors;
3. The true value of an observation is never known;
4. The exact error is always unknown. (Wolfe & Ghilani 17)

These are the errors of perception and cognition. Everything we seek comes with an error that hides. Hills can be vantages or can provide cover:

Geography matters.
It is the plan,
the arrangement of things
that confuses our enemies,
the difference between what
they expect and what they get;
. . . .
deception is
an achievement in ordering the obvious. (*Selected Poems* 20)

Deception is a plausible arrangement of observables and is possible because all observables deceive. (This, though, does not constitute an assent to Kant.)

In "A War Story," the emotional value of the story cannot be reclaimed by an assiduous survey:

Sensation is the impediment to design:
remember this—that was all on Rees Street

which runs East and West exactly
doesn't intersect the North-South transit
missing by one block the playground;
extended it would span the earth,
to this table was parallel,
or, rather, being square on any side,
either parallel or perpendicular (*Selected Poems* 49)

Because perception can be an "impediment," the narrator trusts orientation "that this was all on Rees Street / which runs East and West exactly" (49)—perhaps even more than recollection. The story told in the poem is fragmented, even though its setting can be marked. The "I" can be located, but not the sequence of events, "at this date exact order is impossible" (48). To errors of perception are added faults in memory. The observation points—Rees Street, playground, a studio couch—situate but do not conjure the original sensations. The value of the experience is outside measure. Appropriately, there is a death at the center of the narrative.

If the outside is the sender and the mind the receiver, messages lose information in transit. In addition, the mind can confuse, even when the senses are clear. The fifth section of "Riversongs" is composed "As Meriwether Lewis" where mental errors accrue:

the river has neither course nor current;
the last point of the relative compass,
upstream/downstream, falls away; the duet
of waterfowl and waterfall, complimentary
virtuosi of distances untaken or taken
and forgotten, is joined to dissonance. (*Selected Poems* 68)

On an unmapped river, Meriwether's mind receives the tumult around him. Waterfowl join their music with falling water and distance. In the unsettled auditor, all becomes noise; there is nothing to fathom.

These error types account for the elegiac mood in Anania's poetry, which is reinforced by autumnal settings. Perception and memory fall away. But if the poet is a disciplined surveyor, well-schooled in things, errors can be minimized. Deception can deceive itself. Noise can be re-absorbed into music. Perpetual change can at least be delineated:

> it is the line of force or the vector
> that sees us through our ambiguities,
> diagrams of rivers, path the semi
> takes among its various winds, turn
> the night makes at neon sign, EATS,
> locus of all points on the lasso's rim,
> itself remembered. (104)

If we know nothing, we can almost always figure out where we are by the intersections that circumscribe our location. This orientation grounds us in the world, allows us to navigate, and read what the landscape signals, like "EATS," ringed with running lights.

2. Melos

Errors occur because our perception is based on a model shaped in and limited by gray matter. The mind is between the world and the poem. What we experience as the world is a nerve cell model of it:

> what passes through us,
> waiting some arrangement
> of our smallest parts,
> a clear space opened
> . . . .
> press of movement, place (*Selected Poems* 124)

The world passes through our mind when we perceive, though it is no longer the world; it is consciousness, an arrangement of our smallest parts. Consciousness is the consequence of perception but is active in that it directs our focus. We can cast our mind where we list. Anania has called this willful casting of intense focus the poet's "moment of attention," similar to the term photographer Henri Courtier Bresson used to describe an essence captured on film, "the decisive moment."

The moment of attention includes not just the object, but the mind that perceives the object—not the poet's sensibility but the poet's consciousness. We can change the direction of the image's vector in moving from modernism to postmodernism. If consciousness is the mind's model of the world in real time, then the image can be a complex of consciousness. In postmodernism (and compost modernism), an image accommodates discourses of the thing and the brain perceiving the thing. Much of Anania's verse from *The Sky at Ashland* has such imagery. These poems are as concerned with *cogito* as they are with *geô*.

An image of consciousness has a wide range of disparate material to turn into poetry:

> the one who scrapes
> a cleated heel along
>
> the inner passage of
> your ear
>
> all movement implies collision:
> raise the temperature,
> increase the pressure,
> and it multiplies.
>
> Supposing as well,
> resonant frequencies,
> diverse harmonies (*Selected Poems* 168)

We start the image in the basilar membrane of the inner ear, where tiny hairs wave from the sound of a cleated heel. This sound signifies movement formalized as thermodynamics, "raise the temperature / increase the pressure." The original sound is then combined with other acoustic waves in lines like "supposing as well, / resonant frequencies / diverse harmonies." The cleated heel is heard through a wall that is also part of the calculation:

> this wall, exactly twice
> the length of a distant

axle, roof pitch an even
fraction of the highway (168)

"Sums" illustrates another characteristic of postmodernism and
compost modernism—the arrangement of multiple scales. This is
not unique to postmodernism (Donne's "Valediction: Of Weeping" is
a good example from the seventeenth century). But it is much more
prevalent in poetry of the latter half of the twentieth century and
continuing through the twenty-first. The poet has many scales with
which to compose, a range from the cosmos to probability tables of
quantum phenomena. Consciousness is able to shelter multiple scales
because it itself is composed of huge collectivities of minute matter. If
we know the little world made cunningly, we know the world.

In the poem "Such Summers," we can see how the image operates
in multiple scales:

2.
nest of twigs
and loose grass,
bits of string
the rainwater
runoff leaves behind

3.
A snag in the river
curls, loops, and spins
away, a branch, a stump,
the crosspiece of a broken
jetty, cloud-play, foam.
. . . .

6.
a tree, a stand of trees,
the shadowed relief of hill
against receding hill
hill as movement (156)

Section 2 is a static image in the usual visual sense. Section 3 becomes more dynamic. We change scale in linear dimension when we move from "crosspiece" to "cloudplay." We can formalize the curls, loops and spins through fluid dynamics. Section 6 starts with particulars, "a tree," then expands outward with "shadowed relief of hill" and in the last line moves from the concrete to the metaphoric, as in "hill as movement." The mind sees these hills as movement while they slip past the field of vision—we move from the outside to its transformation as metaphor inside.

In a poem like "Factum, Chansons, Etc," images are strung together syntactically while engaging multiple scales:

> mulberry stains, the dark
> remnants of mulberries
> in a mulberry shade, green
> against green luster and chalk
> white tracings of mulberry yeast,
> the brief ferment briefly known,
> drawn into the moist grains of
> broken soil like watercolors
> drawn into moistened paper,
> the spreading frayed bands
> of color signifying hill-line
> and bluff fall, the long
> consequences of wind and rain,
> the jagged tumble of vegetation. (225)

The passage begins with a direct treatment, "Grape ivy and blue gentian, / mulberry stains." The image is transformed by increasingly narrow time scale, "the brief ferment briefly known," and space scale, "tracings of mulberry yeast." The particles of yeast are like "watercolors / drawn into moistened paper" projecting the image, through metaphor, onto the mind's eye. The passage resolves by turning the watercolor into an image of the world "signifying hill-line / and bluff fall" and then broadens the time scale via "the long / consequences of wind and rain."

In "The Sky at Ashland," the narrator, after nominating the visual field in a series of names—lambent silo or sweet sorghum, foxtail crown goldenrod silver-rod and ragwort dogbane and star-petalled milkweed, broomsedge and blue stem—asks:

> Are we able to do any more
> than propose distances for this
>
> brown meandering in a play of names?
> If words extend themselves from place
> to place, are their movements less
>
> determined than the course of water
> leveling itself or more diverse than
> what sheathes it here like a plumed skin? (137)

The narrator asks these questions of language. How determined is its meaning? How responsive is its force? What distances can it cover? Is language like a petal that sheathes the flower's style?

In the same way that sight introduces error into observation, language introduces error into rendering observation. Language and the world are always "at odds again." One way to reduce the error is to find a form that eschews the weight of the referent—there is no error where there is no reference. Kandinsky believed that music is unencumbered by content. Just like painting, music works for Anania as an idealization of poetic form:

> 'Neath luna then, all things conspire
> figure and fancy toward song, as the dried grain
> is lifted and thrown, as the light is caught
> along the leeward edge of unbroken waves (173)

The image captures music in matter—the wheat separated from the chaff by the melody of wind, light caught across a score of waves. In "Gin Music," this ideal form is procreative—it grows its own content, i.e., "the song would ease its way out into / the room like a root extending itself / into damp soil and take leaf and flower" (196). The song ends up as a plant.

131

In some of these poems, such as "And So," images invest music with content:

> The foam that curls
> against your ankles, chill morning
> leaves and blades of grass,
> reed wet and trembling, tendons
> your walking plays into view,
> toes finely turned toward humus,
> sky running along treeline,
> the sheer sway of cloud furl
> like music arching into song. (213)

The vibrations of the wet reed, the grace notes of tendon and toes treading on the lively and lovely earth prepare the final figure "like music arching into song."

Music may not hold explicit reference, but it does have content— what beats time against the tectorial membrane in the inner ear. Music is just another form of mind in time and, like all things, it "trembles / hums a while and slips away." The loss in perception is the loss in language is the loss in music:

> We have talked for so long
> about the limits of words,
> all that they can not touch,
> how the song fails us even
> in its delight, things cut
> short by what is said,
> as though the hand could
> be certain, the eye in its
> lifelong fidget, exact. (182)

"Its lifelong fidget" is a description of the saccadic movements the eye uses to take in the world. The certain hand could be painting or writing. No matter how many scales consciousness accommodates, there is loss in each. Does this mean elegy holds sway? These poems say, sometimes as painting, sometimes as music, that there is always some *thing* to talk about. The poet's task is to treat that thing directly, even if that treatment is always incomplete.

3. Propositions

Though Anania clearly can be traced to the image-making in Williams and the place-making of Olson, he proposes as much as he observes. Stevens was a poet of proposal and Ashbery after him. Wittgenstein also figures in, under a desk in "Fifty-Two Definite Articles" and in "Factum, Chansons, Etc" where Prague is a variable name.

Because language is the *logos* of the *geô*, we cannot avoid making propositions. Wittgenstein puts it this way: "in a proposition a thought finds an expression that can be conceived by the senses" (3.1). In other words, the proposition, if it makes sense, is one possible situation to be fulfilled, since "a proposition contains the form, but not the content of its sense" (3.13). A proposition is an image outside in. It is a direct treatment of a thing proposed, a form in the mind waiting for a case to become real in. Stevens and Ashbery use propositions in this way. Of his peers, Anania could be seen working in the same field as poets like Rosmarie Waldrop and Ann Lauterbach. For these poets, the poem is a linguistic field where proposition and image are the components of lyric. I have called this kind of poetry "propositional lyricism."

In propositional lyricism, content does not have to start from the outside and transfer inside. The poem is a transit system between mind and world. Each transfer necessarily involves a scale change as here in "Five Proper Nouns":

> These plains run off the edge
> of sight. Mountains we have
> names for hold imaginary
> distances in place. (*Selected Poems* 203)

The first sentence sets the limit for sight. The mountains in the second sentence are named and remembered. They not only signify specific peaks; they signify distance. The distances are imaginary by being psychic; the mountains real by being physical. Conversely, the

133

distances are real by being physical; the mountains imaginary by being psychic. Mind and world cross and recross. The abstract and concrete re/in form each other. Furthermore, if we look at the second sentence by itself: "Mountains we have names for hold imaginary distances in place"—we recognize it as a proposition.

Poetry's privilege is to move between the spheres of mind and world:

> This
> privilege of voice is pure
> substance. Between this hill
> and any hill is conjury
> of syntax, and this hill
> this steep, an inclination
> bearing substance into time. (222)

Syntax is able to project any image onto consciousness because it is the form of language. And because consciousness is repository of memory, the image is portable; it carries substance into time. Again, if we turn the lines into sentences, [we recognize them as propositions].

> *This privilege of voice is pure substance.*
> *Between this hill and any hill is conjury of syntax.*
> *This steep bears substance into time.*

Anania shares another quality with his contemporaries Lauterbach and Waldrop: he can shape a lovely lyric. The poem "As Semblance, Though" exhibits this quality. The poem begins with an error type of the grandest scale: "the nothing—or the not—supposes, of course / and gestures into some certain absence" (*In Natural Light* 16). This is a proposition straight out of the via negativa. But the *via negativa* is not a tenable way for an imagist:

> More than zero, always, and more than one,
> the self and its selves edging along successive
> thresholds, sill after sill, a blue contentment
> as certain as the sky, washed over hillside

and treeline and all those distances it recedes
from as the land slips past you or the river (17)

The self is "more than zero" but never coherent, "more than one."
The self changes on the threshold of each perception and dissolves into
a "blue contentment certain as the sky." Because each iteration of self is
timebound, "it slips past you." Nothing eventually claims the self as the
body becomes some other thing. The poem ends with music excavated
from other things:

the cuttlebones of giant squid, tentacles, beaks
and ink drawn off into the soil, river
only briefly stained, time counted out in longer
intervals than intent has patience for; tree
lilt, silt swirl, the earth's long hush humming. (19)

Matter accrues in a time scale that is geologic. The proposition:
Time counted out in longer intervals than intent has patience for is
answered by the sprung rhythm of "tree / lilt, silt swirl, the earth's long
hush humming." The answer is rich in sound and O Montale! it is
lyrical.

Propositional lyricism is a nexus where a number of lines in
American poetry meet. Pound and Williams provide theory and
practice for the image. Olson provides a way to map the image in
relation to place and other discourses. Stevens provides a model on
how to turn propositions, images of mind, into music. After Stevens,
The New York School provides a model for composing propositions
as painting. Michael Anania has received his schooling from all these
poets. To this education is added precise vision, sure line stroke, and
sensitivity to beauty in the world, mind and language:

the descending intention

of color, however casually
chosen; and what is said
in time is always temporal,

> hence song and dance
> swaying from axis to axis,
> words like gauds, spun and spinning (55)

In Michael Anania's poetry, experience is given voice in multiple scales, "from axis to axis." It is a site that gathers images and attempts to make sense of them by arranging their relations in space and time, like a map or a painting. When sense is not enough, the poet makes propositions to extract meaning from the mind. When meaning doesn't suffice, the poet, "spun and spinning," makes music.

Note

It is noteworthy that both Albers and Olson taught at Black Mountain College in North Carolina.

Works Cited

Albers, Josef. *Interaction of Color.* Yale UP, 1975.

Anania, Michael. *In Natural Light.* Asphodel Press, 1999.

———. *Riversongs.* U of Illinois Press, 1978.

———. *Selected Poems.* Asphodel Press, 1994.

Bergson, Henri. *Introduction to Metaphysics.* Translated by T. E. Hulme. Hackett Publishing, 1999.

Kandinsky, Wassily. *Concerning the Spiritual in Art.* Translated by M. T .H. Sadler. Dover Press, 1977.

Pound, Ezra. *ABCs of Reading.* New Directions, 1960.

Stevens, Wallace. *Opus Posthumous.* Knopf, 1989.

Wolfe, Ralph and Charles D. Ghilani. *Elementary Surveying.* Prentice Hall, 2002.

Wittgenstein, Ludwig. *Tractatus Logico-Philosophicus.* Translated by D. F. Pears and B. F. McGuiness. Routledge, 1995.

Looking Back at Michael Anania's
In Natural Light

Reginald Gibbons

Predominant sometimes in Michael Anania's work is a reverence for and linguistic enactment of the act of seeing and of becoming conscious of seeing. If we are tempted to think of this in relation to the unmistakable qualities of light over the prairies and in prairie cities, we might also regard it as a quality inherent in English-language poetry, a quality of English itself that is also keen for visual images.

Why should the act of seeing matter so much in poetry? In English-language poetry, in particular? The Romantic shift in consciousness and poetic practice—in poems by Wordsworth, in the everyday descriptive detail of John Clare, and the work of other poets of that time—enhanced a greater attention to the uniqueness of objects and nature and persons. And such descriptive specificity is still the measure of much of the poetry that's written in English today. New awareness of the artistic problem of making our sense perceptions vivid in the English language, and especially the sense of sight and of detailing lived experience, did not diminish poetry but instead brought new materials into it—a specificity of the qualities of objects and events that was found less often in earlier English poetry and in attitudes and feelings also new. Never mind that all poetry is inescapably not itself the reality it may describe or suggest. For most poets even today, to gesture toward a credible relationship between concrete language and the experience and even the exhilaration of perceiving is a kind of artistic honesty.

And for a poet to gesture toward admitting the impossibility, finally, of such a credible relationship ever being fully achieved, is also a way of acknowledging its having been desired. One impulse (or even wish) of the postmodern literary era has been to insist that language is almost entirely an unreliable construct and that poetry can only be an ironic manipulation of that construct. But to some degree, this is old news, so long as we don't expect this conviction to be absolute (the "inexpressibility topos" goes all the way back to Virgil and before). And there's scarcely a good poet in English of any period beginning with the Renaissance who doesn't manifest the frustration (yet without at all eviscerating poetry itself) of working against the limitations of what we human beings can articulate. Yet at the same time, another aspect of our very complex use of language is that there are some things we perceive *with* language, not just "representing" things, etc. with words but apprehending certain feelings and ideas unique to what poetic language and structure do "things" (in the most general sense) that cannot be otherwise perceived at all. By poetic structure I mean simply the way a poem achieves its movement from one idea, feeling, image, moment, to the next, and how it organizes all of those movements into a (perhaps complex) train of thought, feeling and perception.)

An important aspect of poetic technique that comes into play in English is the relation of the particular "music" of our English-language consonant clusters and rhythms to our lived experience itself, to sensation. If I mention the "thwacks of a dull tarnished axe on logs not yet fit for fires," then I am putting it this way because it seems to me I cannot only think but partly *sense* what I'm saying because this sort of language so vividly evokes the physical world in our imagination and subtly even in our bodies.

And this brings me to Michael Anania. With keen perceptiveness and self-awareness as a user of language, and also with enormous skill and thoughtfulness as a practitioner of poetry, he opens a path of poetic thinking. Faithful to the innumerable attempts since the poetry of the 1790s to make language seem a representation and even an enactment of *seeing*, he has perfected signature style with a commodious capacity for articulating experience and thinking and feeling, and with a lively, jazzy, improvisational mastery of language. He creates an illusion or dramatization of seeing with his use of vivid literal *imagery*, makes a discerning and very characteristic *selection* of what he describes, and he articulates a poetic *discourse about* seeing.

His visual powers of language are characteristically attentive to the fine detail made visible by prairie light—the clear edges of every petal or brick; his poetic style transformed perception into the language of uncannily clear perception, and it conveys a clear (as in "clear light") sense of the reward of paying attention, of perceiving. To notice is to begin to feel and think. Of course, however concrete a poet's imagery, light can almost never escape our reading it as a metaphor. Anania writes in "Some Other Spring," "'You know how it goes,' / he said—the quick shift / of light and dark" (27). And attention at its most intense is a kind of nondenominational, even nonreligious, spiritual practice in itself, thus not at all unworthy as one focus of a poet's work.

Anania has been the exemplary artist of the poetic pleasure of visual, kinetic, auditory and emotional perception in and with words. In his volume *In Natural Light* (1999), the subtleties and delicacy of his language of perceiving also lead to a more emotionally freighted attention, and to a more problematic, and no less interesting, pondering of how it might be that "the eye is now the problem, imperiums / of sight, one after another, glance, gaze / or glare" (61).

In Anania's poems, urban scenes, gardens and wild places continually play their energies and attractiveness against each other: the natural, and especially the vegetal, for its beautiful freedom from possessing a will like that which leads to human striving and suffering; the urban, the social, the historical aspects of human life, for the beautiful range of narratives and incidents of human action and experience. Also, only one phoneme separates Anania's title, "in natural light" from being "unnatural light." This implied substitution might suggest that the flowers are in the natural light and the city is in an unnatural light, but it's more complicated and paradoxical than that: "We walk / the dark's bright crevices" (one also hears "crevasses") (44). In "Incidental Music," Anania writes cities

seem so purposeful,
their musics half-formed,
urgent as traffic;

lake effect snow—
the day not quite cold
enough—brightens

the pavement only
momentarily, laughter
and exhaust plumes,

their sudden clarities
passing (45)

In both the natural light of sky and the unnatural illumination of street lights we are so often oblivious to what is.

To Anania, music, "Mozart, then Horace Silver" (45) is human solace and exuberance, and it too is one of the central materials of his poems. In his words, it can sometimes seem almost tactile [as in "And This Is Free"]: "at the curb a man extends three fingers / toward the music, feeling its edge spill / toward him as though it were a subtle / property of the air, a Braille he reads" (23). That is, Anania can perceive the sound of music as almost tactile and almost made of words. Responsiveness to sound is like reading (i.e., that other seeing that allows us to imagine visually). This complex metaphor repeats the "edge" that figures elsewhere in these poems—something that suggests the effect of clear light on things, but then turns the air-that-is-light to an air-that-is-text, allowing this man, and perhaps others of us, to improve our imaginative seeing (at least while reading). (There's a big essay to be written about music, especially jazz, in Anania's poems—it's thoroughly woven into his work.)

From the very first poem of *In Natural Light*, I think a heightened awareness of human damage—experienced and inflicted—informs the clarity of perception that we already knew to expect in Anania's work (and which he himself announces in his epigraphs to this volume). Anania is not a "political" poet except in the sense that any poet attuned to the range of human experience cannot avoid at least implying the contexts of human experience. The large-scale chaos, accomplishments and failures of our incomprehensibly complex world and our American cultures have been overwhelming, especially in these last four contradictory decades of political darkness, cynical use of power, and ever-present financial corruption. (The sometimes savage American sophistry, denial and piety, to an ear that has not been seduced or cowed, makes the sound of an evisceration of language as poet[s] would want to use it.) Anania's poems seem to make the honorable and humane claim that a careful, fully responsive and humble attentiveness of and to language must be paid to the reality that surrounds us—from love all the way to "terrorists in New York" (10), as Anania wrote, even before 2001 or 2021. While not as torqued as the work of such poets as Paul Celan and not as plain-style as George Oppen, there is in Anania the sort of serious play of language that one finds also in Lorine Niedecker.

The sorrow expressed in "A Place That's Known," the first poem of *In Natural Light* gives us a delicate energy for elegy, and does not insist too much on grief yet is saturated by it, is given to the reader as a moment of taking note of small things—dangerous or assuaging or celebratory—of the physical world. These things, evoked in English words orchestrated with nuance of sound and connotation, in turn "speak" without their own words (but in Anania's words) of what is going on in the human beings nearby. The poem begins with "American elms opening a span of western sky" and quickly moves into memory and mourning, and a sense of human desperation whether in wars or neighborhood brawls; it ends with description of brutal suffering. At its center is the poet's mother:

> "Your father," "your grandmother," "my dad,"
> she said into the broken night, sirens edging
> toward us, the fight across the way spilt
> down the steps onto the Plaza's hopscotch,

knife flash or skillet lid, a razor's band
of blue darkness moving across soft skin
as smoothly as sweat, blood quick as a tear. (5)

The lines below show Anania's ear for densely physical language—vigorously evocative monosyllables (and the repeated phonemes that improvise the poem like a particular melody of word-sound: "wavefoam or waveform," "eddies ... seaways," "oartip slips ... our ship's," "frothy ... both," and then the allusions to Homer and Pound "So-shu" ("a Chinese mythological figure" in Canto II). Anania can also give us the phonetic pleasures of a jazz musician's sly ability not only to allude to someone else's riff but also to playing it in someone else's style, as in the following section of "Fifty-Two Definite Articles":

wavefoam or waveform and what eddies
from this oartip slips away into
our ship's own frothy past; seaways
are strange both here and in China:
water and wave mechanics, their random
certainties make some Homeric moments,
some So-shu more or less inevitable (77)

The particular American poetic genealogy to which Anania belongs also reaches back along a somewhat parallel path to Pound's opposite-yet-comrade William Carlos Williams, who mostly praised not Europe's old texts, ancient gods and glorious buildings, but the flourishing American weeds that grow in the waste ground behind a hospital for infectious diseases, the ordinary child in a workingman's household in New Jersey, the woman on the sidewalk looking for the nail in her shoe, a big scrap of brown paper tumbling in the winds of the street. Anania bows slightly to each of these two master craftsmen. Without Williams' example, there would be no poems in Anania's book like "December Commonplace" or "Things Ain't What They Used To Be," nor the use of three-step lines. And in response to Pound's famous imagist couplet set on an underground train platform, Anania writes a miniature "Eclogue," as if one might tease not only a modernist poet but also, with this title, the whole ancient tradition of setting poems in idealized sheep fields:

How sudden they seem,
the gradual lives
of flowers, or the faces
you see in the brief
light of a "B" stop
taking, as you always
do, the "A" train. (8)

("A" and "B" stops used to be the station scheme of the Chicago El from downtown through the North Side to the northern border of the city.)

Anania sees and evokes many more blossoms. In the very first poem of this volume he mentions "a dance spun / across the linoleum's worn flowers" (4). These blossoms in particular—doubly represented in both linoleum and words—seem to encompass all of Anania's complex attention both to our worn humanness and to nature, to both the human experience of the damages and fulfillments of time, and also our sensations of how the unnatural (here, the linoleum) has its own way of trying to outlast time. In this poem, the linoleum flowers are more affecting than real ones could be because of how they evoke obliquely the everyday life of ordinary people. Throughout *In Natural Light*, Anania also names foxgloves, cosmos, those flower-faces on the "A" train, the "tufted nylon rose / upholstery city sunset," "smoke trailed petals" of wind, "mums / and white statice," periwinkle, "iridescent birdflowers," "flowers trembling / against their buds," and "a desire for roses." Of "Psyche and Eros" he writes, "His sepal wings and her arms petalled / upward" (58). He writes of "red picot cream colored petals recalled / more than seen," of lilacs, of "the great bearded iris," and he asks the elegiac question—as if the poet of now, here, on a rainy everyday street, might offer a remembering gesture to a dead friend at a T'ang Dynasty festival at which poets float celebratory wine in cups placed on lotus leaves to float down a river. Some of Anania's poems are also like funeral offerings of poem-blossoms from another culture—"mullai, kurinci, maratum, neytal"[1]—down the Ganges:

143

what flowers should we
drift along this course
of dampened asphalt

in your memory, Raman?" (46)

(My guess is that "Raman" was short for Anania's friend, the Indian poet and translator A. K. Ramanujan, who taught at the University of Chicago.) Anania's question leads to the unavoidable thought of "the fifth region, flowerless, / a place of separation" (48). Flowers in a time of mourning remind me again of the first lines of the first poem, in which Anania names flowers. And almost as if to define a poetics, he writes, "an accident / of flower and poem" (77).

The repetitions of light, a diction of physicality and images of flowers are only part of what a reader may respond to in Anania's work—especially in this book. The relation between every poet and every reader is that the poet may evoke more than any one reader will see or hear. Amidst Anania's color, physicality, light, scenes, music, leaves and trees, which are all part of the character of *In Natural Light* and of his other books, I for one find myself mostly pondering Anania's flowers, which are so illuminated, so much for the mind's eye. To me, they suggest not only what is out there beyond the poet but also his inner landscape, registering the pain and the vividness of life as if his attentiveness were evoked by real and imaginary flowering of feeling and thought, memory and personal human histories. This book takes pleasure in flower names,[2] nuances, implications, associations of beauty, ephemerality and more. But the flowers face inward, too—in this book, especially at the implicit feelings which in the very first poem circulate around the mother.

I was not entirely truthful, above, when I wrote that the linoleum flowers were the first that Anania mentions in this book. Rereading the book, I see that what I first saw (the linoleum flowers) was what I—for whatever unconscious reasons—wanted to see or was able to see; but of course Anania sees more than I do. In fact, at the beginning of the first poem he writes

Out on the front step fifty years ago,
my mother beside the four o'clocks
smoking her last Chesterfield of the night (3)

The importance of the flowers' metonymic name (four-o'clocks bloom at the end of the day) is that the hour stands for the flower itself, and the flower stands for a lateness that is emotional. In this book there is a subtle configuration of flower, mother, and the impulse to memorialize.

About the mother herself, standing "in natural light," one could say that although she may be explicitly mentioned only once, in this opening poem, as if she were the guardian of a metaphorical doorway through which we pass only once (because we are born only once), it also might be she who hovers unnamed and out of sight in the backward-looking "Songs Intended for Familiar Places," or in "De Kooning," she who is the

blank space
that urges space
along, the way
in music silence
drives the song. (65)

Or she who seems to appear repeatedly, but again never named, in "Fifty-Two Definite Articles," or she who stands behind stanza X of "What Are Islands to Me Now":

sighting across her upper arm, the way
it was turned toward him and her breast
his first horizon, the room a focal haze;
a snarl of sunlight among carnations (63)

Carnations: in the inner space of our incarnated responsiveness as we read, Anania's flowers seem to be marked as something like what is finally said in the little part iv of "Sequence Composed on Gray Paper":

warm breath on cold fingers,
cloud cupped there, voiceless,
between thought and sound (31)

145

That is, the moment of passage between thought and sound—while we may normally only notice it when we cannot find the word we want, when language cannot represent what we know intuitively that is too elusive, too subtle, too ephemeral, to be articulated—is articulated here by poetic thinking. Much poetry is—but most often only in its depths, where part of its nature should be, like nocturnes and symphonies and string quartets and lieder—about itself.

So for Anania, the flower, the mother and the moment "between thought and sound"—a moment of evanescent remembering seem like elements of a profound but only implicit configuration deep in the psyche and thus also in the poems. A light along the edges of an object, a person and a moment of almost preverbal thought: this is very illuminating, in just the way that poetry throws its light-of-words and light-of-movement. Language has eyes that see what our physical eyes cannot. Our eyes and the mind's eye see what language can suggest but cannot bring fully into words. Great poetry does not settle for approximations or familiar wording; it brings here what can be articulated and is all the more valuable to us because at least it brings nearer to us what remains elusive in our being and in the world. A poet of great gifts and mature imagination and thought can get hold of such discoveries. To have done it with grace, modulating through so many pleasures of language and thought, is what Anania has done.

Notes

1. "mullai, kurinci, maratum, neytal": convention symbolic landscapes of classical Tamil love poetry. See en.wikipedia.org/wiki/Sangam_landscape. And from an earlier web source I can no longer access: "The life found in Literature is termed as Literary life. It is divided into two: *Internal-life (aham)—Internal-life (aham) talks more about the love and passion between the hero and heroine of the literature which are felt and known only to the couple and not elsewhere. Internal-life comprises of five ThiNais. Kurinchi—togetherness of hero and heroine. Mullai—heroine awaits arrival of the Hero. Marudham—short temporary misunderstanding between the pair. Neydhal—heroine depressed since the hero has not returned. Paalai—departure of the hero from the heroine for the purpose of earning money ... *External-life

(puRam)—The portion of life that is declared publicly." *Tamil Design Guide* 8.2.2. tdil.mit.gov.in/TamilDesignGuideOct02.pdf.

2. Flower names: such *names* in themselves have appealed strongly to poets, especially since Coleridge and romanticism made us start looking, in poems, at flowers for what differentiates them from each other. To emphasize generality rather than uniqueness, Dr. Johnson advised fellow poets of the eighteenth century "to examine not the individual, but the species," because the poet "does not number the streaks of the tulip" (*Rasselas*, 1759)—i.e., does not seek to represent any individual real flower. But the romantic poets reversed this preference for the general over the specific, the idiosyncratic, the unique. When Coleridge (or rather Sara Hutchinson, on his behalf), transcribed into his notebook several pages of alphabetized vernacular names of wildflower species, the effect was not of generality but of a world marvelously crowded with differences and with words for those differences (entry number 863, written probably in early 1801, *The Notebooks of Samuel Taylor Coleridge*, vol. 1, 1794–1804, edited by Kathleen Coburn, Princeton UP, 1957).

Works Cited

Anania, Michael. *In Natural Light*. Asphodel Press, 1999.

The True Troubadours Are C.B.S.: Land, Sea, Light and the Poetry of Michael Anania

Michael Antonucci

In his essay "On Michael Anania's *In Natural Light*," Reginald Gibbons brings particular attention to the way that poems from Anania's most celebrated collection of verse engage with the sense of sight throughout the volume. Gibbons speaks to the poet's investment in "ways of seeing," focusing on Anania's use of observation, description and other approximations of vision and sight. Situating verse drawn from both *In Natural Light* and the poet's project at large against this framework, Gibbons discusses poems from the volume as being invested with "appropriate self-awareness and self-doubt" that allow the work to demonstrate Anania's "enormous skill and thoughtfulness as a practitioner of poetry" (98). To extend his argument, Gibbons goes on to suggest that "language has eyes that see what our physical eyes cannot. To make such a discovery is one of the things that poetry and perhaps no other medium of human communication, can do" (103).

As the critic extends this discussion of Anania and *In Natural Light*, he ultimately suggests that the poet's work in this volume underscores his commitment to a literary project that is, at once, devoted to examining questions of space, location and observation. Discussing the poet and his work in these terms, Gibbons describes a "particular" set of visionary practices that inform "English language" poetry. He writes that Anania's verse employs "the concrete language and the experience and even exhilaration of perceiving" in ways that connect it to a "descriptive specificity," which he regards as the principal "measure" of literary value in Anglo-American poetic tradition. Further refining his claim, Gibbons suggests that Anania's verse focuses its "attention on the uniqueness of things" rather than understanding "unique objects as belonging to general categories" (97). Measuring the acuity of the poet—paying homage to the deft precision and clarity of the images that Anania delivers through his verse—Gibbons writes, "In a number of poems, he creates an illusion or dramatization of seeing with his use of vivid literal *imagery*, the highly characteristic *selection* of what he describes, and his poetic *discourse* about seeing" (98).

In our collaborative essay "South Loop and Flat Water," which appeared in a special volume of *Valley Voices* dedicated to Anania's literary project, Garin Cycholl and I explore the poet's engagement with a set of geo-poetic impulses rooted in the landscape and possibilities of the Great Plains. Our essay identifies the fluid series of movements that inform Anania's verse as it surveys, marks and maps features evident in the Plains' blend of Western and Midwestern motifs. Interstate 80 serves as the central corridor of our study. It runs through the essay—just as it runs through Anania's native state of Nebraska—connecting poet, place and image. Considering this segment of the Eisenhower Interstate System facilitates our reading of Anania's poetry by intersecting with our discussion of Charles Olson's study *Call Me Ishmael*. I-80 and Olson help our essay to present the poet's project as maintaining connections to both the "dug in" and "mounted" positions that Olson regards as the binary "alternatives" for fruitful literary engagement with an American geography that he describes as a "hell of a wide land" (11).

From its outset, "South Loop and Flat Water" works to establish a sense of the distances, depths and details that Anania collects and measures with his verse. The essay seeks sources for the poet's insistence that there are ways of seeing in Nebraska that allow Olson's claims for the existence of both the "wide land" and an "American SPACE" to find a point of convergence. Tracing pathways to this site, the essay presents evidence for this reading, identifying the poet's capacities to produce a body of work that—at once—incorporates multiple elements into its discussion of human and natural geographies. "South Loop and Flat Water" moves into these environments with the poet, breaking, entering, searching, seeing and recording their features: "SAC Headquarters. Carnival rides towed across the prairie. Rivers running channels of grass. A playground outfield positioned behind a young Bob Gibson" (136). These sites become Anania's poetry retained and compressed as "Dirt. Flat. Water. Plain. Song" (136). Cycholl and I develop this line of inquiry into the poet's work with the help of Olson's critical investigation of SPACE in *Call Me Ishmael*. We hear Anania's verse respond to Olson's study by repeatedly asking and addressing the question "How do I bring my voice into the space supplied by geography?"

In "South Loop and Flat Water" we suggest that Anania makes these entry points evident to his readers, recognizing that it is "a brutal American SPACE" (136) that generates both demands and expectations for narrative and song. The poet knows that this terrain is, after all, the North American Great Plains: colonized, occupied and bloodied by nation and desire, recognized in "manifest destiny." He is aware of the genocide against indigenous peoples that transpired throughout its expanse and works to find a voice that speaks the Plains, in poem or as story. Our essay observes Anania's capacity for maintaining this distinct mode of literary return, especially as he treats objects (of occupation) that demonstrate or proceed from decidedly "dug in" positions. In "South Loop and Flat Water" this list includes, "A kitchen table. That truck cab. This motel parking lot. The prairie night" (136). To underscore these complementary impulses in the poet's work, we offer a reading of "Return," a three-part poem from the final section of Anania's break-through-volume *Riversongs*. Our discussion of "Return" identifies Anania's ability to write, simultaneously, from both the "mounted" and "dug-in" positions. In this way, "South Loop and Flat Water" recognizes the poem as demonstrating the poet's commitment to a literary project that affirms Olson's assertion that "SPACE" is "the central fact to man [sic] born in America" (11).

The intricate relationships between SPACE, place and poetry that shape Anania's project come into focus in the first section of "Return." This impulse becomes evident as the poem opens and four unrhymed couplets allow his speaker to announce that

> The distance back is greater
> each time we settle on the journey;
>
> it is a game of chance, this play
> of time against the lay of the land,
>
> the hills stretched flat, wheatfields
> spread thin, abrupt highway towns,
>
> brief irregularities of line, sloped
> now like telephone wires at the window (78).

The poet's movements in this section of "Return" align with the posture Olson understands as "mounted." They convey a set of observations the speaker makes, looking out from the bus, wagon, train or car that transports him towards his undisclosed destination. In this way, the poet narrates his initial steps along a path "back" into the Great Plains. Surveying the territorial boundaries of Olson's "American SPACE," the poet's (re)entry or return to the Plains identifies the topographic and cultural features he sees in/on/of/upon a landscape that is at once "spread," "stretched" and "sloped." Riding mounted into this open expanse, he takes notice of its "brief irregularities," emerging as "wheatfields" and "telephone wires" rushing through his line of sight (78).

Even as specific details, such as these, emerge from the Plains, Anania's readers do not receive information orienting them with respect to the poet's journey. They are left to ask, "What is he leaving? Where is he going?" Whether bound for or departing from the homestead, a fort, his hide-out, the reservation or elsewhere, each of these possibilities stand as an equally likely site of terminus for the speaker's travels in "Return." All options offer a distinct set of potential outcomes and

FROM THE WORD TO THE PLACE

thereby present discrete leverage points for the poet to grip what Olson refers to as "the fulcrum" American SPACE in *Call me Ishmael* (12). In this way, Anania allows his audience's imagination to guide and direct their reading of the poem.

In the second canto of "Return," Anania's speaker repositions himself as he dismounts and assumes Olson's "dug-in" position. Speaking from this vantage point, the poet works to dispel some of the ambiguity surrounding the circumstances of his journey. These clarifications become clear as this section of the poem opens and Anania's speaker states, "How will it begin" (78). Despite being left unpunctuated in the poem, the line delivers the question that motivates and guides the poet's movements in the course of the work. The response that follows offers readers a sense of the SPACE that he has entered. Anania makes this vision evident by writing

> How will it begin,
> second by second,
> the strum of a taut cord,
> an accumulation of swirling in
> late snowstorm drifting long
> shapes, snow fences bellying
> like sails to its weight (78)

These lines shift the orientation of the poem's speaker and his journey. As he is gradually buried beneath layers of drifting snow, in Olson's terms, he becomes "dug-in." The speaker is, quite literally, impressed by the transformations and movements shaping the SPACE to which he has returned.

As such, the speaker's position is the mirror image of the one he maintains in the poem's first canto: rather than the swift rider moving across the Plains' vast expanse, he is bound to a single location. The poet addresses his readers, rooted in place. More like a blade of grass or corn stalk than a tumbleweed, he is harnessed by and subject to the dynamic and unpredictable conditions governing the Plains. Having assumed this fixed stance Anania's speaker answers his question "How will it begin?" in the final eight lines of the poem's second canto. He offers an additional set of possibilities by describing his static condition as

> built up, day by day
> like the glow of a glaze painting,
> the light coming back through
> layered strokes as luster
> and curve from the still-lifes
> expected oranges and bottles,
> or raged up like silt and rubble
> with spring floods. (78)

Both answers allow the speaker to further articulate himself from a "dug-in" position and, with that, the temporal parameters of his answer expand. In the first stanza of the second canto, snow sweeps and shifts the landscape. It is a becoming or a beginning that moves "second by second." Yet, with the environment continuing to be "built up" around the speaker and his lines of sight, it, too, is not left unchanged. For this reason, throughout the second stanza of the second canto in "Return," ambiguity swirls in the winds of this blanketing storm. Its effect on the Plains SPACE is far from certain. The poet understands that these unyielding and unpredictable forces may transform portions of the Plains SPACE into placid still-life that glows in painterly curves and brush strokes. The landscape may also be left to stand, subject to the rough, uneven forces of a spring flood "raged up like silk and rubble." Ultimately, given the inevitable passages of time and changes in season and temperature, Anania's speaker acknowledges that the SPACE he enters in "Return" is and will be both possibilities.

The poem's speaker alternates between these two distinct perspectives in Canto I and Canto II. Shifting from the sensibility of a tumbleweed (detached, impersonally pushing through this territory) to that of a cornstalk (localized, subject to the force of a storm as its power comes and goes), the poet projects an ambivalence that eventually begins to yield as Anania's speaker approaches his destination. The immediacy and complexity of SPACE and circumstances becomes increasingly evident at the outset of the third and final section of "Return."

His heightened sense of urgencies becomes evident when the poet proclaims

> We know so little of weight
> she said, since we've come
> to believe in flight
> casually, as though lift
> could measure anything at all
> Go to the corner, watch your
> shadow lengthen as you pass
> the streetlight, edging into
> the next darkness, You push
> your own contingencies before
> you, carry those distances, also. (79)

At the outset of the third canto, the poet takes a stance that is, at once, both "mounted" and "dug in." Readers find a speaker who is equally dedicated to exploring the possibilities and propositions invested in the project of mapping a journey as well as the environmental features that define the course and direction it assumes. To align himself within this position, Anania's speaker records evidence of these seemingly contradictory circumstances and conditions. He describes the "weight" of this movement he encounters within the territory. Speaking to an unnamed female interlocutor, the speaker attempts to construct a system for measuring the scale of his return.

To frame this exchange, the poet positions a metaphysical investment of lengthening shadows against the hard science of "lift," presenting a counterargument against better-known notions of SPACE and movement. By doing so Anania's "return" to the visible and observable realities of the Plains SPACE finds a measure of completion. His speaker, having been informed that he is "edging into the next darkness" in order to "push / [his] own contingencies / before" presents readers with a measure of poetic relief (79). Bridging the psychic and physical ambiguities that arrive throughout the "Return" in the course of its three crisp cantos, the poem's final section extends its confirmation of the "both/and" possibilities that Anania considers as his poem and its

155

speaker come to "carry those distances, also" (79).

Throughout the entirety of his body of work, Anania recognizes that a sustained journey, such as the one he records in "Return," is maintained by an inwardly directed motion that is, at once, being broadly conveyed. His poetry offers an odd duality where the kinetic act—in this case his speaker's "return"—becomes and arrives as something Olson regards as a "meeting edge of man [sic]" in which "the world is also his [sic] cutting edge" (*Collected Prose* 162). From this perspective, the image is open to the manipulation of commerce and propaganda. These fusions render what Olson calls "the true beginnings of nothing but the Supermarket," and become manipulations that he sees proceeding from a "sick mouth" (*Collected Prose* 121).

In "Flat Water and South Loop" Cycholl and I follow Olson's efforts to link the Old English word "muthos" (mouth) to "mythos." Along one portion of this pathway, we understand Robert von Hallberg as identifying Olson's critical work as staging a confrontation with "the common, public deprivations of a culture suspended in cold war" (*The Scholar's Art* 80). Cycholl and I make the case that "these enactments of place—whether manifest as Plains SPACE or Supermarket—generate confrontations and become the interest of other Black Mountain poets" (Antonucci and Cycholl 141). We locate both sacred and political impulses as informing these sites of moral confrontation, identifying them in the poetry of Denise Levertov, for instance, as well as Olson's body of work. The project of establishing sites such as these oases of alternation and opposition—both the "mounted" and the "dug-in"—finds Anania's verse, too. Setting his poetry against a "suspended" cold war culture, we see his poetry seeking a sense of freedom through its enactment of alternatives that is firmly rooted in notions of place. The possibilities emerging from this dynamic occupy space both in the poet's mind and on the Nebraska plains. Their expanse constitutes an archipelago, manifest in islands composed from this poetic listing of suspensions and made connections, which serve as the dueling pathways of the poem "Return."

In *The Special View of History*, Charles Olson writes, "History is the new localism, a polis to replace the one which was lost in various stages all over the world from 490 B.C. on until anyone of us knows places where it is disappearing right now" (24). Olson makes this claim while outlining "a course of study which proceeds on the level of history and of a concept of man [sic] with the dynamic first proposed in *Projective Verse*" (13). Throughout his inquiry into intersectional engagements between history, place and self, Olson identifies a critical contradiction that he sees informing elements of Western tradition, particularly the way it treats meeting points between literary culture and SPACE. According to Olson, having adopted the polis of history as its home space, Westerners seek exemption from its demands and strictures. To make his case in this volume, the poet asks, "What are we to do but break the egg of history and get outside?" (25). In the course of this study, Olson refines his thoughts from a series of lectures delivered at San Francisco and the Black Mountain School in 1956 and 1957. He suggests that spatializing history—locating its influence within places, bodies and minds—is a distinctly Western project which, ultimately, invests history with "the intensity of the life process" (17).

Finding this reified "special view of history" to be both troubling and troublesome, Olson opens his exploration of this phenomena with two epigraphs. In the first of these, he employs a one-line dictum drawn from Heraclitus: "Man is estranged from that with which he is most familiar." The second epigraph comes from John Keats's efforts to develop the concept of "Negative Capability." Specifically, Olson brings attention to Keats's desire to move toward a possibility of proceeding, freely toward "uncertainties, mysteries, doubts, without any irritable reaching after fact and reason." Positioned between these limits— where Heraclitus becomes "dug in" and Keats is "mounted"—Olson's study proves to be informative for reading Anania's "What Are Islands to Me Now." Like "Return," this poem provides readers with another example of the poet's efforts to counteract what he regards as the more restrictive aspects of Western dualism. As a poetic sequence found in the third section of *In Natural Light* and dedicated to poet Barbara Guest, "Islands" allows Anania to execute a series of guerrilla-style, hit-and-run, literary maneuvers across various of spaces and circumstances. In his homage to this first-wave New York School predecessor, Anania pursues a list of targets, pushing past the binaries and limits that vex and constrict Olson, ultimately investigating the West and its construction of a "special" history.

Reading Anania's "Islands" as a chain of ten seven-line cantos, the poem charts and locates new terrain within the discourse of "Western Tradition" that recognizes—even embraces—the ambiguities and contradictions that Olson regards as tarnishing the defined relationships that maintain boundaries between history and geography in the West. By bringing an adaptive and improvisational approach to both his mode of inquiry and his subject matter, the poet effectively releases himself from the particularized authorities and acute authorizations that converge and clash, creating hazardous crosscurrents on Olson's mapping of this territory. Anania's poetic project gains a sense of differentiation by rendering a series of variations on Olson's thematic challenge to a notion of "history" that encompasses and eclipses the past. To navigate these temporal and philosophical straights, the poet pursues a course guided by continuity and connection. Shuttling between the canto/islands that comprise this archipelago, the speaker of Anania's poem is buoyed throughout its alternating uses of repetition and concordance.

It is, therefore, not surprising that water becomes the controlling metaphor for the verse in "What Are Islands to Me Now." The poet brings its ebb and flow—the tidal regularities invested in these patterns—into sharp focus with the third and fourth cantos of his poetic sequence. These observations become a matter of record as the poet concludes Canto III by writing, "objects are picked up and moved around / and others may be gone entirely, stolen" before opening the fourth canto with the lines "stolen moments, it was a song they heard / long after everyone else had gone below" (63). The undulated repetition of the word "stolen"—the closing and opening words of each canto—serve as Anania's poetic skiff; he uses it to cross the linguistic channel separating these two poetic islands, effectively acknowledging that the cantos form a chain that is, at once, separated and connected by the waters surrounding it.

In order to successfully make this crossing, the poet must recognize the scattered poetic(land)masses as islands and regard the waters between them as a stream of historical indeterminacy. Understanding this environment and these conditions, having fashioned a seaworthy craft, Anania works to skillfully avoid the shoals of Olson's totalizing claims. Maneuvering beyond the limits of the "special view of history," aware of its rocks and tides, Anania guides his language skiff into and through the straits of historical convention. He is propelled by reverberations from *The Special View of History*, in which Olson asks, "when the estrangement is over, when the familiar is known, who isn't up against the face of God like a wall or a mirror where the shadow or the cut-out shape off the light is the reflection or the light of the figure of himself in species?" (26). Olson's admonitions echo in the pointed confessions that his speaker makes in the poem "Maximus, Himself" when he proclaims

> The sea was not, finally, my trade.
> But even my trade at it, stood estranged
> from that which was most familiar. Was delayed,
> and not content with the man's argument
> that such postponement
> is now the nature of
> Obedience (*The Maximus Poems* 14)

In these lines, Olson's speaker would appear to have intentionally run himself aground: taking refuge in the perceived certainty and security of dry land. However, discontent with the outcome of his experiment, Maximus resolves that "the sea [is] not, finally, [his] trade," adding that "it could be, though the sharpness (the) / I not in others / makes more sense / than may own distances" (14).

In Canto V from "Islands," Anania's speaker takes his place among Maximus's "others." Examining the "consequence" of his movements on the open waters, which lie beyond the rocky coastlines of Olson's "Special History." The poet, sailing into this uncertainty, writes

> consequence might as well say it
> and event of single consequence; imagine

> the mire of occasions and our habits
> of attribution, the more or less troubling
> accidents of speech, collisions of all sorts;
> dear rushing heart, is there less to us
> or more or simply just what meets the eye (61)

Yet, as the poet addresses history, the past and the consequence of their "collision" in these terms, he effectively doubles back on Olson, moving inland, returning toward the Plains. This gesture becomes apparent, as Anania's central engagement with the question of history in "What Are Islands to Me Now" grows increasingly diffused as the fifth canto draws to a close. Like the receding horizon on the plains, "events," habits and "a mire of occasions" merge and blur in "accidents of speech and collisions of all sorts."

Boundaries distinguishing solid from liquid, sea from shore, wave from beach fail as the poet's craft approaches this canto/island. His empirical doubt and "its consequences" become clear as the speaker asks, "dear rushing heart, is there less to us / or more or simply just what meets the eye"? Addressing these questions to his "dear rushing heart," the poet aligns himself with this body part and its perceptive powers. By privileging the heart's structure of feeling over the eye's powers of observation, Anania's poet moves boldly to penetrate the layers—the "mire of occasions"—that envelop human experience. As such, "What Are Islands to Me Now" stands as an affirmation of the vision Anania's fellow plainsman Ralph Ellison articulates when he describes the American landscape as a storehouse of "limitless possibilities."

Read through this sort of Ellisonian lens, Anania's project in "Islands" emerges as an experiment with the structural relationships of time and space; it resonates and harmonizes with the impulses driving Plains SPACE refugee Charlie "Bird" Parker and his musical engagements with the "Dionysian urges" that Ellison identifies as the guidelines of an "underworld of American culture" (227). With these connections made, received notions of order and perspective dissolve in the poem's fifth canto, where Anania's speaker appears to be "dug in" and ride "mounted." His vision branches off and breaks out in extended riffs on a "single event of consequence" like changes in the flatted fifths, eights, and sixteenths that propel Parker into his bebop odyssey. The poet thereby offers his own set of "both/and" solutions to questions he raises about sensory and perceptual reality in the poem's fifth canto. Penetrating this set of interior spaces, Anania moves "underground" announcing his break with the dual straitjackets of positivism and scientific history. Anania thereby finds Parker and his ancestors and samples the blues-rooted tradition of the territory bands. The poet, thus, like Bird, grants himself permission to, as Ellison writes, "play the thing [he'd] been hearing"(229) in order to come alive.

Anania continues probing issues of perception and evidence in "Islands," with Canto VI. Extending his poetic examination of the eye and its powers of perception, the poet addresses Olson's discussion of Herodotus, the West and the "special view of history," scrutinizing the concept of the eyewitness and its reliability. The poem's line of inquiry becomes fully evident in this canto, as it opens with the speaker announcing, "the eye is now the problem, imperiums / of sight, one after another, glance, gaze / or glare." However, after addressing these vulnerabilities in the "imperium of sight," the poet abruptly shifts focus, from the physical act of seeing to matters of memory and the archive. Making this reversal midway through the third line of Canto VI, his speaker asks, "do you remember the orange itself, some other orange, or paint curling light into a skin of apparent brightness"? The implications of the poet's inquiry become more pointed as he continues, asking his reader/interlocutor to reassemble, "incidents of touch, not merely recollected or assumed but edged into the space between canvas and pigment" (*In Natural Light* 61).

Canto VI concludes with the poet continuing to fill the spaces between the island/cantos, striding toward this balance point between what is and is not available to both sensory and cognitive recall. In this way, "What Are Islands to Me Now" embraces the possibilities that inform Keats's Negative Capability and are stored by Heraclitus's idea of "estrangement." Throughout the poem Anania invites readers to accept or simply consider these propositions and their validity as a way of being in the world. In effect, "Islands" responds directly to Olson's dictum that, "Reality is unfinished business" (*Special View* 26). The poem follows this heading throughout its final four cantos. By doing so, "Islands" presents an active model for the free-flowing notions regarding "history" and perception that Olson interrogates and advocates for in *The Special View of History*.

To pilot his craft—and his reader—into these uncharted waters, the poet's success depends on adopting a frontiersman's wariness of formulaic responses to matters of perception and appearance. As plainsman and navigator, Anania would have it no other way. Standing watch in the captain's tower, through his weather-eye, the poet confronts any undercurrents of empirical doubt in Canto VIII when he states

> of course, we have a sense of destination,
> that a line of green trees, underscored
> with white sand inevitably awaits us,
> a shore against which all these moments fall (*In Natural Light* 62)

Aware that as "moments fall / fall like light across her outstretched hand," Anania's speaker finds "sight" and "sightings" to complete his circuit in the islands in cantos IX and X. To conclude his voyage, the poet renders an image of indeterminate and fluid movement, in "red picot cream colored petals recalled / more than seen, the moment hanging there" (63).

As Anania extends this vivid reconsideration of culture and its suspensions, jazz extends a valuable link in this discussion. In "Flat Water and South Loop," Cycholl and I recall that following his return from Europe, Coleman Hawkins entered the studio in October 1939 to record "Body and Soul." Hawkins' recording begins with an exploration of the tune's melody and then wanders through a series of rhythmic pathways, varying tempos and sometimes blowing eight notes to the beat. The whole trick in this rhythmic experiment is working through the piece without returning to the combination of notes that define the original melody line. Two months later, at Dan Wall's chili parlor, Parker begins working through the upper reaches of "Cherokee" and finally, in his telling, is able to "play the thing I'd been hearing. I came alive." Considering these mythic geographies, Ralph Ellison writes

Parker operated in the underworld of American culture, on that turbulent level where human instincts conflict with social institutions; where contemporary civilized values and hypocrisies are challenged by the Dionysian urges of a between-wars youth born to prosperity, conditioned by the threat of world destruction, and inspired—when not seeking total anarchy—by a need to bring social reality and our social pretensions into a more meaningful balance … a reaction to the chaos. (229)

Parker *hears* and plays; the poet hears and *speaks*. Both acts are guided by breath that moves with the "Dionysian urges," as defined by a racist, cold-war America. Through this "chaos" they become, primarily, a matter of unsorted history, that dross and detritus that has been plastic'ed, repackaged and sold back to the land. Bodies pinned to place by a jingle. In Olson's formulation, "The true troubadours are C.B.S." But such "chaos" is simply an overgeneralization of the human being's position. According to Olson, "Spectatorism crowds out participation.… Passivity conquers all.… man [sic] reverts to only two of his [sic] components, inertia and gas." The situation becomes the artist's starting point, where "the skin itself the meeting edge of man and external reality" (*Human Universe* 8). From this point, where the artist recognizes that the work is about "reenacting kinetic," we understand this task as ultimately comprised of breath. Geography and the dead will have the last words. Until then, the musician licks his reed; the poet sits down at his desk. The jazz player's breath is part of the kinetic act that defines place, pressing back against the surrounding culture. As for Olson's figurations, places become and are enacted *here*, with meetings of breath and ear or sight and sound. These unions stand and are supported by Anania and his poetry, where voices speak in and from place as well.

Work Cited

Anania, Michael. *In Natural Light.* Asphodel Press, 1999.
———. *Riversongs.* U of Illinois Press, 1978.

Antonucci, Michael A. and Garin Cycholl. "Flat Water and South Loop." *Valley Voices*, vol. 16, no.1, 2016, pp. 134–44.

Ellison, Ralph. "On Bird Watching and Jazz." *Shadow and Act*. Vintage, 1994, pp. 221–40.

Gibbons, Reginald. "On Michael Anania's *In Natural Light*." *Valley Voices*, vol. 16, no.1, 2016, pp. 97–104.

Olson, Charles. *Call Me Ishmael*. Reynal and Hitchcock, 1947.

———. *Collected Prose*, edited by Donald Allen and Benjamin Friedlander. U of California Press, 1997.

———. *The Special View of History*. Oyez Press, 1970.

———. *The Maximus Poems*. U of California Press, 1983.

Borrowed Music, Borrowed Time

Mark Scroggins

Sometimes a fully realized poem, long or short, is at the same time an *ars poetica*, a medition on the art itself of poetry: "Out of the Cradle Endlessly Rocking," "Tell all the truth but tell it slant—," *Un coup de dés jamais n'abolira le hasard*, "Peter Quince at the Clavier," *Briggflatts*. Such self-reflexive moments are nothing new—Horace, after all, wrote a verse *ars poetica* two millennia ago—but it's perhaps an index of the social marginality of poetry over the last century that so many of its great poems, like Michael Anania's "Borrowed Music" (from *The Sky at Ashland*, 1986), are at least in part parables about the fashioning of poetry and its relationship to time—its durability.

Poets, of course, have never been able to resist crowing about their own makings and telling us how their word-constructions will withstand the ravages of all-devouring time. Horace begins one ode (3.30) comparing his work (favorably) to age-old funerary architecture—*Exegi monumentum aere perennius / regalique situ pyramidum altius* (I have made a monument more lasting than bronze, and taller than the royal pyramids)—and boasts how his writing will preserve some of his identity from the coils of Libitina, the goddess of funerals: *non omnis moriar multaque pars mei / vitabit Libitinam* (I shall not entirely perish, and a great part of me will escape Libitina). A millennium and a half later, Shakespeare (sonnet 28) explains to a beloved how his verse praise is more than immediate flattery and it will, in fact, render some part of her immortal:

> But thy eternal summer shall not fade,
> Nor lose possession of that fair thou ow'st;
> Nor shall death brag thou wand'rest in his shade,
> When in eternal lines to time thou grow'st.
> So long as men can breathe or eyes can see,
> So long lives this, and this gives life to thee.

Art, like the human beings who make it, exists in time and in relationship to time. The finitude of human life is the central constant within that relationship. For Horace and Shakespeare, individual mortality is a boundary that art can overleap as mortal beings; we make poems in order to make some part of ourselves, or the things we love, immortal. When we poets are dead, as one day we inevitably will be, we'll still be speaking through our poems.

As readers of poems we may be conscious of this relationship—that we are in some measure hearing the voices of the dead, of Keats or Shakespeare or Dante or Homer, voices that have been heard and responded to by generations upon generations of readers. More often, however, the intensive engagement with art has the immediate effect of taking us *outside* of our immediate timeframe, suspending us in a realm impervious to the clock (which otherwise is ticking down the moments toward our demise).

This, I take it, is the gist of the notorious "Conclusion" to Walter Pater's 1873 *The Renaissance*. We live, Pater reflects, with a constant "sense of the splendor of our experience and of its awful brevity":

> A counted number of pulses only is given to us of a variegated, dramatic life. How may we see in them all that is to be seen in them by the finest senses? How shall we pass most swiftly from point to point, and be present always at the focus where the greatest number of vital forces unite in their purest energy? (60)

"[S]uccess in life," Pater argues, is to "burn always with this hard, gemlike flame, to maintain this ecstasy" (60) of vital forces united in pure energy; and the surest path to that flame lies in the experience of the arts: "[o]f this wisdom, this poetic passion, the desire of beauty, the love of art for art's sake, has most; for art comes to you professing frankly to give nothing but the highest quality to your moments as they pass, and simply for those moments' sake" (62).

This conclusion scandalized Christian readers, outlining as it did an ethos of pure aesthetic experience (if not outright hedonism) that took no notice of moral obligation, religious duty, or the possibility of a life after death. His career at Oxford was stymied, and he excised the "Conclusion" from the second, 1877 edition of *The Renaissance*.

New to that edition, however, was a bit of aesthetic theory rather more remarkable than mere "art for art's sake" (which the French had been going on about for some decades). It arrives in the essay "The School of Giorgione," where Pater discusses the notion of *Anders-streben*—German for "other-striving," each specific art form's attempt to "pass into the condition of some other art." Pater pronounces, *"all art constantly aspires to the condition of music"* (54–55). This is because music—and one assumes Pater has in mind instrumental music—is the ideal *formal* art. In music, we have the ultimate fusion of "form" and "matter," a distinction that all the other arts only strive to achieve.

I will pass over the central importance of Pater's "condition of music" for later formalist theories of art—suffice it to say that it is indeed central, and still provocative—in order to linger a moment on its cruel temporal implications. We immerse ourselves in artworks, the "Conclusion" to *The Renaissance* claims, in order to heighten the intensity of our experiences, to make as rich as possible the "counted number of pulses" we have been allotted. Artists, conversely, bend their craft and energies to fashion "monuments" more durable than bronze, outlasting time, capable of awakening and energizing the senses and minds of their beholders when their makers are long dead. But music—in contrast to painting, sculpture, architecture and to poetry especially—is (with dance) the most evanescent of the arts: we hear it, and it is gone; it lives only in its living performance, and is bound up with the timespan during which it unfolds and vanishes.

Anania's "Borrowed Music" is a series of evolving meditations on landscape, sculpture, history, music and time—and the art of poetry, conceived of as the making of a "music," tenuous, vibratory and vanishing, out of the experience of the present. The poet is locked in a paradox: marooned on the moving line of the present moment, contemplating the stretches of experience and art that have come before, simultaneously mourning and celebrating the glorious and futile *"dur désir de durer,"* [to use] Paul Eluard's phrase: the hard desire to endure.

*

"Borrowed Music," in seven-line stanzas, has five irregular sections: 105 lines in all. At its beginning, we find ourselves in a landscape that may be observed reality or may be a painting, so precisely does the poem's voice follow the details of the growing darkness:

> First, the green line blackens, under-
> leaf silver becomes shadow and blue sky
> fails into vermillion like a vein opening. (51)

"Like a vein opening"—a vivid, Ruskinian simile, at once capturing how the evening sky shifts from blue to red and introducing a note of mortality.

With the third stanza, however, we are firmly within the realm of art: a statue of the nymph Daphne transforming into a laurel tree as she tries to elude Apollo's pursuit (see Ovid, *Metamorphoses* 1.452–566):

> Laurel bark sheathing the fugitive, thighs
> grown rough and darkening, sinews tendrilled,
> the first twig vibrating from her finger (51)

In classical mythology Daphne is the very emblem of lively motion arrested into art; she flees the god's embraces and is transformed by her river-god father from a moving, lively subject into a rooted tree. And as such she is named Apollo's favored tree, the source of the laurel crown that designates the "laureate."

What the poem presents is not Daphne's story, but a stone statue of the scene: the moment of metamorphosis from running nymph into static tree has been captured in an even more motionless, permanent material. (Bernini's Baroque seventeenth-century treatment is only the most famous such scupture.) But such permanence is only relative; even the stone from which the figure has emerged is the product of "the slow / press of centuries she struggles into and from" (51). And in letting his attention play over this emblem of simultaneous permanence and metamorphosis, the poet hears both the story of Daphne and Apollo and the narrative of a sculptor at work, "the cry of a young girl in blown branches / or the ring of the mallet along emerging limbs" (51). These sounds make a "song" that "has already slipped / away like pale lips beneath distant waves": to capture that song, to fully realize it, "the mind" must be able to "jump without building" (51).

We see something of what this mind's movement involves in the second section:

> One thing, as relation to one thing—
> numbers curl, and what should be a simple line
> is a succession of waves. Between zero
> and one, that space or the next, the slope begins,
> advances and turns back, as though hearkening,
> as though each point were its own occasion,
> something to be remembered or acted upon. (52)

As in Zeno's Paradox, the distance from one point to another is potentially infinite: "what should be a simple line / is a succession of waves." "Between zero / and one, that space or the next" bristles with intermediate points, each of which is "its own occasion, / something to be remembered or acted upon." The mind must learn to "jump without building" or (as the previous section has it) "each step is its own politics, each word / its own forfeit" (51).

From this abstraction the poem moves back into the phenomenal world: we are in the night now, where a "wooden bow-piece"—a carved figurehead on a boat, another female scupture—is "lifting and falling beside a wet stone wall" (52). Each detail is a *grace note*," a musical ornament to the unfolding "song" of the poem. The bow-piece reappears crucially in the poem's third, central section. We are in the poet's dwelling, where he can see

> The clear air
> above the streetlamps darkening the sky
> toward lapis, the leaves of the sacred lilies
> at my window pressing pale veins to the glass. (53)

His thought moves to the ocean, to "kelp lines scrawled across / littered sand," to the "years" and various "landscapes" he has witnessed "drawn up, drawn out like fine wire, / drawn and turned" (53). And he imagines these moments of intense perception as a song exhaled by the bow-piece herself:

> This is the song her breath might leave
> if she were moving over a staff of waves,
> moment to moment, as the night air moves its
> bright molecules across the surface of your eye. (53)

(The "staff," in a masterful touch evoking Pound's Canto 82, is that of musical notation.) Song, then, forms itself in a perpetual succession and recombination of sensuous experiences. It is like the bow-piece moving over the waves and cannot be held or lingered upon:

> 'Neath luna, then, all things in things conspire
> figure and fancy toward song, as the dried grain
> is lifted and thrown, as the light is caught
> along the leeward edge of unbroken waves,
> or these jade-green leaves tumble against glass.
> Listen, listen. Nothing here is closely held,
> this dream or the next and their uncertainties. (53)

Were the poem to end in this nocturnal moment, it would be something of a paean to evanescence, to beautiful song woven out of moments of intense observation, song which is blown away by the sea-breeze as soon as it is uttered. That's not what Horace and Shakespeare, Ovid and Bernini sought to make in their art; they sought rather to forge permanence out of evanescence, monuments out of moments. The morning dawns in the poem's fourth section, revealing "The world and its massive variety"—the Chicago lakefront of skyscrapers, sailboats, "the park's double row of indigenous trees" and morning automobile traffic. And the sun falls upon one vast monument to memory and permanence, a museum:

> Behind a concrete portico,
> the reconstructed spine of a mastodon
> offers its airy permanence. All that was
> or is, case after case of moths and butterflies,
> edged flint, geodes opening like crystal seeds. (54)

The museum is a vast archive of time and relation, a kind of physical model of the poet's mind, filled with memories personal and cultural, perceptions. What he seeks, what he finds himself perpetually losing, is the precise order of his mind's contents:

> One thing in relation to one thing, quickly,
> or a sense of loss, as though the field you paused
> in once, slow river slipping under exposed
> roots and memory's dire complexities,
> revolved around you. (54)

He must move quickly, make the single connections to achieve the "music," or he will sink into the marshy field of "exposed / roots" and memorial "complexities," a morass of self-regarding nostalgia in which all chance of song is lost. Like broken potsherds in the museum, each refers back to a now-lost entire vessel, "These bits of time spindle / and turn, each numbered shard coded to the arc / its shares with a probable amphora" (54).

Section II of the poem had advanced a Paterian notion of moments of intense subjective experience, "as though each point were its own occasion, / something to be remembered or acted upon." In the poem's fifth and final section, the poet muses on quotidian, relatively unintense moments of the sort that fill up the majority of our lives; nothing seems to "animate this moment / I sit in." Does this mean that it all fails

> the play of possibilities, count
> down counted out, cecropia, viceroy,

> pebble tools by the basket full, numbered bones
> wired carefully into place, the sorted bins
> of unassembled jars, vain antiquity? (55)

[Or does this mean], that the entire project of assembling memory and culture into a whole, of shoring the fragments of experience into a musical order, is an empty dream?

A lesser poet would provide us with a definite answer; Anania refuses. The middle stanza of this last section offers a pair of axioms:

> Sorrow is
> a kind of order, loss a proposition
> exaggerated by our faith in beginnings,
> the sense we have that each of these surfaces
> is a commemoration in time. (55)

These axioms underline our desire to make order of our experience, even if that order is only a desire for order, a perhaps illusory sense that our ephemeral experiences have lingered as some sort of "commemoration."

The poem ends with a brief return to immediate experience: in the wind, "trees stiffen, then relax; before it falls, / the petunia manages a brief parody / of itself and its flowering" (55). What might the poet make of this? At first, he would seem to make nothing, but as the final sentence unfolds, we find him making all:

> It is no
> more emblematic than the lake's recurrent
> surge or the palm print of a squall line, traffic,
> conjecture, adroit leaves signing leaf veined mud. (55)

"No / more emblematic"—but no *less* emblematic, either. The "lake's recurrent / surge," the "palm print of a squall line" (the disturbance on the water caused by a brief storm) and "traffic" are all ephemeral phenomena: they are there, and then they are gone. But they are precisely recurrent, rhythmic. "Conjecture" as well passes through the mind and is gone, but is a moment in a series of conjectures, the sequence of "impressions, sensations" that for Pater constitutes our conscious being. There is a permanence in the recurrence of these phenomena's ephemeral appearances.

The poem's final phrase—"adroit leaves signing leaf veined mud"—is, in its gnarled sound-texture and ambiguous syntax, worthy of Basil Bunting. The juxtaposition of "leaf" and "mud" reminds us of the metamorphoses of the first section, where the nymph first becomes a plant (a tree), then is transfigured (as statue) into mineral form. The leaves, once nimble and "adroit," are pressed into the mud, leaving their signature like a Chinese chop-mark: they "sign 'leaf,'" as it were, leaving the impression of their veins. (Alternately, we reflect that the leaves, part of a tree's complex system of processing the sun's energies and the soil's minerals, are in a sense "vein[ing] mud.")

Mud will one day be rock, and the print of the leaf will become a fossil, just as the mastodon's "scattered / vertebrae" will be "compressed to stone." And here we return to a striking detail of the first section, where we see the "the first twig vibrating" from the nymph's marmoreal finger—or rather,

> found in the fault lines of the stone
> itself as mere stone was cut away, stipule,
> some quirk of vegetation caught in the slow
> press of centuries she struggles into and from. (51)

The twig is the emblem of the flesh-and-blood nymph becoming tree; but it is as well a fossilized fragment of actual vegetation, the evidence of the tree becoming stone. From flesh, to wood, to stone—levels of greater and greater permanence, durability.

Hovering over all these levels of matter, however, is the consciousness of the artist who has "cut away" the stone to reveal the twig and the finger. The artist, whether sculptor or poet, works in time, balances and navigates the degrees of temporality, from the quicksilver transience of a wave or squall line to the relative permanence of stone. The "song" of the art emerges above, on a different plane than, those degrees—"the ring of the mallet along emerging limbs" we hear when we view Bernini, the "cry of a young girl in blown branches" when we read Ovid.

Anania's poem has indeed "borrowed" its music, in a sense both like and unlike Pater's *Anders-streben*. (And I speak here not of the actual aural qualities—the "melopœia," to use Pound's term—of his verse; that would take another entire essay.) He has taken his themes and motifs from landscapes and seascapes, from the cataloguing practices of museums, from Ovid and Pound, from both "high art" and vernacular sculpture, from his immediate experience and observations, from memory and from careful contemplation. And he has woven them into a "song" of recurrences, repetitions and developments that is audible when we bring our attention to bear on the lines of "Borrowed Music."

Whether or not this song braves time is not at issue in the poem itself; Anania makes no Horatian or Shakespearean claims. (Monumental boasts, as Shelley's "Ozymandias" tells us, have a way of ending badly.) One implicitly challenges time whenever one fashions a poem, or a statue, or a drawing; but all human marks, from the pyramids to one's signature on a credit card terminal, are in some senses challenges to time, attempts to overcome inevitable transience. "Borrowed Music" meditates deeply on the matter of time and durability; whatever conclusions it may arrive at or eschew, its lines burn throughout with a "hard, gemlike flame" of concentrated intelligence and thoughtful musicality. And as we concentrate our sensibilities on Anania's densely interwoven lines, we may find ourselves—at least for the space of reading—lifted into a timeless moment where "vital forces" unite in music-like energy.

Works Cited

Anania, Michael. *The Sky at Ashland*. Moyer Bell Limited, 1986.

Pater, Walter. *Selected Writings*. Edited by Harold Bloom. Columbia UP, 1982.

On Michael Anania's *Nightsongs* & *Clamors*

Philip Nikolayev

This book of poems closes with an essay, "An Afterword in Response to a Query about Gardens," a perfect conclusion because it provides an entryway into Anania's poetics "from within." The ostensible point, that gardens are in some ways like poems, conversely means that poems are, in turn, like gardens: "So gardens have different valences just as poems do, differing values, some of them very similar to the differing values of poetry—symmetry, harmony, disorder, wildness or any and all of these mixed together" (91). Anania's reflections on gardens recall Andrew Marvell's classic poem "The Garden" (published in 1681 and explicitly acknowledged here) as well as Kantian aesthetic theory. The garden was Immanuel Kant's favorite metaphor of the work of art: both the garden and the artwork impose order and purpose upon natural, wild growth. But Anania goes beyond this, adding a temporal dimension to the metaphor. Gardens change in time and so do, though less obviously, poems. Both gardens and poems are caught in their distinct ways in a Heraclitean flux of being and perception. You cannot dip into the same poem twice; a great poem evolves in perception every time you approach it, always sprouting new shades of meaning. "Insistently so, gardens are surfaces in time" (93) concludes the essay.

These insights provide a fitting key to what we may call the gardenesque poetics of the book, with its delicately balanced control of form ordering a sensuous wildness within. These are poems of the temporal surface, of the interface between experience and the mind; they are all about "how we hold / the moment against its lapse / into time." Listen to the soft hiss of "against its lapse": that is the noise—now white, now pink, now musical noise—of lived moments dissolving into oblivion. Not chiefly driven by explicit plot or cerebral logic, many of these texts are like a sonic gliding in time, a study of time's phonetics, as it were. They orchestrate time, camerata style, occurring and passing as musical moments, with no other truth status attached to them than that they are moments of the poet's lived experience. The poems make recalled experience come alive as a kind of music. This poetry treats life itself as a sensory phenomenology of spacetime, where all things that have a beginning dissolve upon their end. The poetic process consists of listening, observation and reflection—reflection, not in the sense of authoritative pondering, but as neurons firing, along with the consequences of such firing. The visible flows with sound, and sound resonates through the visible: two aspects of time conjoined by the brain.

The poetic ear habitually parses the world's cacophony into music, into chiseled lines and stanzas. But a poem, just as reality itself, sounds either fine-tuned or jarringly out of tune, depending on where one happens to stand with respect to it. Sometimes the reader's ear must adjust, attune itself, playing catch-up to the poet's. Helpfully, tuning forks are placed at strategic points in the work in the shape of literary and artistic references, allusions and direct quotations, some attributed and most given in quotation marks. This densely allusive web of intertextual and cross-cultural references is impossible to miss, with examples too numerous to list (a good many are revealed in the volume's endnotes). Anania's grasp of cultural history is vast, and he expects—but gently, without pressure—a similar dedication to literature and the arts from the reader. His poems are for the connoisseur. This is culture appropriated, filtered through a strongly invested personal taste, passionately assimilated and made deeply personal.

I began by mentioning the book's closing essay as a handy distillation of (some of) its poetics. Of course, one need not read the book backwards for best results. Placed at the end, the essay retroactively refocuses the reader's mind on the reading experience, which begins with "Nightsongs & Clamors, I–VI," the volume's title sequence. The arrangement of the texts in the book is highly deliberate with the opening sequence and the concluding essay acting like the framing prongs of a horseshoe magnet aligning the poetic particles around them along the geometry of the magnetic field that they generate. The title of the sequence highlights the tension and ambiguity between music and noise with the ampersand standing as the elusive boundary between them. Indeed, the sounds in question seem to be both nightsong *and* clamor simultaneously, the point being a likening more than a contrast. The combined epigraphs—"I hear a cry of spirits, faint and blind" (from Philip Sydney's "Farewell") and "the chance of night" (from Thomas Campion's song "What If a day, or a Month, or a Yeare"; "a chance of a night" in the original)—alludes subtly to the ancient themes of the vagaries of fortune and of the death and transience of all. A night is inevitably a *memento mori*, a mild hint at death. This nuance subtly sets the tenor of the whole sequence but without making the minor key too ostentatious: the chords do not come in heavy clusters of notes but are contrapuntally arpeggiated, as it were. The six poems deal with six categories of sounds. I read them as follows.

Poem I of this sequence meditates on the rustling noise of leaves, specifically of leaves that "the live oaks / are dropping / this March night" (3). It starts on a modality—"*and if I tried*" (Anania's emphasis), which is then confirmed (try he did)—and it dwells on the ear's attempt to discern a code (read "song") in the murmurs of nature, finding none. The rustling remains "a rasp not quite / like breath or song" as the poem itself proceeds, by lines of similar but irregular length, with an audible pulse that nevertheless always shies away from becoming a verse meter, "a kind of absence / milled from loss" (3). Here the tone briefly hints at the poignantly existential, then turns soft and soothing again—"a game perhaps"; "hide and seek"—as "we" (note the sudden "we") sink into sleep, "the day / still hissing in our ears" (3).

Poem II carries us away from the sweet whispers of nature and into the deafening din of metallurgy. Here, we vicariously experience the noise of a drop forge, which is a device for forging metal between two dies, one of which is fixed while the other is dropped by either gravity or by propellant pressure. The drop forge has been operating all night, and now the poem is "between 4 and 4:05 a.m." (are we asleep or insomniac?), when the mind returns to its characteristic dwelling to modalities: "'I wish I may, I wish I / might' see the sun," etc. (Contrast this with seeing the first star of the night in the old folk song that the lines allude to). After suffering this manner of night clamor, the mind's ear wants to "hear nothing for just / a short while, listen/for my self returning" (4).

In parts III and IV, we are at last exposed to music proper, pop and baroque respectively. In III, we hear (of) "Joe Turner, / Ruth Brown, The Drifters, / Little Walter and Otis Rush," (5) names that are markers of a period and of a generation, pop culture being a context and frame of reference that for so many American poets seems to define a large part of who they are and what they mean. The poem provides an insight into why this is so: it is because the relevant "nightsongs" connect deeply with bodily experience: "breathing, / its measured rise and fall" ("breathing," a thread of breath, is the natural bass drone that is heard throughout this collection, always associated with music) and "the moment swaying." (5) What does one do "all night, all night long," (5) an allusion to a Lionel Ritchie song of 1982? Well, dance, of course: this is a dancing culture. Here, we have moved from a "drop forge" to a "drumhead pulsing" with an equal boom, rock music being of a piece of the rhythms of industry and of urban life.

In poem IV, we eavesdrop on the speaker tuning into Baroque "nightsongs"—Robert Jones's Elizabethan song "And Is It Night" (published in 1609) and Jean-Philippe Rameau's "consoling symmetries"—meaning Baroque counterpoint and specifically the way that Rameau's brief variations are held by a strong tonal base. These melodies are associated here with dusk, "residual city light, / its ingathering ash" (6). The poet is obsessively aware of time and how things move in it. Sensory experience—this poetry's organizing principle—comes in measured syntagms and punctuated rhythms reminiscent of musical time. Anania's somewhat unconventional punctuation goes pleasantly well with the highly stanzaic and enjambed regularities of form. He is a frequent user of the semicolon; the period is rarely seen. Apart from the pronoun "I," capital letters occur only as initials in the titles and of proper names.

Part V of the "Nightsongs & Clamors" sequence connects the contemplation of nocturnal sounds with a philosophic purpose, "to find a pathway / through a field of doubt," from Lucretius, which is pursued in a musical tempo in the well-coordinated manner of a dance: "one measure at a time"; "heel and toe, / a step in prelude," guided by none other than Calliope, the Muse of epic poetry, as the sounds of "words / and weather" … / move the night along" (7). The "sparks our eyes flash / against the darkness" stand out as bright signs of life against the background of night and of all that it stands for metaphorically, yet this symphony resolves, negatively, into echoes of emptiness:

> empty is its own space
> defined by what surrounds
> it, tremors and memory (7)

An underlying void winks behind the phenomena; the world seems empty beneath its surface.

In the last, sixth poem of the title sequence, dissonances suddenly grow to an emotional crescendo as catastrophe and death enter upon the scene without being explicitly named: "voices splinter against / brickwork like shells," human speech becoming fragmented; "sirens we know by heart" (presumably of ambulances) "coil and strike"; elms flail in the wind amid a chorus of rain as cries for mercy and cries of despair are heard, and even "the pavement's breath" becomes "slow and uncertain." The sequence ends on a note of unrelieved alarm, with the image of a "mobile / stretcher, chattering by" (8) onomatopoetically in the night downpour, any "consoling symmetries" (6) now gone and forgotten.

Consolation does not return until the next poem in the book. Quiet, spare, downright minimalist next to the preceding sequence, it gently modulates into a major key, and we emerge into it as if after a troubled dream. Here it is:

Morning Poem

an eyelash,
yours, brushes
the close threads
of a pillow-
case, mine (9)

A comforting scene is implied, barely indicated here: two people, a couple, awaken peacefully together in the morning. (The speaker's head must be on the pillow next to his partner's, to notice with such precision the microscopic detail described.)

Although the writing foregrounds its attention to the life of the senses, there is a great deal of intellectual substance to it. The poet's mind is alive on all the pages, often engaging with outstanding art. From part II of the poem "Tin Tin Deo," I learned of the American composer Louis Moreau Gottschalk (1829–1869) and of his work "A Night in the Tropics" ("La Nuit des tropiques"—literally, "of the tropics"—a.k.a. "Symphony No. 1," a sweet listen), which uses some 600 musical instruments "sound[ing] like dense foliage, / banana tree and plumeria" (48). The triptych "Three Poems with Max Beckman" comprises the poet's interpretive responses to three well-known paintings by the artist, a kind of art criticism in verse. Another poem responds to Vincent van Gogh's 1888 painting *The Poet's Garden*, revisiting the theme of gardens and poetry. The poems are often in dialogue with other poets. One poem, "Always the Surfaces," dedicated to Diane Wakoski, reflects on the title's phrase from her poem "California Eyes: A Meditation from Poitou-Charentes."

The idea of surface is central to Anania's poetic concerns. Surfaces can be immensely deep in some sense, e.g., the surface of a painting, to say nothing of the surface of the world. Phenomenologically speaking, all our experience of the external world are experience of surfaces. The perceived world is skin-deep, while the Kantian *thing-in-itself* remains elusive, impenetrable. On this view, poems are necessarily about surfaces, and they are themselves surfaces. A work can address only the surface of experience. Things can be loved or hated, spoken or written about only at the surface; what lies beneath it—their very being—is ungraspable and inexpressible. Anania's poetry does not relish or celebrate this surfaciality, but rather comes to terms with it, vulnerably and bittersweetly. (Among the most moving and beautiful in this book are the poems of love and loss commemorating the poet's late wife Joanne Oliver (1939–2012). I asked Anania which poems they were, and he told me: part I of "Nightsongs & Clamors," "lulled with flowers," "Shake off your heavy trance," "Away So Wears" and "Things Forgotten," all worthy of the reader's attention.)

Yet we know that a surface is not all that there is to the world. We know this by knowing ourselves, through introspection. In ourself, we are able to connect the internal and the surficial. In the book's last poem, "Tampa, March 2018," the speaker, who is giving a poetry reading, notices that he is bleeding from a paper cut. A drop of his blood lands, seemingly symbolically, next to the lines from Lucretius which we have already seen: "to find a pathway / through a field of doubt." The body's surface is compromised: "I bleed easily / these days, my skin as / frail as onion skin" (90). And he concludes

> Time in the body,
>   in aging skin, is
>   another form of time. (90)

Works Cited

Anania, Michael. *Nightsongs & Clamors*. MadHat Press, 2018.

Field of Uncertain Dreams: Memory and Invention in Michael Anania's *Nightsongs & Clamors*

Cynthia A. Davidson

In his 2018 book of poems *Nightsongs & Clamors*, Michael Anania uses dreams to recall and reinvent his career-long journey as a poet, revisiting the labors of working as an American writer born into uncertain beginnings with a voice forged out of the modernist assurance of Pound, Frost and Williams. Through memories of dreams, photographs, paintings, everyday events and scenes, he confronts the possible failure of voice to tell a coherent story in the face of uncertainty, loss and change both personal and societal. His poems tell us to take our time nonetheless, to depend on our ability to witness, to experience and to use our recollections to invent whatever dreams will move us through our lives without the pressure to force any particular outcome or agenda. Anania's lifelong documented passion for understanding, witnessing and writing about and through the inventive and constructed nature of memory puts him squarely at the center of what Robert Pinsky called America's poets' "fragile, heroic enterprise of remembering" ("Poetry and American Memory").

Anania grew up in the heartland—the center geographically—of the United States, with blues, jazz and the Beats, learning his craft as the modernists of the first half of the twentieth century veered into the extremes in the latter half of impassioned social performance versus radical visual linguistic experimentation. In its midst, Anania has developed a signature style that some might find restrained, even conservative, in its approach to both lyric and long-form poetry. He has consistently and patiently distrusted grand narratives and eschewed reliable narrators in his work, which includes seven volumes of poetry, a book of essays and an autobiographical novel. Writing primarily in a period between the 1970s and the present, he provides strong continuity between the bold late modernism of William Carlos Williams and the often bewildering, fractured evolution of postmodernist society, locating meaning in usually ordinary (in the non-fantastical, non-surrealistic sense) recollections of people and things, scenes, dreams, photographs, music and paintings.

This distrust of reliable narration can perhaps most clearly be seen in Anania's 1984 autobiographical novel *The Red Menace: A Fiction* as made evident by the enigmatic title. A series of more or less linear vignettes on growing up poor in Nebraska and meeting a series of interesting people along the way in the shadow of the Cold War, the ending disrupts expectations of continuity with a chapter devoted to descriptions of automobile accidents the narrator was involved in or witness to that seem to shift and change with multiple retellings, described with a glamor that demonstrates an attraction to catastrophe. There is a reasonable, trustworthy, analytical single narrator (named Michael Anania, like the author)—and then, at the novel's end, the narrator crashes his car, an echo of William Carlos Williams' poem "To Elsie" (also known as "The pure products of America go crazy"). This selection from *Spring and All* concludes:

> It is only in isolate flecks that
> something
> is given off
>
> No one
> to witness
> and adjust, no one to drive the car. (*Collected Poems* 219)

There are narrative gaps, partial mental erasures of events, that cannot be bridged with explanations supported by the narrator's experiences. Anania, like Williams, acknowledges that at some point reason and order will fail—and something else must "drive the car," since in unstable and inequitable times even trustworthy drivers are often more infatuated with the possibility of crashing, or at least transfixed by the possibility that something will break the boredom of safe predictability and/or social and economic depression, than focused on staying safely on the road that may, indeed, lead to nowhere preferable.

The theme of memory, which is frequently visited in his poems, concerns this project of isolating these flecks or shards, a project which causes introspective examination of what memories are, time and time again. There is seldom certainty that these memories are representations of a real past that existed. *The Red Menace: A Fiction* spells this out for us: the title of a prose volume depicting the author's autobiographical details, using his own name and place of birth and known details of his early life, is labeled a fiction. In the Derridean sense, the writing of this "fiction" stands on its own; it does not need its author to *speak* for it. This recalls formalism, a modernist method of reading, but it also gestures toward the dilemma of postmodern uncertainty about naming what is "true" about experience. While the experience of writing may belong to the writer, and while the experience of reading belongs to the reader, the writing belongs to itself; and these experiences and belongings do not necessarily overlap. The real fiction is believing that they do. The relationship between living and writing is called into question, and this in fact might be the long-lingering source of uncertainty that is central to the poems I discuss in this essay (along with the inevitable loss and uncertainty that come with advancing mortality).

The poems of *Nightsongs & Clamors* strive to locate memory in a personal and philosophical sense, reflecting a search for the American identity that Pinsky talks about in his essay. The book bridges several fundamental general themes: the poet's life as both personal and public, private and political, physical and mental, of earth and spirit and an intellectual journey. These poems also provide an opportunity for readers to reflect on the transition of poetry from the modernist to the postmodern era in the sense that this can help us to understand who we were, who we are, and who we may be becoming.

The book's title sequence, "Nightsongs & Clamors, I–VI," begins with a melancholy reflection on dreaming, the imagination, sleep, and memory, utilizing references to industry and factory—a kind of particularly American industrial age idea of the imagination or "dream factory." This is an America that is on the decline, since America is post-industrial and factories are often abandoned, fodder for urban exploration, having laid off many workers who must be retrained or relocated or relegated to the welfare state that "rescued" Williams' Elsie. In the dreamscape of factory America, we encounter an exhausted poet narrator, writing of a "precinct" we curl into during sleep (a space where police would patrol, but with no mention of police presence) which also invokes authority and protection of the factory's workers and the outlying community—if anyone else is left. It is a space left by absent industry, haunted by the narrator and his memories. This is what he has to work with. Like an urban explorer, he and readers can go into these factories and view the raw materials that are left, the stuff that the spaces are constructed of. The space of imagination and dream is shaped by the dwindling, inactive industrial society that shaped the poet.

A bit on, he calls out:

To find a pathway
through a field of doubt,
   one field at a time. (7)

This setting can be seen as the shell of modernist America. A task of the poems in this book is to find a path through this field of dreams, which is a field of doubt—to recover glimpses of something "given off," as Williams wrote in "To Elsie," to light a path in this abandoned factory of memory and dream. The poet/narrator is combing, scanning, exploring and excavating for flecks in that abandoned factory. There is a precinct, but there are no police. There is a shell of authority, but no one left to enforce it. This is a postmodern dreamscape. If the environment has stories to tell, they are not grand narratives of national progress and identity, but something much more personal, local and necessary for survival. It is "a pathway," not *the* pathway. Conceivably, it is the one that seems most likely to let the writing move forward. There's no pride in choosing a good path or a correct one or even Frost's "road not taken / that made all the difference," no pretension to a grand design or impact, just a desire to keep moving reminiscent of Mark Strand's movement through a field in "Keeping Things Whole":

> We all have reasons
> for moving.
> I move
> to keep things whole.

One difference between Strand's narrator's experience and that of the narrator of "Nightsongs & Clamors, I–VI" is the presence of a clear agenda. Anania's narrator makes no effort to keep things whole, nor does he seem especially bent on escaping those things. Like the subjects of the photographs and paintings that he scans in other poems in the collection, the narrator is simply recording his movement, and that is contingent on finding a path (or a road).

The poet calls on the classical muse, Calliope, to help him forge the path out of doubt. That is a grand gesture, as Calliope is the muse of epic poetry and eloquence. This is also a romantic notion and a supremely hopeful—or desperate—one. He even suggests that what he's supposed to hope for is "pleasant dreams?"—the question mark underscoring his doubtful condition. But the romantic spell is quickly broken: "voices splinter / against brickwork like shells" (8). Perhaps this isn't going to work. Perhaps poetry isn't reliant on eloquence, or at least, eloquence does not need to be epic—or perhaps the entire process needs a revolutionary change. Perhaps the path needs to move through the fields of doubt instead of rushing to get out of them. The narrator will instead witness and record what he finds along the way. That is the essence of urban exploration.

If "voices splinter," then the narrator will turn to sight, to witnessing made possible by light and shadow, as the foundation for this writing.

He will be examining the nature of visual memory primarily. Visual memory occurs in dreams, in reflection of the past and also in material form as photographs and paintings. In one poem, "Composition in Metallic Grays," we view the first photograph:

> we stare into its varied
> grays and its archaic
>
> magics. the first photograph
> . . . .
> light is a hammer, earth
> its forge, bitumen asphalt
> welled up, Hephaestus (16)

The poem becomes a memorial to a lost classical god of industry and then quickly ends with his naming. There is no fanfare, but the photograph gives off traces of the memory of a god in a captured moment of light and shadow. Memory, here, includes the recollection of classical mythologies that blur the line between history and invention—a theme that is recurrent and important in these poems.

In "Away So Wears," our narrator confronts waking from dream to a different uncertainty:

> its voices, so clear; still,
> the light through your east
> window silences them;
>
> this is the other you, my
> second self; speaking
> as always, out of turn (17)

Light wins against the voices; light silences the voices of the dreams. The waking self is the one who bathes in light of day, but "speaking / as always, out of turn" is not comfortable with its own voice, remembering the clear voices of the dream world. This is ostensibly a poem about an absent loved one, taken through death perhaps or through separation of another kind—or a remembrance of a more fecund and rich time of life, a time when the voices were a part of everyday life. But it could just as easily be about the separation of voice from light, or of voice from writing itself. One thinks of Derrida and how postmodernism views writing on its own, not dependent on speaking, to consider how the tension between speaking and vision (Reynolds) in these poems reflects the journey of a poet from modernism to postmodernism—a journey mirrored by processes of aging and the promise of loss and death, but also marked by finding new pathways of considering subjectivity and identity. If writing is not dependent on a speaking subjectivity, it may find other ways of asserting itself. Separated from Calliope, it might begin to depend on its own vision as muse.

"As Seen" addresses painting, the sister art of poetry but one that privileges vision over voice—in particular, the still life, a staple of artistic practice and a genre that has endured many civilizations. Still life focuses on things, and so evokes Williams again, in *Paterson:* "no ideas but in things" (9). It was Williams who insisted that abstract words cannot create images, hence the focus on "things." In this poem, however, it's the way that the things are seen by the painter, and third-hand by the poet, that take center stage. Seeing is an action, although a quiet one, akin to witnessing, and painting and writing what one witnesses is certainly active and an act of agency. Seeing invites light and keeps the voice in check, invoking another American identity—the mystical philosophers, the Emersons who meditate and the Quakers who bathe in silence. The dynamic qualities of looking come to life on the page like a tiger relaxing in the sun:

> consider the still life, not dead, certainly,
> or even inert but rather, color poised,
> at once liquid and solid, color raised
>
> as the orange's edge, brush and band implicit:
> light, its light, not yours, caught in the bristles track,
> an occasion of form and matter held there (21)

This energy is underscored by a cycle of activity within the thing made by the artist's witnessing:

space accedes to color, color to motion,
motion to gesture, each the other's moment,
each moment a force arced and snared and made still;

a table of ordinary objects oddly
skewed, as though each thing acquired a kind of force
sharing in the painting's equilibrium

so we stand before a cascade of causes,
arranged, the table set, light from an unseen
window crossing from left to right, each shadow

darkening edges (22)

Anania makes more explicit the fields of energy that Williams pitches at his readers in things. There is no need to foreground the agency of the painter, but there is a humming energy in the made thing. The scene is created from ordinary everyday objects bathed in light and color. It does not demand our attention because of magic or heightened emotional attachments or even through a compelling story. The real-life source of the current scene's light is identified. The source of the painting's light is made distinct from the viewer's: "light, its light, not yours, caught in the bristles track, / an occasion of form and matter held there" but even so, this "given off" quality is what a reader gravitates towards, a fragment of artifice with its own vitality. As the viewer of a painting, the poet/narrator is able to address its internal momentum: "space accedes to color, color to motion, / motion to gesture, each the other's moment, / each moment a force arced and snared and made still" (22) without reifying the internal light of it, and perhaps this leaves him free to sense not only its light but its movement. If a still life can move like this, then surely the dreamer can find a path to move through fields of doubt. Perhaps it can even teach a dreamer something about how to move within a very limited field, how to in effect move while fixed in the space of frailty, confinement, or sleep.

We need to pause here to reassess the relationship between vision, remembering and invention in these poems. All of these can be considered part of the process of witnessing, and witnessing cannot happen without the poet's body, which creates the narrative. The body is always a felt presence in these poems, even though it is seldom drawn to our attention. The elder poet is the witness, the one who has witnessed more than others and who understands that the changing body changes what is witnessed. "Poem for Akira Blount" is another regarding a work of art, this time a "spirit / in the guise of a doll":

> She comes to us, arrayed,
> in twigs and branches,
> a figure, not of change
> but of what change
> might leave behind,
> ragged, stark, and as certain
> as the darkening season,
> winter's brittle
> dryad, a spirit
> in the guise of a doll. (31)

There is a certainty in the coming of winter and decay; change leaves behind a husk. There may be subjectivity in the doll, since she is haunted by a spirit, but her thoughts if any cannot be known. However, she can be seen. What change leaves behind is often rendered invisible, ignored. Blount's ability to craft a dryad out of a doll is marked by her ability not to create not a representation of a powerful magical being, but the husk that one might leave behind. The doll, like Williams' Elsie, gives off "isolate flecks" of something that could have been powerful in the proper season. While Williams' poem might have been a treatise on the failure of class and entropy in American society, the story here is one of what change leaves behind—not a story of failure, but the gibbous stage of success, what occurs after the execution of some powerful act.

Like this doll is invented, as well as the still life paintings, in reference to representations of the past and present, the work of memory is a hybrid blend of recollection and creativity akin to Pound's supposed admonition to "Make it new!"—the battle cry of the modernist poet

(North). "Conjectures for an October Evening" returns to the problem of memory, but now considers if it is actually a problem. While vividly reconstructing the titular eveningscape, the poet pauses to reflect if this is really what happened:

> not merely
> remembered but inventions
> out of memory
>
> things reached out
> for and persistent change. (43)

An invention out of memory is neither a faithful reproduction of something that occurred nor an original scene, but something else. It is a new permutation of difference, perhaps. It is certainly a kind of pun on experience—a pun involving memory as Derrida's *différance* is a pun involving language (Reynolds), but not a new idea for Anania, remembering his autobiographical *The Red Menace: A Fiction*, where memories were made new and were not to be entirely trusted, but thoroughly recalled as multiple retellings. "[T]hings reached out / for and persistent change" more or less resolves the ever-present issue of doubt, certainty, and finding pathways without making any grand philosophical narrative statement. If memory is the factory of dreams, it exists not to simply record experience but to create new experiences. The word "persistent" here is perhaps most interesting, given the invocation of the dream factory, this abandoned modernist trope and place—factories were meant to turn out products, in this case, to turn out imaginative work, tangible dreams, the stuff of writing. Memories must always be constructed in the mind or in media; even a photograph is a work of artifice, even as it strives to be a reproduction, and it is also vulnerable to overt manipulations.

A great dream cannot be chased after. Or rather, it can be, but it owes us nothing, and it does not owe poets either. If one has a dream factory, one will probably have dreams given the raw materials (sleep, food, memories, a body, a working brain), but that does not guarantee a great product every time. In the case of a poet like Anania, dreams are and must be poems. One dreams to simply move to the next morning and wake up. A sensei meditates in order to experience enlightenment with more regularity, already knowing that enlightenment exists in an "out there" that is actually internal. "In Time" is a nearly perfect poem, bringing together previous tropes of light, speech, memory, representation and invention—in this case, invention of an Icarus-like narrator who does not fly too high and fall. There is no longer any mention of doubt, although there is also no seeking after certainty either. Balance of forces is key to flight, and steady movement:

> what we read there,
> as the wings lift
> and fall, light caught
>
> hold of, occasions
> of self, futures;
> is there a past that
>
> is inherently avian,
> something that moment
> by moment, point
>
> after point, offers
> us a line we can
>   follow to its end,
>
> to our endings (68–69)

This is memory again, but it is also the possibility of multiple lines (paths) of memory or perhaps of invented memories. We can relate this back to the dream factory and the path through fields of doubt. This might be where multiple memories are in fact invented. The narrator seems to realize that there might not be one real memory, that the dream might be the source of memory itself, or that it doesn't really matter whether it is remembered or invented in the dream. Here is the stuff again of postmodernism and emergent sciences that at once embrace reason and move beyond it. If we are co-creators of our realities, then the factory of dreams is more than a record of the past, and more than a laboratory of effervescent immaterial visions. If one past is "avian," this could be evolutionary; it could be an ideal Platonic past; it could be that we have memories of being birds or angels. But what matters is the memory of flight. This isn't myth, the story of some god, goddess or superhero. Likewise, it is not ordinary and certainly not reflective of the modern (now decaying) industrial settings of "Nightsongs & Clamors, I–VI;" this scene is outside of our history, our industry, our towns, our streets, our factories, our farms, our cities. There is a remembering of

> filaments recalled
> merely, relied on,
> their purposes, ours (69)

This is the moment of certainty, even if fleeting, even if it will disappear with waking.

> I
> return to the curves
> they draw in air,
>
> filaments recalled
> merely, relied on,
> their purposes, ours,
>
> lift and glide, one
> arc after another;
> the river furls its
>
> slowly gathered soils
> from bank to bank;
> clouds, sun-swept (69)

The next stanzas fold in light, flight, art, writing, and speech into an effortless lyric invention of memory:

brighten the day
with shadows, flight
compels both hand

and breath, word
and picture; if you
could draw on water,

write on air, if speech
and flight remained
suspended there:

desire, love, sorrow,
the sudden rush of
wings in aging hands (69–70)

Possibly the avian narrator is flying in dream over the field of uncertainty that once perplexed his movements. In his essay "Poetry and American Memory," Robert Pinsky writes of another field in reference to Abraham Lincoln's poem "My Childhood-Home I See Again":

> The poet's connection with the field is elemental and personal rather than historical—this is not the field of any national military glory, or the field any poet sang, or the field of any ancestral meaning, because the human meaning of it is recent, and also perhaps tenuous. It is not quite, or is only just becoming, a cultural field, with a people who recall its stories.

This kind of poem, only developed "In Time," is not only elemental and personal, but constructed over time and *through* uncertainty, via movement:

> These spaces are intimate,
> then, time's reckonings
> shared, colored radians,

breathless, you might say;
already with us, light-quick,
bunting, hawk or swift,

the reach of live oaks,
their leaves trembling
between sun and shade. (70)

This is what has been created. It was not sought so much as encountered along the way of witnessing, reflecting and writing. In his essay "Poetry and American Memory," Pinsky [names "a characteristically American form of memory" that "haunts" our poetry]:

> memory concentrated on ... the fragility of community, the mystery of isolation, and a particularly elegiac quality that is almost self-contradictory in its yearning toward a past that in one way seems forgotten and sealed off, yet in another way is determinant, powerfully haunting the present. Perhaps as a corollary to that double sense of the past, another aspect of the poems ... is the defeat of reason—even the threat or presence of insanity.

All of these traits are present in *Nightsongs and Clamors* in abundance, except perhaps for the threat or presence of insanity. Anania is one of the sanest American poets. But this is not for lack of haunting by the failures of reason and its concomitant certainties. Only through the discipline of persistent engagement with our surroundings, real or imagined, can we hope to write our paths forward—even when we are limited from speaking or unable to find an audience for our expressions. And, through persistent writing, we can continue to seek the "isolate flecks" of Williams' "To Elsie" that will guide us on the path to another day.

196

Work Cited

Anania, Michael. *Nightsongs & Clamors.* MadHat Press, 2018.

———. *The Red Menace: A Fiction.* Thunder's Mouth Press, 1984.

Frost, Robert. "Stopping by Woods on a Snowy Evening." *The Poetry of Robert Frost,* edited by Edward Connery Lathem. Henry Holt & Co., 1969, pp. 224–25.

North, Michael. "The Making of 'Make It New.'" *Guernica,* 15 August 2013. https://www.guernicamag.com/the-making-of-making-it-new/.

Pinsky, Robert. "Poetry and American Memory." *The Atlantic,* October 1999. https://www.theatlantic.com/magazine/archive/1999/10/poetry-and-american-memory/377805/.

Reynolds, Jack. "Jacques Derrida (1930–2004)." In *The Internet Encyclopedia of Philosophy.* https://iep.utm.edu/derrida/.

Strand, Mark. "Keeping Things Whole." Poetry Foundation. https://www.poetryfoundation.org/poems/47541/keeping-things-whole.

Williams, William Carlos. *Paterson,* edited by Christopher McGowan. New Directions, 1995.

———. "To Elsie." *The Collected Poems of William Carlos Williams,* vol.1. Edited by A. Walton Litz & Christopher MacGowan. New Directions, 1986, pp. 217–19.

Consoling Lines: The Edged Vision of Michael Anania

Sarah Wyman

Angled in, crevacing
the edged places where
darkness shapes itself
    —from "Bell Sounds," *In Natural Light* (36)

Michael Anania's decades of reading, writing, editing and living poetry keep him in conversation with the poetic traditions of late modernist writing in Europe and the Americas. His often jazzy, always intensely visual lines capture everyday objects encountered and moments deeply felt in the Midwest USA. In his early work, scenes of local color, memories of family, and the pioneer myth resonate with the broader human experience. This essay looks at later works that demonstrate Anania's connection to twentieth-century modernism in the West. In these poems, he expands upon the traditions of imagism, or he deploys words for their sounds in ways that mimic musicians he knew growing up in Omaha and later in The Stroll section of Chicago, where he lived near Chess Records. In both modes, the imagistic and the more loosely musical, he employs the rhythms of painters who shattered conventions of traditional realism. These visual artists took the recognizable things of the world and heightened their formal qualities for emphasis and abstracted patterning. *In Natural Light* (1999) and *Heat Lines* (2006) demonstrate Anania's poetic utterances as synaesthetic acts of expression in the lyric mode. His words come across as bits of spoken language that echo in the ear with their repeating sounds and circling themes.

1. *In Natural Light*

In Natural Light builds up multi-layered images in a painterly way by selecting and combining natural objects with an eye to their formal similarities. One finds remnants of James Wright's poetry of the "deep image" with its origins in Spanish symbolism, as Anania takes objects and saturates them with the intensity of visual exploration.

> December Commonplace
>
> Bare foxglove stems
> and remnant cosmos
> sketched across this
>
> morning's snowfall,
> sunlight fissured
> among seed crowns;
>
> we are tilting past
> solstice; dead plant
> shadows, like blue
>
> veins in pale skin,
> branch through crystals
> and course and grow. (7)

This poem reads as a visual painting, connecting the shapes of withered stems to winter sunbeams and veins that penetrate prismatically. The lyric persona speaks with the inclusive first-person plural "we" to invite the reader's eye through a scene. The temporal move intersects the winter solstice, about December 21st, and becomes physical, with a visceral tilt to mimic the earth's axis. As though the poet is William Carlos Williams' own "Solitary Disciple," he places objects in relation to each other and thereby lets them speak through their positionality. Similarity and contrast between shapes produce harmonies and tensions that afford significance beyond the neutral view. Here, one finds dry flowers in silhouette against a new snowfall in the manner of Williams still life or an Ansel Adams photograph. The poem takes a turn from the purely imagistic, however, as Anania develops a conceit and objects speak metaphorically. He has moved far from Ezra Pound's (and Williams') concept of the "direct treatment of the thing" to pivot on simile "like" and overtly invite comparison between dead stems and ostensibly human veins in light skin to suggest the passage of time, vulnerability and transformation. The augmentation of the "cr" phoneme from "crystals" to "course" expands the line and the unabashed repetition of "and" creates an almost cinematic depiction of unexpected growth and accumulation despite deep winter.

Anania's attention to language saves him from the merely decorative. His images are often tactile: nylon thighs rubbing against each other, the mind's eye tracing movement in a physical way. This orientation to the materiality of the medium, language, becomes self-consciously meta-textual in this passage from "Sequence Composed on Gray Paper":

> At the curved line
> wind hones along
> the snow's extended
> edge, the sound
> of a glass bottle
> spun on smooth stone. (30)

As in a lithograph by Ed Colker, Anania's frequent collaborator, it is the edge, the limit between layered tints, that generates meaning. The poet borrows "the comparison of objects implied by juxtaposition" technique of Pound, as he layers snowfall and glass, tossed by the weather in a visual soundscape. The reader intuitively reads the shaped snow and the bottle's grating friction in terms of each other as image: "An intellectual and emotional complex in an instant of time" (Pound

100). The mind logically connects the kinetic images of wind carving snow and the similarly smooth elements, glass and stone in contact. Simultaneously, emotional associations keyed to tactile sensation— cold, sharp, smooth—combine in an energetic, affective image. Despite the passage of time implied by objects in motion, the poem operates according to the supposedly timeless or instantaneous moment of a painting.

Again, fierce attention to qualities of language pulls this visual curiosity to the realm of affect, to work on the reader/listener in ways that surpass the merely logical. The open o's illustrate the wind's drone and its force until reined in by the alliteration of "s" in the ultimate line. Anania thus paints forcefully with phonetic sound, landing on end-stopped, accented syllables with the exception of the third line that describes its own enjambment, "extended," and linguistically mimics this gesture. Critics have often noted such attention to gesture that distinguishes Anania's work as a whole and typically accounts for its most emotive aspects.

Despite the poet's ventures beyond strict imagism, Anania stands firmly against poetry that smacks of sentimentality or partakes of another major movement of the twentieth century: the confessional. He strongly disparages that which adheres to the "poetry therapy movement" (*In Plain Sight* 117). In fact, in his own version of T. S. Eliot's "escape from personality," Anania claims that poets are "feeling impaired" and rejects all poetry of the "evolving self" (Graham, "A Range" 8). Worst, in his opinion are feigned poems that take advantage of every conceivable poetic license toward sentiment and cliché.... Reading through several is like being trapped in the linguistic aftermath of a thousand encounter groups: "I believe in you / You need me. / You believe in me. / I need you"; "I want to get back to the Harmonious Us"; "I mean I really do have some fears"; "You and that special May day." (8)

As vehemently as Anania disparages the overtly personal and shamelessly exhibitionist, the sensitivity of his own best poetry discredits his claim of disability when it comes to feeling. The repeating motif of driving while listening to music, a specific tune pinned to a remembered view, engenders nostalgia. Many of Anania's poems are dedicated to friends, souvenirs of conversations or encounters, presented as affectionate gifts.

Throughout Anania's oeuvre, one finds the limit situation, the edge, the boundary, the location where one must remain or transition to something new. This obsession is remarkably constant. The world sees itself delimited and we witness these lines, smooth surfaces, finger resistance, register friction of glass on stone. As wind sharpens itself on the edge of snow, leaves its mark, we have moved beyond Williams' things as they are and ventured to the realm where the imagination distorts familiar reality and the expression becomes dreamlike in multivalent ways, often generalized and circling about the imperfectly remembered, "going home or nowhere / in particular" (*Heat Lines* 11).

Anania allows the world to exist as found object, nevertheless. He takes familiar things of the world as they appear, then permits the imagination, informed by rational logic, to deepen the images. This, again, constitutes no "direct treatment" as per Pound's directive, nor an instance of Williams' "no ideas but in things," but is informed by both practices. The ideal of imagism, a dream of the objective, inspires the early twentieth-century poets Anania reveres to return to the everyday object, but rarely restrains them from interpretation. Although the comparison between blowing wind and spinning bottle in "Sequence Composed on Gray Paper" is "implied by juxtaposition" rather than simile, it only approximates Pound's strict imagist rules. The full poem from which it comes involves personification, conversational interjection "I think," and the interpretation of urgency, all rhetorical features that dissolve the poem's connection to imagism. Intense, affective elements energize Anania's best poems, honed on the lessons of concrete poetry, that venture into more contemporary rhetorical venues.

Reading Anania's poems, one often feels as though the poet is alongside, speaking the poems aloud. The poet's musicality and his capacity to reproduce language as it is spoken tie him to U.S. modernists, especially Walt Whitman and Williams, but also solidify his work as lyric, as actively expressive rather than simply representational. Jonathan Culler has insisted that the lyric "characteristically strives to be itself an event rather than a representation of an event," in a way that captures the immediacy of a good Anania poem, keyed to time and place (32). As Anania the professor explains, Williams and the objectivists' "desire for the vernacular" and their "concurrent interest in the stuff of perception, the 'thingy-ness' of language and the distrust across several poetic schools of abstractions created a set of compositional practices in poetry that made its ordinary language a very limited version of speech" (*In Plain Sight* 129). In this way, Anania's poetry consistently marks "an event in the lyric present, a time of enunciation" (Culler 12) and thus fulfills the lyric requirements of the contemporary critical school of Culler, Charles Altieri, Heather Dubrow, Robert von Hallberg, Virginia Jackson and others.

In this essay's epigraph, "Angled in, crevacing," Anania presents another image, with noun turning verb as stones seem actively to assemble before the reader's eye to build the darkness they shadow in. As the poem progresses, sea foam piles upon sea foam in a gestural expression of weightless augmentation. Instead of setting objects on the page in a neutral, imagistic way, however, the poetic voice and eye remain painterly and productive, using ambiguity to produce meaning. Natural elements as found objects operate in ways that suggest both ruin and the building up that ruins imply. The poet crafts the descriptive collocation "edged places" rather than "edges placed" that might evoke an unseen hand, in a more typically nineteenth-century mode. Instead, the abstracted affective qualities of sharp angles, closed spaces, and darkness build space. Anania distinguishes between image and consequence as he undoes the predicated opening, a done deal at the beginning, monumental and imposing. Found objects faithfully portrayed are hardly neutral; they evidence prior activity, their construction a consequence of transformation wrought by wind and water. Nothing is simply found untouched but is rather weighted with its own history.

Why would Anania move away from the ideals of imagism so evident in aspects of his work? The poet explains, "The most extreme of these experiments seem to me to proceed not out of a lack of faith in illusion ... but rather from a conviction that certain artistic conventions are too firmly implanted in the audience, to the point of being entirely confused with reality," (*In Plain Sight* 78). Anania understands the machine of the new, perhaps capitalism's appetite for novelty, as Frank O'Hara would put it (Blasing), and knows that eventually even the most "experimental" becomes a conventional language of representation.

As both poet and critic, Anania understands the potential pitfalls of writing within any tradition: "It is embarrassing and not a little frightening to notice how often good, accomplished poets can be bad and how easily the modern virtues—terseness, physical images carefully rendered, plain diction, and surreal surprise—grow conventional and dull … as the 19th-century excesses they replaced" (117). The rigor of Anania's deep images saves them from such cliché and allows his best work to evoke the memorable and lasting associations that stem from a "set of objects, a situation, or a chain of events" as prescribed by T. S. Eliot ("Hamlet and His Problems" 100), another poet who took on the job of explaining his own craft with the objective correlative.

2. *Heat Lines*

In *Heat Lines*, a volume dedicated to printmaker Ed Colker, the fascination with lines and limits continues as names serve as "connectors," according to Lea Graham, and the things of the world become more tightly anchored to place and time ("Like Hands" 1). In "Summer Night," for example, dated circa 1957, Nebraska, the "thin line" of Gil Evans' or Miles Davis' trumpet "draws along the horizon, / one darkness defining / another, and clarity" (10) as musical elements delimit a landscape. Anania captures the local color of the pastoral environment as might Louise Bogan in one of her vistas, yet eschews extensive philosophical conclusions. In the manner of Richard Wilbur, Anania lets adjectives pass as verbs and plays with the subtle metamorphosis of linguistic sounds: "the night air / greened with cooked alfalfa" or "each measure measuring / out its own place" (11) as one rides along with the poetic persona, again driving while music plays on a car radio.

In "Certain Variations *for C. S. Giscombe*," Anania takes language's visual potential to the end of the line. He situates objects in landscapes like a painter building up scenes of rural or urban Midwest USA through a locomotive's window. With repeating rhythms and clever modulations, he retains the attention to objects of earlier imagist-inspired work, but now employs looser modulations and increased experimentation with the graphic disposition of lines on the page. These formal choices create a sense of forward movement to echo the theme of the journey or of the discovery of people and places in time. The reader attends as much to what the poem does as to what the poem says, another feature of the true lyric, according to Altieri. The work seems less self-consciously poetic and more reminiscent of overheard snippets of conversation, musing memory or musical exploration. According to Altieri, this lyric orientation to musicality in not only theme but in sound serves as a link between poem and world via the reader's own experience (12). Anania rigorously distinguishes his own writing from language poetry, yet the increasing stylization of his formal structures and the heightened attention to sound narrow the gap (Graham, "A Range" 18).

Spreading his lines across the page in regular tercets, Anania builds momentum to mimic the "beginning," the "first stage," the "journey opening" moments his lines describe. As in Gary Snyder's iconic "Riprap," words tumble over words, as the train lurches through. Yet Anania's ontologies of being are more modest than Snyder's, or certainly those of Wallace Stevens. Objects are again carefully situated as found, "the space / between one hill and the next," and prepositions mingle with the disorientation of rapid speed through a landscape: at, ahead, under, into, etc. Amid this fixation on the positionality of the parts, other tensions arise such as those between "Apprehension" and "holding," between the "clutch" for stability and the "jerk" of the train car. Despite this confusion, syncopated rhythms push the lines onward: "carriage jerking the car, your / spine" (*Heat Lines* 26–27). The poetic voice remains unafraid of repetition because it prepares for modulation in a mode reminiscent of blues musical forms:

all that you are passing is past,

moment by moment.
>   Moment is the arc of one
>   force exceeding another,

implying movement.
>   Moment is your place
>   in time, is stillness, then. (27)

With the simple insertion of "ve," "moment" becomes "movement" and ties the hurtling train to the passage of time and the transposition of bodies through time and space. And here and there, a lull, as assonance slows and opens up sounds: "neither here nor there, / like sound boxes, hollowed / out and deeply echoing" (29).

Anania's *ars poetica* spins out in such poems as "Such Much" and "Now and Then." "Such Much," an ekphrastic based on a scene from the film *Casablanca*, holds one instance of the title phrase, "heat lines," as it presents a meta-discursive meditation on words, playing them against each other in windy swells reminiscent of "Sequence Composed on Gray Paper" and the cinematic scene set in a desert. The poet dedicates this poem to a German couple, Yaak and Ingrid Karsunke who, like the actors in the scene, practiced speaking English in anticipation of their immigration to the U.S. as World War II refugees. In "Such Much," discrete sounds are personified, multiform and surprising as they merge with a rapid catalogue of terms that describe them in a way familiar to language learners. The poet melds phonemes and meanings to bring us to *things*, through the delightful discovery of defamiliarized ease, "hair across fresh linen." Or sounds, "some wingéd, some gilled, some lidless and strange," (40) return us to the deep image and a poetic version of synaesthetic expressionism. Anania admires ekphrastic poet Frank O'Hara's "complete absorption into the stuff of the poem," which he manages here (Graham, "A Range" 6). As wind simultaneously whispers aurally and grates with tactile determination, an interlocutor recalls "the slim margin of damp sand hissing / between the long desert and the persistent sea" (41). Thus, the measured strip of land feels moist and sounds off as it both connects and separates land and water in a variously sensational and memorable image of crossing borders.

The penultimate poem of *Heat Lines*, "Now and Then," holds that the partial or interrupted view outshines any fully imagined perception of the world. Since we can only know our physical environment in fragments available to our senses, we continually compensate for the limited by imagining wholes. Yet the parts have value in themselves. Even the liminal spaces between form and ground come into focus again when the third-person persona (who may stand in for the poet) "thought the edges of things mattered." Lines themselves are "consoling" as "horizons of all sorts" allow objects and forms to define each other: "the sea's lift against morning or evening, one / color giving shape to another" (106).

In this poem of poetic philosophy, the speaker returns again to Whitman and Williams—of whom all poets are "heirs" according to Anania (Graham, "A Range" 18)—to the vernacular world of *things* and the mixed sensations they offer: "light, tension, moisture" (*Heat Lines* 106). Again, the "solitary disciple" looks at the world and sees intersectional objects in relationship:

> The pipe fence, for example,
> against the privet hedge's uneven greenery or the
> water tower's side cut out across the afternoon
> sky, sycamore at sunset, the city's motley of
> rooftops (106)

Like a painter with her many brushstrokes and choices, the speaker knows "things are conditioned in multiples or by mul- / tiples" (106). And these objects are connected, embedded; although they may be named individually, things belong to the landscape of a room or the view framed through a window. The "thing in itself ... wish[es] for ... an idea warmly wrapped around it" (107). Anania ultimately leaves Williams' and Pound's dream of the self-sufficient *thing in itself* behind as his persona acknowledges the way things bring us to concepts, to life, through lyric art, which is probably what his great mentors knew all along.

Works Cited

Altieri, Charles. "The Lyrical Impulse." *Journal of Literary Theory*, vol. 11, no. 1, 2017, pp. 12–21.

Anania, Michael. *Heat Lines*. Asphodel Press, 2006.

———. *In Natural Light*. Asphodel Press, 1999.

———. *In Plain Sight: Obsessions, Morals & Domestic Laughter*. Asphodel Press, 1991.

Blasing, Mutlu. *Politics and Form in Postmodern Poetry*. Cambridge UP, 2010.

Culler, Jonathan. "Lyric, History, and Genre." *The Lyric Theory Reader*. Edited by Virginia Jackson. Johns Hopkins UP, 2014, pp. 63–76.

———. "Lyric Works, not Worlds." *Journal of Literary Theory*, vol. 11, no. 1, 2017, pp. 32–39.

Eliot, T. S. "Hamlet and His Problems." *The Sacred Wood: Essays on Poetry and Criticism*. Methuen & Co., Ltd., 1920.

Graham, Lea. "'Like Hands Raised in Song': Proper Names in Michael Anania's 'Steal Away.'" *Valley Voices*, vol. 16, no.1, 2016, pp. 91–96.

———. "A Range of Experience: Conversations in Place with Michael Anania." *Paper Street*, Spring 2006.

Pound, Ezra. "A Few Don'ts by an Imagiste." Poetry Foundation. https://www.poetryfoundation.org/poetrymagazine/articles/58900/a-few-donts-by-an-imagiste.

Williams, William Carlos. "To a Solitary Disciple." *Collected Poems of William Carlos Williams*, Vol. 1: 1909–1939. Edited by A. Walton Litz and Christopher MacGowan. New Directions, 1986, p. 104.

"Energy held in elegant control": Vortex Anania

Lachlan Murray

The First World War brought an end to the short-lived Vorticist movement, during the early modernist era a proposed cross-disciplinary enterprise encompassing painting, sculpture and literature. The mass death and dehumanization that modern technology had enabled suddenly made the artist's relation with modernity and technology acutely ambivalent. Perhaps the cold, geometric abstraction and urban industrial ethos of prewar and early wartime Vorticist painting, and the bellicose rhetoric of the Vorticist vehicle *Blast*, now felt unseemly to its creators. For Wyndham Lewis and Ezra Pound, however, the movement's two key figures, the governing concept of the Vortex still exercised a powerful hold. Some critics suggest a Vorticist aesthetic underlies all their subsequent work. In this view, *The Cantos* and the novels of Lewis develop a more slowly evolving literary Vorticism that was only embryonic at the time of *Blast* but would subsequently become more influential than Vorticist painting or sculpture.[1] Certainly some interesting affinities exist in the work of Michael Anania, whom Robert Archambeau has described as a contemporary modernist ("Michael Anania" 3–4).[2]

So what constitutes a Vorticist aesthetic? Following the second and final issue of *Blast* in July 1915, Lewis was reticent about the matter in public. The writer Douglas Goldring, a contemporary of Lewis's and a supporter of *Blast*, provides some insight:

211

> The meaning of the Vortex and Vorticism as propounded by Lewis, was simplicity itself. "You think at once of a whirlpool", he explained. "At the heart of the whirlpool is a great silent place where all the energy is concentrated. And there, at the point of concentration, is the Vorticist." (65)

By contrast, Pound was effusive, but his tendency to hyperbole, generalization and the cognitive leap makes encapsulating his ideas about Vorticism difficult. His various statements about the meaning of the Vortex are further complicated by the fact that he was attempting to bridge imagism and Vorticism at the time and not only for aesthetic reasons. Within two years of its formalization as a movement in 1912, Pound had come to realize imagism's limitations along with its benefits. But he may have been more eager to publicly articulate the limitations and play up a successor because his leadership of the imagists was being successfully challenged by Amy Lowell. Three months after the first issue of *Blast* in which Pound declared "The vortex is the point of maximum energy" ("Vortex. Pound." 153), he published "Vorticism" in the *Fortnightly Review*, which contains the following well-known paragraph:

> The image is not an idea. It is a radiant node or cluster; it is what I can, and must perforce, call a VORTEX, from which, and through which, and into which, ideas are constantly rushing. In decency one can only call it a VORTEX. And from this necessity came the name "vorticism." *Nomina sunt consequentia rerum*, and never was that statement of Aquinas more true than in the case of the vorticist movement. (Gaudier-Brzeska 92)

Pound seems to be arguing that an image and a vortex are one and the same.[3] In the face of an imagist movement that Pound felt had deteriorated into routine recitations of static visual imagery, he was in fact reasserting his earlier definition in 1913 of an image as a "complex"—"An 'Image' is that which presents an intellectual and emotional complex in an instant of time" (*Literary Essays* 4)—described here as a "radiant node or cluster." While reasserting his definition he was also extending it, deepening its implications. Closely following the paragraph describing the Vortex is another in which Pound states, "The organization of forms is a much more energetic and creative action than the copying or imitating of light on a haystack" (Gaudier-Brzeska 92). Although the Vortex is only implied, Pound went even further in *ABC of Reading*:

> The defect of earlier imagist propaganda was not in misstatement but in incomplete statement. The diluters took the handiest and easiest meaning, and thought only of the STATIONARY image. If you can't think of imagism or phanopoeia as including the moving image, you will have to make a really needless division of fixed image and praxis or action. (52)

Pound is not arguing that the image and the Vortex are one and the same, but rather that the image is the result of the Vortex. The whirling forces of a vortex and the still point at its center, the perfect embodiment of a dialectical relation between motion and stillness, are an analogue for the "creative action" or "praxis" of the artist and the resulting "forms" or "fixed image." Both action and form are suspended in the work of art, although as Paul Edwards points out with regard to Vorticist painting, not necessarily as a recognizable vortex—the Vortex is analogous, not literal (102). The energy and force required to arrive at a Poundian image, by which Pound meant not simply a visual representation, but an Aquinian essence, a "radiant" form (*Nomina sunt consequentia rerum*, names are the consequence of things), is by necessity a permanent part of that image. Evidence of the generative tension, the form-giving force moving within a work of art, must remain. In Hugh Kenner's memorable description, "the vortex is not the water but a patterned energy made visible by the water" (146).

Writing about his old friend, John Matthias observes, "Anania admires energy, even deadly energy, held in elegant control." Matthias uses energy to draw a parallel between some of the specifically rendered objects in Anania's work—the pistol owned by Anania's father, the hot rods that populate *The Red Menace*—and "the textures of Anania's verse and prose" (32). I would extend Matthias's observation by suggesting that in Anania's work the pattern of at least some of that "energy …

held in elegant control" is vortical, often with an accompanying radiance or central light. This vorticity and the energy it represents manifests itself in different ways: in the repeated appearance of words that describe vortical motion; in precisely rendered moments that evoke vortical motion; and in a recurring fundamental panorama that exhibits a vortical structure. Words that describe vortical motion, appearing repeatedly over a period of five decades, beginning with Anania's first book publication in 1969 and continuing through *Nightsongs & Clamors* [2018]. [These] include spin, swirl, eddy, turn, circle, furl, churn, curve, curl, bend, coil and twist. Often constructed as verbs that help create kinesthetic images of water, silt, air, dust and wind in involuted or vortical motion, these words are the charged particles of Anania's poetry. Precisely rendered moments that evoke vortical motion and its central stasis provide some of the most striking images in Anania's work. They include the mushroom cloud, "a light at the center" that results from the atomic test in *The Red Menace*:

> the cloud ... stood still, or seemed still except for the constant enfolding of smoke shadows at the top and sides, and the constant pumping of smoke into the crown from the column below. (9)

[And again in] "the catfish dance" in "The Riversongs of Arion":

> when catfish feed
> in quick channel waters,
>
> they move upstream, angling
> into the surface just as
> the curling wave is pulled
>
> back. Rivermen call this
> the catfish dance because
> from the banks they seem
>
> stationary....
>   the river itself,

The river's wavelets,
thick with sewage, move,
it seems, upstream against

final deposit in some
widening delta. Illusive.
It is the rush beneath

speeding as the deep
channel bends; the surface
moving more slowly, inertial,

is curled back and downward. (*Riversongs* 6)

[Anania's vortical motion and central stasis continue in] the planetary wobble of a toppled Winesap in "Apples":

Perhaps, it is always true that each
occasion is its own center, that in
its moment the wobbling Winesap's stem
is the axis to our irregular pasts,
motions that curve inward as they fall
across contending radians (*In Natural Light* 12)

Typical of Anania's poetic method, these moments briefly coalesce then as they disperse, like eddies or small vortices in the river that has long provided Anania his dominant motif. Fleeting conjunctions in time and space, "each occasion" with "its own center" paradoxically fuses motion and stillness, life's ceaseless flux and transience momentarily suspended in Pound's "instant of time," as well as in an instant of the poem. Archambeau sees Anania as "fundamentally a poet of transience and change" ("Michael Anania" 8), while also noting "a kind of will to stability and permanence ... despite the poet's knowing such stability to be illusory" (6).

The fundamental panorama which occurs in different guises in Anania's work depicts Anania's childhood home as a still point infused with light and warmth, surrounded by darkness and apparent chaos. In "'A Place That's Known'" the most immediate chaos is "poverty's continual rage" just beyond "the front step" in the Omaha housing project where Anania grew up—"the Plaza's hopscotch" (*In Natural Light* 5, 3), also recreated in *The Red Menace*: "Fires, scaldings, wife-beating, arms, legs, heads broken, old people and children carried away, sirens and flashing lights" (44). Beyond the familiar "clamor" of the plaza the Second World War occasions much greater conflagrations, but beyond even the war, the "Summer night" with "American elms opening a span of Western sky" (*In Natural Light* 5, 3) suggests the essential chaos of all creation that "Missing Matter" directly addresses:

> Of course, it is improbable
> that in all of this endless turning
> things do not simply fly apart;
> stars uncluster
>
> . . . .
>
> the day's accumulation of objects
> turned out into the impending night
> like dust and lint swept across a door sill,
> the door, backing into the evening's shadows,
> itself a proposition. Hold on, fast, back,
> your eyes pressed open by the sheer rush of things,
> though nothing past this threshold is defined. (39–40)

Although "nothing ... is defined," "Missing Matter" suggests, like chaos theory, that a pattern may exist, however "improbable." The pattern the poem suggests is "endless turning," the "sheer rush" of a cosmic vortex (reminiscent of Pound's "constantly rushing") surrounding "a radiant node or cluster" of stars—the condition that must exist if the stars are possibly to "uncluster." Within the threshold, Anania's childhood existence is more defined, establishing a brief stability at the center—an evanescent safety and happiness—despite the omnipresent whirl of uncertainty and danger without. The transition between without and within in "'A Place That's Known'" is "a dance spun / across the linoleum's worn flowers, / her hair pressed into his chest." Anania's parents present a vortex on a human scale, one that surrounds the central radiance and stasis of "the Zenith's / pale dial" on the family radio (4) while also recalling "the catfish dance" that makes visible the transition between "deep" and "surface." This center also has a center—appropriate given the double sense of "zenith" as brand name and central or highest point in the heavens. The stanza continues to spiral inward from dance to radio dial to the "words of the song that stopped / the dancing, everyone staring into / the music." The popular song that everyone dances to, here and in *The Red Menace*, is "Let the Rest of the World Go By." The song's lyrics supply "'A Place That's Known'" with its title, and the line, the last of the stanza, that stops the dance: "I'd like to leave it all behind and go and find" (4). Or it almost supplies the line, for Anania substitutes an ellipsis for what is central to the lyrics:

> With someone like you,
> a pal good and true,
> I'd like to leave it all behind,
> and go and find
> some place that's known
> to God alone,
> just a spot to call our own.
> We'll find perfect peace,
> where joys never cease,
> out there beneath a kindly sky,
> we'll build a sweet little nest
> somewhere in the west,
> and let the rest of the world go by. (Brennan and Ball)

Here is the implied still point of this particular turning world, the axis to Anania's irregular past, a popular cultural equivalent to T. S. Eliot's mystical oneness with the divine in *Four Quartets*. ("At the still point of the turning world. Neither flesh nor fleshless; / Neither from nor towards; at the still point, there the dance is" ["Burnt Norton" II]). Cosmos, "the long dusty / tilt of the world," "war" (*In Natural Light* 5, 4), Nebraska, Omaha, the Logan Fontenelle Homes, the plaza, the

217

family home, the dance, the Zenith's dial and the song title that conjures "the sheer rush of things" "curve inward" to the point in the lyrics that briefly, tremulously, holds out the stillness of "perfect peace" to people for whom life is anything but perfect or peaceful.

The lyrics locate that perfect peace "somewhere in the west," the words with which Anania begins the next stanza, creating an opening out after the spiraling inward, a whirlpool that gently carries the reader inward and down before a release into something new, in the words of the song "Across the Great Divide."[4] The transition between the two stanzas is the only one in the nine-stanza poem not coincidental with a transition between two sentences; the second of the two stanzas is also the fifth or central stanza of the poem. By disrupting a pattern of stanzas ending with full stops, and instead constructing one long sentence that encompasses two stanzas, Anania subtly accelerates the poem's rhythm, propelling the reader toward and then through the still point—an example of the "creative action" that Pound felt should be evident in the completed work of art. By positioning the still point at the center of the poem Anania further emphasizes the vortical structure. In a review of *In Natural Light*, Archambeau also suggests a vortical structure emerging from "'A Place That's Known'": "Memories spiral out of this moment, and image modulates into image in an almost cinematic montage" (134). Archambeau identifies the center point as the portrait of Anania's mother dying in hospital rather than "perfect peace" (although the two are related), and as the vortex dissipates and reforms throughout the poem there could be other centers as well— the "white chenille" bedspread for example (*In Natural Light* 5), under which the poet may have been conceived, the fundamental panorama perhaps also originary. But regardless of where the center is temporarily located, Archambeau's structural observation seems consistent with my own, and "montage" is a kinetic instance of collage. It imparts the sense of movement Pound envisioned in a poetics that evolved from the image or images juxtaposed as a compositional imperative to the Vortex.

In *The Red Menace* the vortical structure of the fundamental panorama includes an additional component, one that I speculate may derive from Pound's idiosyncratic choice of *The Unwobbling Pivot* as the English title for the *Zhong Yong*, one of the classic Confucian texts Pound translated. Dasenbrock points out the similarity between the pictograph of the Vortex that appeared in *Blast*, and the Chinese character *zhong* (meaning "middle").[5] "Both have a line passing through the middle of a circle and both attempt to represent a point of stability in the midst of motion and flux" (226). Dasenbrock argues that Pound merged Vorticist, Confucian and ultimately Taoist ideas in *The Cantos*, the equilibrium and detachment characteristic of the sage in the *Zhong Yong*, essential qualities for Pound's notion of the Great Ruler—and for Lewis's conception of the Vorticist artist.[6] In the section of *The Red Menace* entitled "The death of Mrs. Rich—a musical interlude," the radio and the dancers have moved outside to the plaza, where an impromptu party takes place on a summer evening after a group of men from the project and the surrounding neighborhood return home drunk, Anania's father among them. Having served as pallbearers at Mrs. Rich's funeral, the men reward themselves for the respect paid their neighbor with an afternoon spent in various taverns. Their reappearance takes the form of a vortex:

> It was past seven when the pallbearers finally roared back, boisterous and disheveled. They laughed up the stairs and into the backyard like a winning team, jostling one another as they walked, arms draped over one anothers' shoulders, backslapping, recoiling with laughter, then regrouping again.... The group reassembled, surrounded almost immediately by a dozen children, wheeling around, tumbling, darting back into place like pilot fish, tugging at arms, belts, pant legs, and sleeves.... They moved around the yard, propelled, it seemed, by their laughter. Sometimes the group fractured and reassembled, and there were occasional sorties to kitchen steps, where the wives watched, nervous and resentful, a little afraid of the size and abandonment of the gestures that were filling the yard.... Slowly the women were drawn out, pulled along by their husbands or caught up as they ran after stray children imperiled by boisterous arms and legs. (49–50)

Dissipating, reforming, progressively gathering strength, drawing

219

in others, the vortex grows into an emotionally charged party with the adults dancing and drinking. Again, the panorama spirals inward to a point at which "The radio play[s] 'Let the Rest of the World Go By,'" and "All the adults [are] quite still." In the midst of the activity is the unwobbling pivot, a still point with a luminous core, as the narrator/Anania tells us:

> My friends and I took turns shinnying up the telephone pole guide wire just outside Mrs. Rich's door, hanging over to watch it all upside down—agitated beer sprayed up into the lamplight ... jitterbugging, real jitterbugging with legs kicked up high, skirts swirling ... the lamp above me shaking from my weight on the guide wire (50)

If we agree with Matthias's hypothesis that "the author and narrator [are] one" (37), *The Red Menace* as much autobiography as it is novel (in autofictional fashion, Anania identifies the narrator as "Anania" in the novel's final passage), then not only is the radiance ("the lamp") located at the still point/axis/pivot ("the telephone pole") but so is Anania. Adopting the position that Lewis claimed for the Vorticist, Anania gazes out at the flux, detached, and yet part of it. In fact, he orders it (the Confucian approach), or finds the order in it (the Taoist approach).[7]

The two versions of the fundamental panorama suggest further interpretive possibilities that may seem diametrically opposed but in fact are bound together in a dialectical relation. The vortical structure at the center of "'A Place That's Known'" ultimately represents a route or portal to a paradise or heaven. The association of Vortex and route to paradise becomes more explicit in the first "ending" of *The Red Menace*, which also locates paradise "westward ... over the Rockies" (142). The structure of the narrator's peyote-fired vision, revealed as he drives away from the Omaha Indian Reservation at Macy, seems explicitly vortical:

> Coming over a slight rise I noticed an odd fork in the road ahead, a second highway brightly lit that veered to the right and upward, as though following the face of a steep hill that was not there.... There was a pull toward it that seemed at first to be a fault in the car, then I realized that I was edging the car in its direction, or, rather, I felt

the urge to steer toward it.… The second road was lovely, like a silver ribbon that lifted and furled, banking as it turned westward, a finely worked contrail spiraling against the pure lapis of the summer sky. It bent over the horizon, dipping and turning, brightening as it went, as though it were gathering back the rays of the vanished sun as it curled over the converging lines of distant cornfields. (141–42)

In a manner similar to his poetic method, Anania describes "the second road" using language dense with verbs that evoke vortical motion: "veered," "furled," "banking," "turned," "spiraling," "bent," "turning," and "curled." Further emphasizing the road's vortical structure, its "radiant node," the narrator feels an inexorable "pull toward it," and the road progressively "brighten[s] … as though it were gathering back the rays of the vanished sun."

The vortex of pallbearers leads in the opposite direction in "The death of Mrs. Rich—a musical interlude," suggesting a portal to the underworld or hell. For the residents of the project, "unevenly pieced back together" after the war, "as down and out as they had been through the thirties," "A place that's known / to God alone" is revealed to be a "dream" that "fade[s] like a receding light, the dim yellow wedge of illuminated numbers on the radio's face, the only sunset left to dream themselves into" (50). Instead of being gathered back, the celestial light recedes and fades, and the party degenerates into the chaos of a brawl "a few minutes after the song end[s]" (51). The narrator is "hanging … upside down," head pointing earthward, "just outside Mrs. Rich's door," the scene of recent death, and he hangs from "the telephone pole guide wire." In the second ending of *The Red Menace*, which coincides with the end of the book but resists the sense of closure provided by the first ending, "a telephone pole guide wire" is what decapitates a classmate of Anania's thrown from a car wreck (149). Indeed, the whole of "Autoclysms," the novel's last section, can be read as a series of vortices in which violent events and death surround stillness, and time is slowed down or frozen at the point of impact, in one instance a passenger's cigarette embedded in a fractured windshield assuming the role of pivot. Anania labels this inverse world "the hellfire and damnation of the automobile" (144), which echoes his earlier description of nuclear holocaust as "concentric circles of fire," and recalls his portrait of automobile-fiend and Strategic Air Command chief Curtis LeMay, finger on the button, "at the seventh subterranean level of the Offutt Administration Building" (115, 117). The energy of the vortex in these instances is Matthias's "deadly energy," and significantly a deadly vortex is what initially gives rise to the Logan Fontenelle Homes. As the sedentary Mr. King—the sage of the neighborhood, and another unwobbling pivot ("he was one of the few pinnings that place ever had") tells Anania and his friends in the passage immediately preceding the party, "Yawl know … how they come to build this project here? Use to was all houses and tar-paper sheds…. Till the tornado come an blew it all away" (49).

Vortex leading to heaven, vortex leading to hell. This mythical association, its duality, has a precedent in the epics of Homer, Dante and Pound. Odysseus must pass through the whirlpool in order to enter the underworld in Book 11 of the *Odyssey;* with Virgil as guide, Dante descends into the concentric circles of hell at the beginning of the *Inferno;* and Pound invokes both poems when his Odyssean persona proclaims, at the beginning of *The Cantos,* "The ocean flowing backward, came we then to the place / Aforesaid by Circe" (3). The reverse journey, away from hell and toward paradise or heaven, also takes the form of a vortex or spiral in *The Divine Comedy* and *The Cantos.* Dante ascends the progressively narrowing ledges of Purgatory and then traverses the concentrically arranged spheres of Paradise before his fleeting vision of the Absolute. At different points in *The Cantos* Pound vividly depicts a similar cosmology: in Canto C, for example ("Out of Erebus / Where no mind moves at all. / In crystal funnel of air"); in Canto XVI ("In the turn of the hill; in hard steel / The road like a slow screw's thread"); and in the *m'elevasti* passage from Canto XC, which draws directly from Dante.[8] Anania perhaps echoes this latter when he writes: "lift me // homeward, you might have said to the wind— / or into, or against—its vortices curling / their smoke trailed petals across your face" (*In Natural Light* 17).

"From *Many Happy Returns,*" an excerpt from an unpublished novel in which Anania interweaves fictional characters with the aftermath of

Nebraska's Starkweather murders in the late 1950s, he hints at a similar cosmological stance. The protagonist, Henry, is masquerading as a reporter at the trial of the real-life Caril Ann Fugate, who in 1958 was tried in Lincoln, Nebraska for her part in a killing spree that included her own family.[9] Without intending to, Henry quickly falls through the sensationalism and media hyperactivity surrounding the trial to some deep and personal place, becoming mesmerized by the courtroom appearance of the teenaged Caril Ann. The excerpt opens with a disorienting, hallucinatory feel—Henry's stream of consciousness— appropriate for the dissociative state into which Henry may be falling:

> "10–27–58"
>> "The chair she sat in—"
> … sharply underscored at the top of the legal pad, then two full lines of Palmer Method circle exercises. Monday's date, the sign of a momentary, over-earnest professionalism.
>> "The chair she sat in …"
> Two lines of push-pulls. A drawing of a chair. (144)

Instead of beginning his notes beneath the date, Henry inscribes "two full lines of Palmer Method circle exercises.… Two lines of push-pulls." The circle exercises and push-pulls (straight lines) are no doubt a holdover from Henry's school handwriting classes during an era (the first half of the twentieth century) when A. N. Palmer's method of training the muscles of the arm was in vogue. But Palmer Method circle exercises are not discrete circles; rather, they are connected loops that spiral the length of the line, approximating a vortex. The Palmer Method itself emphasized force, energy and continuous, often looping motion.[10] As Henry's fixation with the Eve figure Caril Ann increases, so does the possibility that the vortical circle exercises represent more than just limbering up for a day of note-taking.[11]

A second vortex appears near the end of the excerpt when Henry visits Caril Ann's dilapidated and now empty house standing in a yard full of junk. Another scene of recent death, it is the place where Charlie Starkweather and Caril Ann begin the killing rampage that subsequently spirals outward to surround Lincoln:

He had scuffed around in that yard for a half an hour or so but kept the house and the sheds at a safe distance. Circling the outhouse, he stepped into the coils of a rusted bedspring hidden among the weeds. When he tried to pull his foot free, his loafer came off, and he stood there for several minutes on one foot wondering if it would be possible for him to bend forward and reach the shoe that angled toward him from the spring without falling forward into a snare of rusted wire. He tried it once, slowly, but began to lose his balance almost immediately. Eventually, he decided it wasn't possible and lowered his raised foot to the wet ground, bent over and worked his shoe free with both hands. His sock was soaking wet, so he pulled it off and slipped his cold, bare foot into his shoe. (159)

The precisely rendered and affecting details of Henry's momentary predicament may divert the reader from wondering what Henry is doing at the house in the first place, prowling around, in his own words, trying to "find something of the girl" (159). The answer may come when Henry's investigation is disrupted by stepping into the bedspring, a wire helix that in some configurations can be cone-shaped or vortical. Henry manages to free himself after failing to maintain a Confucian balance, but perhaps part of him does not escape, a particle slowly "circling" that is eventually sucked into the vortex in the yard. Perhaps, like Odysseus and Dante, Henry is about to embark on a *nekuia*, a trip into the underworld in search of the information that will allow one to return home. The two vortices are slyly embedded, akin to elements in a visual puzzle that hides objects in full view within the context of a larger picture. The opposite is true of "the chair she sat in," which is at the center of a compositional vortex, one in which each repetition of the word "chair" is equivalent to an involuted line of force, spinning the narrative tighter around this central image, intensifying and energizing it in the process. The word "chair" is repeated twenty-one times in the space of twelve pages—an incantation that grows in force and strangeness with each repetition. (The effect, when I heard Anania read the excerpt at the University of Illinois at Chicago in the spring of 1992, was riveting.) Each repetition is a re-acceleration of a vortex composed of language, a process that leads to the defamiliarization of "chair," forcing a hyperawareness of the chair's essence upon the reader or the audience at the very center point of the narrative. On the chair sits "unmoving, unmoved, inscrutable Caril Ann," her appearance throughout the courtroom scenes one of charged stasis—"*Rigid*," as Henry describes her (155). During his Vorticist period (1914–17) and immediately prior, Pound used the same analogy on several occasions in his prose to illustrate patterned energy, the effect of force on form:

> If you pour a heap of iron filings on to a glass plate they form a heap; no amount of care and thought would make you able to arrange them bit by bit in a beautiful manner. Clap a strong enough magnet to the underside of the plate and at once the filings leap into order. They form a rose pattern on the lines of the electric force; move the magnet and they move in unison. ("Through Alien Eyes I" 252)[12]

An opened rose bears a visual resemblance to a vortex, but more important to Pound is that both are a pattern or form resulting from the artistic force or energy he feels should be inherent in a work of art. At the end of Canto LXXIV Pound asks, "Hast'ou seen the rose in the steel dust?" (449), a moment Dasenbrock considers pivotal to the entire poem (228). During his drive home from Lincoln to Omaha, Henry passes a "scrapyard … its great electromagnetic crane still turning from one heap of metal to another in a pool of yellow light. Its relentless arm and the charged fist of scrap it handed out over and over always made him think of home" (156). All the elements of the vortex, the pivot, and the rose appear to be present, even more so given the double sense of the word "still," the vortex-like simultaneity of "still turning." But gaining the most from a comparison with Pound's analogy is the startling simile Anania uses to portray Caril Ann at an earlier point in the narrative:

> The reporters … all had intricate theories about the case, and some of them—the hawk-faced guy from Chicago, who had called Starkweather "Howdy Doody," especially—had a finely tuned sense of the girl and her oddly suspended place in the drama—actor, victim, witness, observer—like the last iron filing in the rough cluster that hangs from a bar magnet, loosely caught by forces that

careen invisibly through the filings clumped above it, but solitary and exposed. (155)

Ultimately it is Caril Ann who resides at the still point, who forms the pivot around which the excerpt, and briefly the entire country, revolves, and who may represent for Henry the portal to the underworld. "[F] orces that careen invisibly" seems rich with possibility for the novel's structure, for determining the interaction of the characters with one another and with the larger society, and for mapping Henry's odyssey (perhaps with the goal of a "happy return") through what Matthias calls "the strange intensities and stultifying inertias" of Eisenhower-era America (30)—an odyssey that may include a *nekuia* into some psychological underworld, a pathology both personal and communal, to which Caril Ann holds the key. Certainly the timing is auspicious. Henry drives back to Omaha on Halloween, the evening when the spirit and physical worlds mingle.

I do not want to imply that vortex-and-still-point is the sole pattern inherent in Anania's work, or that an imaginative engagement with some of Pound's ideas is necessarily more important than engagements of another sort. In some important instances the concept of the Vortex describes a pattern in the flux and transience that constitute the work's matrix—"describes" in both senses: creative force finding an inherent structure in, or imparting a structure to, what might otherwise seem an evocation of randomness. The pattern is essentially dialectical, one of tensional opposition and complementarity—stillness/motion, the timeless/the time-bound—which helps generate the energized suspension, the impulse toward spatial form and simultaneity, that characterize Anania's work. Here is perhaps the crux of the longstanding attractiveness of the vortex for Anania: as pattern or concept it provides a means to creatively articulate abstruse intellectual territory, both metaphysical and epistemological, that by its very nature confounds finite articulation. The literary precedent of the Vortex also imbues the work with mythical and divine implications, appealing to a poet of Anania's erudition, while connecting it with a critical strand of modernist poetics. But finally, energy, often in the form of light, rather than any specific structuring device or effect, seems to most interest Anania. The result is poetry and fiction that is an "energy-construct" itself, to use Charles Olson's term (16)—energy born up from Anania's own life. No one is likely to mistake the graceful movement of Anania's poetic line for "the sprawling Olsonian field composition," as Archambeau points out (Review of *In Natural Light* 134), but Olson's belief that a poem should be an energy conduit feels relevant: "A poem is energy transferred from where the poet got it ... by way of the poem itself to, all the way over to, the reader" (16). The sinuous current that bears the reader along from moment to moment in Anania's poetry and prose often achieves this energy transfer, the writing itself the final instance of "energy ... held in elegant control."

Flash forward/afterword

I wrote this essay in 2003–2004, before *Heat Lines* was published, although at the time I was aware a new collection of Anania's poetry was forthcoming. When I revisited the essay in 2016 for inclusion in a special issue of *Valley Voices* featuring Anania, I was both pleased and just slightly irked to learn that ten years after the publication of *Heat Lines* another collection was planned with the title *Continuous Showings*. I'd circled back to the situation of writing about a body of work that would soon expand, in ways that might affect my understanding of the work and what I had to say about it.

The images, patterns and motifs I've outlined in Anania's work, the obsessions both physical and metaphysical, are all present in the three most recent collections. They are again generated by words that describe vortical motion, moments that evoke vortical motion, central radiance/stasis, and in *Heat Lines* the vortical panorama. Section I of "Summer Night," the poem's title appended with "*Nebraska, circa 1957*," provides a good example, subtly interweaving all these elements:

> passing through Elmwood, its
> single amber warning light swaying
> above the pavement; August; stray

> wings and bug smears jewel
> the windshield, the 1948
> Oldsmobile radio clutching
>
> distant musics, its reach
> scraped along the prairie's
> flat water shale; suddenly
>
> empty, this summer night,
> the vague constellations,
> cornrows spinning away (*Heat Lines* 9)

The "single amber warning light" is the central point for a series of concentric circles: small prairie town, "cornrows spinning away" and "the vague constellations" above. The light is "swaying," as if the concentric circles are a magnetic field, large invisible forces that mysteriously impart motion to a single inanimate object, the object in turn the visible indicator of those forces—like "the last iron filing" in the excerpt "From *Many Happy Returns.*" Automobiles "passing through Elmwood" from opposite directions are like particles sucked into a vortex and briefly spun about, before being expelled into nighttime prairie that's "suddenly empty."

While continuing Anania's use of the vortex as structuring concept, *Heat Lines* also develops it further. Approximately a third of the collection uses three-line stanzas, the lines in each stanza progressively indented, creating a regular pattern like the thread of a screw. The effect on the page is to concretize a vortical or helical structure. *In Natural Light* contains four poems that use the same structure, and *Riversongs* contains one poem with a similar structure, but the frequency with which Anania uses this spiral structure in *Heat Lines*, and subsequently in *Continuous Showings* and *Nightsongs & Clamors*, is in marked contrast to the regular, left-aligned stanzaic blocks he has primarily employed for most of his career. The tensional opposition of vortical forces seems to be pushing its way to the surface in these late-career volumes. The structure of the lines remains controlled and regular—more tightly coiled than William Carlos Williams' stepped triadic line—but no longer fully content to be constrained in blocks. The resulting effect is strengthened by the use of enjambment, with few end-stopped lines or stanzas, which creates forward momentum between successive lines and a fluid return from the end of one stanza to the beginning of the next:

Tracked or trekked
        along a river's edge,
                swell, surge, siltlines

shoulder high. Here,
        perhaps, a tracing on
                water, wind's wake

against the bending
        sheen of the brown
                current, wavelets

quick as anything,
        leafshade and sunlight
                changing places as you

go, steps moving
        northward, the afternoon
                intermittent and narrowing. (*Heat Lines* 18)

In the poems with a spiral structure, the lines and stanzas themselves are like "the curling wave … pulled / back" in "The Riversongs of Arion," and are reminiscent of Kenner's "patterned energy made visible" and of Pound's generative artistic force remaining a permanent feature of the finished work. This structural development in Anania's practice accompanies a shift in at least some of the work, from more fully rendered images and moments presented in sequence to something approaching an associative whirl. The familiar components remain— among them, river surface and undercurrent, unpeopled prairie, blue-collar city, childhood panorama, peyote vision, music and dance—but they are touched upon fleetingly before the poems move quickly on, sometimes to return at a later point in poem or collection. The result is a push, in modernist fashion, toward an energized simultaneity, and a more spatial than sequential relation of the elements in a poem, elements that in their brevity become a poetic shorthand referencing Anania's entire body of work, and by extension the fundamental lineaments of his life.

The fleetingness also intensifies the elegiac tone that has long been present in Anania's poetry by suggesting the whirl of a single human life, the poet's or our own, with its particular history, recurring obsessions, dominant images and replayed events all embedded in the swirl of memory. The brief eddy in the river of time that a life randomly generates is a mysterious process, one that Anania continues to fathom, the manner in which each of us embodies a unique energy that coheres for a period, if imperfectly, before the inevitable weakening and ultimate dissolution of the forces that bind us. Anania describes the process in "Ourselves" as "This gathering of chance, / each of us, a swirl of / occasions" (*Riversongs* 77), and forty years later, in "De Un Mundo Raro," as "the whorls / of self" (*Nightsongs & Clamors* 51). "I bleed easily / these days, my skin as / frail as onion skin" (90), Anania tells us at the end of the final poem in the most recent collection, one of the infrequent moments when the poet steps outside his modernist stance to include himself directly. The spheres within spheres of an onion, in cross-section concentric or vortical, suggest the multiple and hidden layers of self that accrete throughout a life, that constitute each of us and our personal *mundos raros* (strange worlds). Moving outward from self in the pre-Internet, pre-social media, pre-mobile device world of Anania's poetic landscape the great wheels of distance, space, time and nature still matter. Reading Anania is to be reimmersed in an older, more implacable universe, a place where we are not all playing the lead role in our own biopic; to be made small again, and to regain something of the particularity of a wide world and lonely cosmos.

Notes

1. In *The Literary Vorticism of Ezra Pound and Wyndham Lewis* (1985), Reed Way Dasenbrock does more than suggest, arguing explicitly for the ongoing importance of a Vorticist aesthetic to Pound and Lewis, and based on their influence, for its wider importance: "so much of twentieth-century literature seems Vorticist without quite realizing it, and notions first adumbrated in the Great London Vortex of 1914 permeate the masterpieces of Anglo-American modernism." Dasenbrock characterizes literary Vorticism as "elusive ... unconscious or implicit" (27), which may be one reason why other critics have tended to imply rather than state explicitly a belief in the influence of Vorticism on subsequent literature. Hugh Kenner writes, "Vorticism remains, though the Vorticists diverged" (251), but does not go on to elaborate. Marjorie Perloff sees the Vorticist aesthetic that Pound worked out in *Blast* and *Gaudier-Brzeska: A Memoir* (1916) as "a turning point" leading to "the assemblage of 'verse' and 'prose' that we find in the Cantos" (163). See also Materer 15–20, 107–08, 133–35, 138, and Schneidau 195–99.

2. While a sound assessment of Anania's aesthetic lineage, we should not assume that Archambeau's description implies a similar social lineage. Unlike the major figures of literary high modernism, Anania did not start life as a member of a privileged class but rather spent his early years among the diverse, proletarian residents of an Omaha public housing project. This experience and an ethnic-immigrant ancestry have tempered Anania's modernism with something streetwise and populist while also liberating it from the ugly political attitudes and beliefs that mar literary modernism's legacy.

3. Alan Robinson claims that Pound's image and Vortex are in fact one and the same. While others view Pound's Vorticism as an important aesthetic development beyond imagism, Robinson sees a continuous aesthetic with a shift in terminology. Furthermore, symbolism, not Vorticism, is what Robinson believes primarily influenced Pound. See Robinson 207–12.

4. The front matter for *In Natural Light* indicates that Guy Lombardo's version of "Let the Rest of the World Go By" appears on the accompanying CD (Anania reading the poems). The song appears on only some of the CDs that accompany the first edition of the book, although the intention was to create "a kind of brief overture to the reading" (Michael Anania, email message to the author, 3 March 2004). Whether present on the CD or not, "Let the Rest of the World Go By" shares an intertextual relation with "'A Place That's Known,'" one in which aspects of the lyrics, absent from the poem, nevertheless comment on it, and magnify its resonance.

5. Dasenbrock uses *chung* and *Chung Yung*, following an older system of romanization of Chinese characters; *zhong* and *Zhong Yong* are equivalents in the more recent Pinyin system. See Cheadle 7, 93–94.

6. My interpretation of the scene in *The Red Menace*, here and in what follows, relies upon ideas about Vorticism, and its relation to Confucianism and Taoism that I encountered in Dasenbrock's study. See 220–222, 226–227, 232.

7. Narrator Anania is "hanging … upside down," a possible allusion to The Hanged Man of the tarot deck, one of the tarot cards in *The Waste Land*, an interpretive possibility WH New alerted me to. On cards, The Hanged Man is depicted inverted, suspended by one foot from a tree or tau cross, with an expression suggesting entrancement rather than suffering, head often surrounded by a nimbus—a merging of temporal and spatial suspension, and a visionary quality similar to that claimed by Lewis and Pound for the Vorticist artist. See Chevalier and Gheerbrant; de Vries and de Vries; and Nozedar.

A further indication of Anania's Vorticist inclinations appears in a short autobiographical essay about his lifelong passion for sailing, in which his description of sailing a small boat is decidedly Vorticist in nature. As a lone sailor, Anania manages tiller and sheet, rudder and sail, and his own bodyweight and position to counterbalance the force of the wind and order the flux ("Messing about in Boats" 151)—the type of fine balance characteristic of one of Anania's poems. In the course of this praxis sailor and mast remain stationary and tensed while simultaneously, and paradoxically, the boat races along.

8. For Pound's use of Dante in the *m'elevasti* passage, see Materer 133 and McDowell and Materer 355–356.

9. During an eight-day killing spree in January 1958, which terrorized Lincoln and the surrounding area, Charlie Starkweather, and perhaps Fugate, murdered ten people, including Fugate's mother, stepfather and two-year-old half-sister. Starkweather also committed another murder seven weeks earlier when he robbed and shot a gas station attendant. Starkweather was executed in the electric chair June 25, 1959. Fugate was convicted of accessory to murder, which also carried the death penalty, but because she was only fourteen at the time of the murders, she was given a life sentence on November 28, 1958. She was paroled in 1976. Questions remain about the extent of Fugate's participation. See Inciardi; Beaver, Ripley, and Trese; and Reinhardt.

10. See Thornton 66–69, 150–152, 188; and Henning 6, 129, 143.

11. Anania also associates Caril Ann with Cleopatra. "The chair she sat in" comes from the first line of section II of *The Waste Land* ("The Chair she sat in, like a burnished throne"), as Catherine Kasper pointed out to me. Anania is borrowing a borrowing; in the notes to *The Waste Land* Eliot reveals he was alluding to Shakespeare's description of Mark Antony's first sight of Cleopatra ("The barge she sat in, like a burnished throne" *Ant.* 2.2.201). Anania also alludes to Shakespeare's description, drawing the connection between Caril Ann and Cleopatra directly: "It was a barge, he thought, 'the barge she sat in,' the whole courtroom drifting" (144). Shakespeare was in turn reworking a description of Cleopatra from Plutarch's *Lives of the Noble*

Grecians and Romans. The Poundian layering of allusion raises the possibility of some interesting synergies in a completed novel.

12. See also "Affirmations II: Vorticism" 277–278; *Guide to Kulchur* 152; and *Literary Essays of Ezra Pound* 154.

Works Cited

Anania, Michael. *Continuous Showings.* MadHat Press, 2017.

———. "From *Many Happy Returns.*" *TriQuarterly,* no. 84, spring/summer 1992, pp. 144–61.

———. *Heat Lines.* Asphodel Press, 2006.

———. *In Natural Light.* Asphodel Press, 1999.

———. "Messing about in Boats: A Plan B Essay." *Ploughshares,* vol. 37, no. 4, winter 2011–12, pp. 151–55. JSTOR, https://www.jstor.org/stable/41441396.

———. *Nightsongs & Clamors.* MadHat Press, 2018.

———. "Re: Song on *In Natural Light* CD." Email to the author, 3 March 2004.

———. *The Red Menace: A Novel.* 1984. Moyer Bell, 1993.

———. *Riversongs.* U of Illinois Press, 1978.

Archambeau, Robert. Review of *In Natural Light,* by Michael Anania. *Chicago Review,* vol. 45, no. 2, 1999, pp. 134–36.

———. "Michael Anania." *American Poets Since World War II: Sixth Series.* Edited by Joseph Conte. Gale Press, 1998, pp. 3–9.

Beaver, Ninette, et al. *Caril.* Lippincott, 1974.

Brennan, J. Keirn and Ernest R. Ball. "Let the Rest of the World Go By." Witmark, 1919. *Historic American Sheet Music,* https://repository.duke.edu/dc/hasm/a2962.

Cheadle, Mary Paterson. *Ezra Pound's Confucian Translations.* U of Michigan Press, 1997.

Chevalier, Jean and Alain Gheerbrant. "Hanging Man." *A Dictionary of Symbols.* Translated by John Buchanan-Brown. Blackwell, 1994.

Dasenbrock, Reed Way. *The Literary Vorticism of Ezra Pound and Wyndham Lewis: Towards the Condition of Painting.* Johns Hopkins UP, 1985.

de Vries, Ad and Arthur de Vries. "Hanged Man." *Elsevier's Dictionary of Symbols and Imagery,* 2nd ed. Elsevier, 2004.

Edwards, Paul. *Wyndham Lewis: Painter and Writer.* Yale UP, 2000.

Eliot, T. S. *Collected Poems 1909–1962.* Faber & Faber, 1963.

Goldring, Douglas. *South Lodge: Reminiscences of Violet Hunt, Ford Madox Ford and the English Review Circle.* Constable, 1943.

Henning, William E. *An Elegant Hand: The Golden Age of American Penmanship and Calligraphy.* Edited by Paul Melzer, Oak Knoll, 2002.

Inciardi, James A. "Starkweather, Charles, and Caril Ann Fugate." *Violence in America: An Encyclopedia,* vol. 3. Edited by Ronald Gottesman and Richard Maxwell Brown. Scribner's, 1999, pp. 215–16.

Kenner, Hugh. *The Pound Era.* U of California Press, 1971.

Materer, Timothy. *Vortex: Pound, Eliot, and Lewis.* Cornell UP, 1979.

Matthias, John. *Reading Old Friends: Essays, Reviews, and Poems on Poetics 1975–1990.* State U of New York Press, 1992. The Margins of Literature Series.

McDowell, Colin, and Timothy Materer. "Gyre and Vortex: W. B. Yeats and Ezra Pound." *Twentieth Century Literature,* vol. 31, no. 4, winter 1985, pp. 343–67.

Murray, Lachlan. "'Energy Held in Elegant Control': Vortex Anania." *Valley Voices: A Literary Review,* vol. 16, no. 1, spring 2016, pp. 33–53.

Nozedar, Adele. "The Hanged Man: Number 12." *The Element Encyclopedia of Secret Signs and Symbols: The Ultimate A-Z Guide from Alchemy to the Zodiac.* Harper Colllins, 2008, p. 204.

Olson, Charles. *Selected Writings of Charles Olson.* Edited by Robert Creeley, New Directions, 1966.

Perloff, Marjorie. *The Futurist Moment: Avant-Garde, Avant Guerre, and the Language of Rupture.* U of Chicago Press, 1986.

Pound, Ezra. *ABC of Reading.* 1934. New Directions, 1960.

———. "Affirmations II: Vorticism." *The New Age,* vol. 16, no. 11, 1915, pp. 277–78.

———. *The Cantos of Ezra Pound.* Faber & Faber, 1975.

————, translator. *Confucius: The Great Digest, The Unwobbling Pivot, The Analects.* New Directions, 1969.

————. *Gaudier-Brzeska: A Memoir.* 1916. New Directions, 1970.

————. *Guide to Kulchur.* 1938. New Directions, 1968.

————. *Literary Essays of Ezra Pound.* Edited by T. S. Eliot, New Directions, 1954.

————. "Through Alien Eyes I." *The New Age,* vol. 12, no. 11, 1913, p. 252.

————. "Vortex. Pound." *Blast: Review of the Great English Vortex,* no. 1, 1914, pp. 153–54.

Reinhardt, James Melvin. *The Murderous Trail of Charles Starkweather.* Thomas, 1960.

Robinson, Alan. *Symbol to Vortex: Poetry, Painting and Ideas, 1885–1914.* St. Martin's Press, 1985.

Schneidau, Herbert N. *Ezra Pound: The Image and the Real.* Louisiana State UP, 1969.

Thornton, Tamara Plakins. *Handwriting in America: A Cultural History.* Yale UP, 1996.

A Range of Experience:
An Interview with Michael Anania

Lea Graham

I arrived at Michael Anania's house in LaGrange, Illinois in my friends' rebuilt Chevette with archaeology tools in the back seat and a plastic hula girl mounted to the dashboard. It was a hot, hot day in late June and driving I-55 to Michael's place from Chicago's northside with Western Illinois stretched out before me, the radio turned up over the wind and traffic of the open windows, the dust from the tools flying and the hula girl swaying seemed to be a perfect way to begin a conversation with a writer whose life's work was about trying to bring all of his experience into his poems. I was reminded of the quote from the poet Charles Boer in describing his visits to Swallow Press in the late 1960s and early 1970s when Michael was editor, the press housed in downtown Chicago on Wabash Avenue, and the offices were only reached by a freight elevator: "You felt more like you were creating a pipe than a pipe-dream." However, upon arriving at the Anania household, I was reminded that the grit and toughness was only one part of Michael's œuvre as we lunched on fruit, cheese and wine out on his patio, in the shade overlooking the garden. His work—like the person—is always a gathering, a ranging from dust motes to the elegance of a Bill Evans song, from the Plaza of inner-city Omaha where he grew up to the forests of Southern Italy.

LG: In "Excesses and Boondoggles" in your book of essays *In Plain Sight* (1991), you say "to live in a city—any city worth bothering about, at least, is to live with a city's past, not as an idea or an academic exercise but as a day-to-day fact of life, something you can brush elbows with or lean up against waiting for a bus." This seems to be very much what "Steal Away" in your new book *Heat Lines* (2006) is concerned with. Can you talk about the confluence of history, place and music in the poem?

MA: Cities change so dramatically. Buildings are torn down changed. Whole neighborhoods change. You were fascinated by the factory building where Swallow Press was housed; that building became a studio for a commercial advertising firm, and now is a very expensive set of condo lofts. Two things happen: the city changes all the time, yet it gives you these recurrent surfaces. You have familiar buildings, streets and sidewalks and a continual economic surge which changes places from one thing to another. When I moved to South Michigan Avenue, the area south of Roosevelt Road still had the vestiges of the great record industry for rhythm & blues music. Chess Records was still there. That gave way to changes in the record industry, and that part of South Michigan then fell into a kind of dereliction. Now it's been revived. Those lofts are quite expensive, but they leave very little of their past except brickwork façades and addresses. These kinds of changes happen in American cities all the time; they exaggerate the presence of change and propose a kind of urban elegy. I also suggested in that essay that economic change, the movements of commerce and trade through the city, means successives of mutations, dereliction and reuse. Sometimes the reuse is wonderful—small clubs, blues bars, galleries, none of which would have the resources for first use or even rehabbed use.

LG: Your use of proper names in "Heat Lines" is stunning in its abruptness and its turns within the poem—like the Jeffrey bus—an early image in the poem—rocks and corners. It seems that names function like that for you in your work—as connectors within the poem, but even more so as a kind of disconnection or more accurately, a dislodging from narrative even as they seem to suggest another narrative.

MA: I have always been interested in names and their weight in poems. The substance they gain is entirely different than what we accumulate adjectivally or in stylish apposition. Modification persuades us toward some episteme behind the poem. Names—proper nouns—simply and emphatically—assert it. Modification argues for the presence of the poet in the occasion being described. Names assert it, along with a community of assent and an enduring presence. These concerns were touched on in *The Color of Dust* (1970) where I used names with reverent familiarity that would not be known by any of my likely readers outside of Omaha. We acquiesce in traditional poems to named places: Penshurst, Tintern Abbey, Westminster Bridge. I was interested in whether or not names in Nebraska could be made to function in the same way, so that book opens "Just north of Clark Street / Grace Street" as a declaration of its significant space.

LG: How far back does your interest in names go?

MA: One of my undergraduate essays was titled "Do Proper Nouns have Meaning?" It's an issue I've raised a number of times in poems. In *Riversongs* (1978), I adopted Saul Kripke's notion that proper nouns are like addresses to which we send meanings to over time. They accumulate significances of various kinds—bundles, parcels, *billets-douxs*—from a variety of sources, some communal, some idiosyncratic. In *Riversongs*, the Plain of Jars in Cambodia is said to be "like a street name or an address," as is the Mare Tranquilitatus on the moon. The Prague poem ["Factum, Chansons. Etc." in *Selected Poems*, 1994] takes up the issue at some length, beginning with that quote from Carnap about "name" languages and what is determined and undertermined in language which necessarily engages, though they elude Carnap's positivism, history, politics, folklore and magic.

LG: Music has been such a central part of your work throughout your career. In *Heat Lines*, you refer to Curtis Mayfield, Blind Lemon Jefferson, Miles Davis and Gil Evans, among others. Can you talk about music as a kind of driving theme in your work—and in this, it occurs to me that the use of the word "driving" gets at both the figurative as well as the literal in that your interest in cars and listening to radio is also recurrent.

MA: Music seems always to be in its own present. We return to it, take our various presents to its present past. This effect is exaggerated, of course, by recordings and is really intense in jazz because of the unique nature of specific performances. To tweak the idiom, it keeps time. I'm especially fond of listening to music while driving; that's the subject, as you suggest, of the Miles Davis/Gil Evans poem "Summer Night—Nebraska c. 1957." The first delight is the music's movement within the car's movement, then in that poem the way that recalling the music recalls the music as it was heard on that stretch of Nebraska highway in 1957 with a 1940s radio and a less than adequate 1950s radio signal fading and re-occurring with the shallow roll of the land, its distances—the music's and the land's both intimate and remote, at once coincident and disjointed. In *Heat Lines'* opening poem, "Steal Away" music is the significant history of the place. The poem is an elegy for Curtis Mayfield who used to visit at the apartment complex where I lived. It also turns out that the space across from my study window had held, before the gas stations took the place of its derelict building, the Plantation Club, where Sonny Boy Williamson was killed in 1948. He's joined in the poem by Little Walter Jacobs and Blind Lemon Jefferson, who were both also killed in Chicago streets, Jacobs in 1948, Jefferson in 1929. But that space was also part of the 1920s Stroll. The Lincoln Gardens, where King Oliver and Louis Armstrong played in the '20s was just two blocks away. Music has a redemptive quality, even when, as in that space, that past it gives present to is filled with violent death.

LG: It also occurs to me in the first few poems of *Heat Lines* that music is a way of creating place. How are the music and landscape linked?

MA: I lived in a housing project in the middle of Omaha. It was an extremely densely populated area. I lived on a plaza where there were 200 kids. So, I had in my life both the sense of living in an urban environment informed on all sides by its rural context, farmland and space, by the cows and pigs in the stockyards every day. We liked to pretend that we were sophisticated—sophisticated and urban, but Omaha was, as Chicago was, a place that was entirely formed by its ruralness setting, and it succeeded Chicago as the edge of the West. When I was a kid you could catch a streetcar to the country. I worked on truck farms on the river silt picking cucumbers and picking strawberries and got there by taking the streetcar. The transition, between an intensely urban environment and an intensely rural environment cost five cents. To get back to your question, though, the music—particularly jazz and rhythm & blues—was a fact of the urban part of my life and was deeply connected to the mostly African American neighborhood where I lived. At the same time, I could go by streetcar to the South Side, to a place called Mandan Park and walk in the space where Lewis and Clark had walked in their trip up the river. For me, the western rural part is counterpoised by the urban, city part. In that sense, the connection between Omaha and Chicago is a pretty deep one. They were both rail centers, both stockyard centers and centers for the exchange of wheat. Omaha had formed itself on the west side of a river. Chicago formed itself around the eastern boundary caused by the lake. There are a lot of similarities. Also, my father was an intensely urban person. He never left the neighborhood without a suit, a tie and a hat. After the war, my grandfather, who had also been a very urban person, bought a farm. And so the farm I went to was my grandfather's, but he wasn't a farmer; he was an ex-bootlegger, ex-foundry worker, who owned a small farm.

LG: And this was your father's father?

MA: [Yes] my father's father. My mother's father had died in Germany when she was born. Her stepfather was a homesteader in South Dakota and then a harness-maker in Coleridge, Nebraska, where my mother lived. My mother lived in that rural universe, but she was born in rural Germany, a very different world. Olson says that "an American is a complex of occasions." Melville said that "an American is a loose fish and a fast fish, also." It's in the nature of what we are, duplicitous almost always, never quite what we say we are. Whatever we say is conditioned by the strange and ambivalent nature of the country. One of the questions I struggled with when I went to New York was "where does the Midwest start?" Is Cleveland a Midwestern city? Does that make Omaha a Western city? Grand Island, just one step west and not a very long one, fifty-seven miles from Omaha, is clearly in the West, no question about it. I went to school with a lot of Native Americans. I went to school with whites, African Americans and Native Americans. We were, are still, I think, multiple. If you are American, you choose what you are. To some extent, I chose to be Italian, although I'm as much German, I suppose, as I am Italian.

LG: How much did surname determine that?

MA: It's true that my surname helped it along, but it was driven by a variety of other things. Italian was, in many ways, more interesting than German, although I speak German better than I speak Italian. My attachment to my father added to this. My father died when I was quite young, so I never had to have conflicts boys have with their fathers, but just had this romantic figure. Also, Italians at that time were still being treated with prejudice; if you had an Italian last name, it pushed you in the way prejudice does toward being Italian. You were Dago ... and proud of it. I am as much German as Italian, and maybe more so since my mother raised me, but that is part of this duplicity I'm talking about—Americans are all very complicated. We are inherently multi-cultural. It's part of our cultural neurosis to either resist that fact or re-contrive it into a farce. There may be a few New Englanders left and a few Southerners who are not plural, but the rest of us from out in the raffish edges of America are never one thing.

LG: Was your father's father born in Italy?

MA: My father was born here, but his first language was Calabrese, the Calabrian dialect of Italian. His second language was Italian. His third language was English. He was probably unlike anyone else [my mother] had ever met, a very spiffy-looking urban Italian. In his fedora, three-piece suit, carefully knotted tie and highly polished shoes, he would have been at home in lower Manhattan or on Taylor Street in Chicago. My father's generation of Italians invented what it was to be an urban Italian. It has its comic side. They were dressing like they thought the bankers and the industrialists who owned America dressed … except that if you were going to get a stripe in your suit, why not get a stripe that showed? If you're going to get a tie, get a wide tie; if you're going to get a hat with a brim, get a large brim. Everything got exaggerated toward self-parody.

LG: This seems connected to the sense of the West that we've been talking about, giving it a different kind of spin and seems part of the duplicity which you've been talking about. I'm reminded of the poet Thomas McGrath and his sense of the West, especially in his long poem *Letter to an Imaginary Friend,* which you published when you were editor at Swallow Press. How were your experiences of the West similar or different?

MA: The McGraths were Irish-Catholics. They settled in North Dakota, and Tom has some Indian ancestry. McGrath's father saw the Wounded Knee encampment. Tom's embedded in that rural America environment in a different way than I was, more confirmed in it. But as you mention, *Letter* starts in L.A. and thinks its way back to that other space on the plains and occasions in Tom's past there. Eventually, at the end of part 2, it wants to reach toward some communal or magical communal life and invokes Southwest Native Americans—the kachina and the circle of light. Tom wanted communism to end in a mystical radiance in the American landscape, in American myth. But in terms of his westerness, he was western in a way that I wasn't, not the cowboy west, but the wheat growing west of the Great Plains. The most vivid memories from his childhood are of threshing machines in the Dakotas. The story about Cal, the Wobbly organizer, who was beaten up by Tom's own uncles for trying to organize the migrant workers, is Tom's political awakening. He runs down the hill and ends up under the stars in a creek among the mulberries. That radiant moment is his poetic awakening as

243

well. McGrath was westerner in the sense that I'm not, although I lived on the margin of the West and had a keen sense that the West was the part of the world I lived in. The Union-Pacific Railroad headquarters were in Omaha. On the first floor there was a museum with the Golden Spike—the spike nailed the East to the West. Also, at the checkout desk in the children's reading room of the Omaha Public Library there was a bell jar that held a scalp. There was a little card explaining that it was one of the last scalps taken in the West. It certainly did make you think that you should bring your library books back in time! [laughter] Like the Golden Spike, it was an icon of the West. My longtime childhood friend Russell, who was called "the Red Menace" in *The Red Menace* (1984) was one of the great-grandsons of Logan Fontenelle, the chief of the Omaha Indians, who made the treaty that created the town. The housing project—the Logan Fontenelle Homes—was named for him. You had a sense, sometimes a burlesque sense, of westerness. When I go out there now and drive west of the city, the sky has a sudden expanse. That moment is for me the beginning of the West, that first sense of almost oppressive expansiveness, a sense of a change of place—West vs. East, rural vs. urban. There are fault lines in the landscape and in cities, like the San Andreas Fault, where the tectonic plates of history, culture and language abrade each other. I think UIC is on one of them; it's the Roosevelt Road fault line between Black Chicago and commercial Chicago. There is another one up towards Fullerton that divides commercial Chicago and the old ethnic residential areas like Logan Square. Those are places where the forces of the city seem to grate against each other. Omaha lies along a major fault line in the tectonics of American culture. It's a poetic advantage, I think.

LG: One of the reasons that I brought up McGrath, besides the fact that you had published him which was part of the work you did during the late '60s and '70s, was that I wondered if you saw yourself as continuing in that tradition, taking up where McGrath left off?

MA: No, though it's a flattering notion. McGrath had different goals. There are only a few great Marxist poets: Neruda, Hikmet, McGrath and probably Hugh McDermott. I can't think of any others. Vosnzensky and Yevtuchenco, we think of as more Russian than Marxist. Tom was always trying to deal with Marxist paradigms. I was never more than a make-believe communist and mostly because it made people mad when I was in school. My yearbook is signed with things about "the Revolution" and the working class, but I was never in the party. I did send for a party card once, but they never sent one back. Tom said that they figured I was an FBI agent, but that they should've sent one anyway. I do owe McGrath, I think, a significant debt because he found a way to take the ordinary materials of the Midwest—weeds, quack-grass, bluestem—and make that stuff an essential part of the poetry. You couldn't get that from Williams. Williams had a different set of flowers, a different set of objects. Williams never traveled to the center of America. Whitman went all the way down the Mississippi to New Orleans, but Williams never dealt with the interior of America. His horticultural book is eastern. Also, I owe Tom the sense that the kinetic image is inherently a part of the politics of any occasion, that part that seems counter-political in McGrath I take away with me. My other teachers … well, Tom was a friend and not a teacher, but I learned a lot from him. Olson was crucial because of his thinking about space and place and the relationship of myth and place to the physical person.

LG: But Olson was actually your teacher when you studied at SUNY-Buffalo. How many years was that?

MA: He was there for two, and I was in his poetics seminar for the first year. I attended the second year, but I wasn't a member of the class. The important thing from Olson was that sense of the relationship of the body and the person to place, that place is an occasion of the self moving in a locale. Polis, for Olson, is the environment leaning in and him pushing out [as in] that diagram of the "Maximus Letter 27," "I compel backward / I compel Gloucester / polis is this," that sense of the body against something, and Olson's sense, which he takes from Whitehead mostly, some geographers, philosophers, is place as defined by movement and movement of the body and in an area of space. Two great American poets of that period were from Worcester, Charles Olson and Frank O'Hara. Both treat American material as though they were the equivalent to Greek and Roman materials. Well, in Olson's case, he actually puts the thing together—text, artifact, evidence and in his own way argument. What O'Hara does is treat the movies and streets of New York, and street signs (the pure products of America)—as though they were the parts of a Pindaric occasion, as obvious as the gods were to the Greeks. So, James Dean and Lana Turner have conspicuous mythic qualities. That's really important. Though there were certainly poets before who wrote about haircuts and Buicks and barbershops like my earlier teacher Karl Shapiro. They used the diction, the status of the poem to distance themselves from the junk that the poem was about. That's the great trope of American poetry of the '40s and '50s, a distancing irony signaled by style, an ironic stance learned from Eliot, of course, that spared the poet the stain of what was all around him.

LG: Because of the banality of it?

MA: Yes, because of the banality of it. It's as though the poem is placing itself at a kind of aesthetic remove from the stuff that it's dealing with. The great invention of O'Hara is that he collapses that space: "O Lana Turner we love you get up" is not, does not do that same thing. "Of course I've been awfully drunk and behaved perfectly disgraceful, but I never actually collapsed … O Lana Turner …" It's the complete absorption into the stuff of the poem that is the virtue of O'Hara. In Olson? Well, Olson is arduous, and the mythic material he moves about is enormous. Olson wants everything in his intellect and experience to be in the poem as a part of its evolving mytho-poetic stuff. To connect back to McGrath— Olson's Marxism, in "The Distances" and "The Kingfisher," say, is different. Olson was in the Democratic Party, quite notably so for a while, not in the Communist Party. The Maoism of some of the poems is engaged with his concern for the communal nature of Mayan agriculture.

LG: I was wondering how I might characterize you as a poet—not just with this later work—like your recent book *Heat Lines*, but in the earlier work. I was thinking about your attention to moment and to gesture and the way you're constantly capturing time, but it's time that's already passed even as you've captured it.

MA: Yes, that's the dilemma of time, which is why we're so easily seduced by photographs. We exist in a curious space between what we think of as the past and what we think of as the future. Everything we see is in the process of becoming as we see it, so to speak of the present is to expand the moment. It's very much like the idea of the relationship between place and space. We think about space in the Euclydian or Aristotelian sense, as empty, as a category—in Cartesian terms by the lattice of coordinates, hence location, or, in everybody's favorite word now, "site" as in "website." But if you think about it, place is really you, in the Platonic sense, in the receptacle; you are "in place," you can "lose your place," "be out of place," you can be "misplaced," but if you are none of those sad things, you are "in place." So place is defined as what surrounds you. That surrounding can be larger or smaller. Is LaGrange a place? Or is my yard with all of the wild stuff that defines the edges of it that holds all of the flowers and the trees, is that the place? Each time we think of place, we think of it defined with a set of boundaries set by ourselves, and as we move, it moves as well. In time, present is place-like in the sense that, if we talk about this moment that we're in right now, it is an area of time that opens up around our conversation. We know, though, that time is continuous, so that if I'm looking at a branch out the window and it's moving, even if I were painting it, as I look back, it would be different. Momentary time, Euclidian time, instantaneous time is not something we experience. We experience this area of time around ourselves, and even that area once defines suffers change. Place is really the area of space around us in time. I think place only exists in conjunction with time. It's not separable. You can separate it out as space in the Aristotelian or Euclidian sense, but organically it is always engaged in time and process. Poetry has a unique ability to hold an instant in remarkable clarity. In my poems, that clarity is both essential and steeped in illusion. It is a gesture that you try to capture. The bright moment is something we extract from the flux of things, wonderfully susceptible to the image. The poem is uniquely capable of doing this because it can hold its place in a resonant instance of piction, music and myth.

LG: For example?

MA: A friend of mine in Paris—we were in a restaurant and the light was reflecting off the crystal of the wine glass and creating little diamonds on the table. Because the wine was moving, refracted bits of light were moving, and he said, "These are your poems." I think it was meant to be a criticism [laughter], and I said, "I don't mind that ... if they are that significant and vivid, and if they can be made to accept all the complexities of this occasion." We look for something in time to extract from time, but the poem is itself, like music, quintessentially temporal, its structures, music gives a kind of architecture to time in space. My interest in space convened as place in time is a substitute for what in a lot of poets is a sentimental attachment to the evolving self. I don't like that, I've never liked that in poetry; it's never interested me. I think it's elitist in the worst possible way. If you can paint better than anyone, there's the painting, but you can't "feel" better than anybody. I don't think poets have particularly better feelings. In fact, I think poets, by and large, are troubled in that area; they're feeling impaired. Well, I mean, somebody dies, and you set out to write an elegy. Two lines into it you've forgotten the person who has died and are thinking about how good the elegy is. You just don't wail, you write, and writing is a different kind of process than screaming and keening and rending your garments and tearing your flesh. The poet's response to write always engages all those other poetries. Somebody dies, and you're at war with Theocritus, passing Shelly and Tennyson and closing in on Milton. Suddenly, the whole history of the elegy comes into play and then you're thinking "How close can I veer to this; what do I do about that ... can I make this guy a shepherd really or...?" So poets are feeling impaired, writers in general are, I think.

LG: In the beginning of your career when you began dealing with place in place of the whole development of self and that sort of thing, were you conscious of what you were doing—in terms of who your influences were?

MA: Yes. I was very conscious of writing about place. I had left Nebraska and gone to Buffalo. I had written a number of poems which were influenced by Eliot at one point. I have this early poem called "The Revelation" which is this very long, complicated thing that [got] published … and I wrote sex poems influenced by Dylan Thomas, like everybody. In Buffalo, I began to think about Nebraska. I knew a lot of people who had grants and had been to Italy and wrote these Italian poems. There were New York poems and Boston poems, and I thought I'd write Nebraska poems that would be every bit as poetic and exotic because they were about places in Nebraska nobody had ever been to. Then I began to investigate some of the things you touched on concerning proper nouns and their relationship to place. So I began to use the names of places and streets in Nebraska with absolute familiarity. I used them as I would use them in that place—that's not directly Williams, but you can take it from him. Place is the largest area of the idiom of individual experience, so that [for example] Paterson is the idiomatic spread of Dr. Paterson. In that kind of idiom there is an absolute consistency between place and name, between location and speech. So there is an early poem of mine that says "so with a thin, green field over Charles Street." Well, that's Charles Street in Omaha, Nebraska, two blocks along the edge of the projects.

LG: One of the things that interests me is the way in which you have maintained a thirty-three-year collaboration with the printmaker Ed Colker at a time that the art world is about "the flavor of the month." Can you talk a bit about this partnership and the ways in which you've sustained it?

MA: Well, I'll tell you how it started. I met him at a party. He was teaching at UIC and was the head of the Art Department there. He said he was thrilled to meet me—can't beat that—and had my book *The Color of Dust* on his nightstand. He said he had done some work with Marianne Moore, with a Robert Frost poem and a Stevens poem. He asked if I'd be willing to have him work with one of my poems, and I said sure. He chose "The Fall," for which he made three separate lithographs, a dazzling piece, 24 by 36 inches, just beautiful. I was overwhelmed. Then we began talking; we talked about art and music, mostly. The advantage for me is that he is, as I've sometimes described myself, an "unreconstructed abstract expressionist." His very gestural and fluid art, action-filled. At the same time, it's absolutely scrupulous, craft-ridden. He's a print-maker—one of the best ever—and printing is an exacting process. I became entranced by what he was doing, and we talked through the connection between his interests and mine. The second collaboration was *Esthétique du Râle*. That poem really emerged from a series of conversations we had in a studio he had in those days on Ohio Street in downtown Chicago. The old Museum of Contemporary Art was just a block away. That was the period in which Chris Burden was lying on the floor under a plate of glass in the museum and, just before his wife shot him as an art piece, putting tin foil over kitchen matches and firing them like rockets at his wife who was naked on a large piece of lavender paper. She and the paper both received scorch marks. "*Esthétique du Râle*" is the aesthetic of the death rattle. That poem is a collaboration in a way the first one wasn't. The first one was a response on Ed's part to a poem that was already finished and published. *Esthétique du Râle* [the book] was really a kind of engagement in which we both did work surrounding a conversation. It's wonderfully disjunctive and strange because of that, and then we went on from there. I sent him what I did—still do. Sometimes he calls about a special occasion. I wrote "Pochades" for a portfolio he did when he was at Cooper Union. There's just been a whole range of work over the years. His work for the *Adami* poems, which you saw today, has a very different palette. But it also has the essential feature of all of Ed's work, an enormously elastic, fluid, almost watercolor-like flow from image to image in prints. I showed the proofs for *sounds/snow* to a friend of mine, a painter and sculptor in Wisconsin, and he said, "This can't be done." Which is exactly what Lester Young said about Charlie Parker. Ed was involved with jazz music and was part of Fantasy

Records in San Francisco. He's a good friend of Dave Brubeck's and was close to Paul Desmond. He's a wonderful resource because those musics interest me as well.

LG: There seems to be a consonance to what you both do in this sense of the tactile—the papers and printing on his part and the way that you name things.

MA: The thing about Ed is you've got two directions going on at once: his drawings which are action-oriented, fluid, always about movement, improvisational, kinetic things ... even the fruits and vegetables that are in that painting [*In Adami*] are very fluidly moving from one part of the thing to the other. All of that fluidity is then counter-posed to the absolute care of materials, printing, handmade French papers, the whole nature of making lithograph. The great area of compatibility between Ed and me is that I want my poems to feel spontaneous, sometimes even improvisational, and at the same time, to feel crafted and precise. I want there to be a sense of the forward-moving, impelling quality of the poem, so as you read it is as though it were being invented in the moment, and at the same time, to have that sense of accumulated knowledge and craft and complex musicality. Ed seems to me to have invented a way to have the same divergent qualities at play in ink and paper. That's also one of the reasons we're both so attached to jazz.

LG: That tension between improvisation and craft strikes me as what you always emphasized as a teacher: trying to get students to think about improvisation and spontaneity in poems while still honoring craft. Can you elaborate on that tension?

MA: Williams said at one point that the real matter of technique is saying what you want to say rather than what you didn't. There is a tendency on the part of students to treat all mishaps as though they were creative acts. "Why did you drop the baby on the floor?" "Oh yeah, that's want I wanted to do. Kids can learn from suffering." Typically in class, I insist that if you mention a tree, you need to know what kind of tree. I would ask questions: "Now do you mean the sidewalk that has quartz in the sand and sparkles or is it more limestone colored?" The pressure was to get them to think about the nature of what they were putting in the poem then ask the same questions about language: "Is this the word you mean?" "What does this word mean?" What's the background of the word? The first stage of craft is clarity. Then you can talk about matters of craft in terms of poetic technique and line.

LG: I remember that one time it was "What kind of socks?"

MA: You're asking people to bring an attentiveness to the poem. It doesn't have to mean that you name the brand or size of the sock in the poem, but you need to know. My other question is: "Where were you standing when you were looking at this?" In the simplest sense ... where is the camera in this shot? And students don't know. How you describe something is dependent on where you're standing. The discipline of location—and here we are back in "place"—the discipline of location is the great lesson of imagism and of Pound and Williams—that objects are not merely names, that it's not a nominal universe in which trees stand for all trees, that the poem is reaching for a kind of particularity in the world. Creeley, in his lectures and in comments around poems, would often talk about the poem's particularity. Strangely enough, Creeley's poems are not full of particular places, but he'd always talk about the poem's ability to illicit particular occasions as opposed to the general one.

LG: Could you talk a bit about your work as editor at Swallow Press? That was about a decade of your work?

MA: About seven years. I had been an editor before that. When I went to Buffalo, there was a magazine called *Audit* which had been started at Harvard and was moved to Buffalo. It had separated itself into two parts: *Audit*, a general magazine of essays and poetry, edited by Ralph Maud, who is an Olson scholar; and a fiction magazine called *Audit Fiction*, edited by David Galloway. Galloway has been in Germany for years, teaching American Literature. The magazine came back together in '62, and Galloway asked me if I would be the poetry editor of *Audit: A Quarterly*. Galloway took his PhD and got a job in Europe, and I fell heir to the magazine, but I didn't have any money. Albert Cook had just come to Buffalo as head of the department. Albert Cook was a poet, scholar/critic and translator and had edited a magazine of his own called *Halcyon*. Albert said that the department would help support the magazine, give us an office and a telephone, but he wanted me to take on Charles Doria as associate editor. Doria and [Charles] Boer had both been students of Albert's at Western Reserve. Doria is a really bright guy, but not strong on the practical side of things. Betty Cohen, who was an old friend of Al's, became the managing editor. It was one of those interesting moments—we sat down and decided that what we were going to turn *Audit* into a poetry magazine, *Audit/Poetry*—it was the first of those slashes—and not do fiction at all. Fiction seemed beside the point in those days. It was a high poetic moment—Olson had just gotten to Buffalo, Cook was there, Creeley wasn't on the faculty yet but was visiting, Duncan visited, so did Dorn, Kelly, Wakoski, Corso and Baraka. Mac Hammond was there, and George Starbuck worked in the library.

LG: So this was post-Black Mountain?

MA: Yes, this was after Black Mountain College and after the great Vancouver reunion on Olson's part—that had been the previous summer. We decided that we were going to favor long poems and that we were going to feature individual poets in every other issue. We decided would do an issue with the work of Frank O'Hara. Now remember at that point—this is in 1963—O'Hara hadn't had a book in trade publications since *Meditations in an Emergency* which was '57—so six years. *Second Avenue* had been published but in very limited edition in '56. *Lunch Poems* had been accepted by Ferlinghetti at City Lights, but I think he was enthusiastic about O'Hara when he met him, but not afterwards because the book was stalled there and nothing happened. *Love Poems* hadn't even been put together at that point. I called O'Hara on the phone, a cold call, as they say. The issue with essays by Kenneth Koch and Al Cook was a huge success—we printed 1500 copies and they sold in no time. Then there was a portmanteau issue and the notable poets in that were Mac Hammond—that was the first publication of his poem "The Horse Opera" and Robert Kelly. And then the next of the single author issues was Robert Duncan. I did the editorial work on the Duncan, but by the time it came out I had moved to Chicago to teach at Northwestern University. I came to Chicago in '65. The Duncan issue came out in '66. In '66, Allen Swallow, who had been a college friend of Tom McGrath's at LSU and had been publishing books of poems in Denver, including all of McGrath's early work, died. In the winter of '66–'67, four guys from Chicago bought the company. One of them, Durrett Wagner, who had been in Ideas and Methods at Chicago, was a Western American historian. Durrett became the press's senior editor. Swallow had a great list of books in Western Americana. People in the West tended to know the press for its Western American History; if they lived in the East, they knew it as a poetry publisher. The poets published were McGrath, Allen Tate, Yvor Winters, J. V. Cunningham and a long list of conservative poets from Winters's circle. In fiction, the press published Anais Nin and Frank Waters. Wagner came to see me at Northwestern—he was the Dean at Kendall College in Evanston— and we talked about the press. Gene Wildman was at the University of Chicago, the editor of the *Chicago Review*, which had just published the first *Anthology of Concretism*. When Wagner asked me what he should do, I said, "publish this as a book." He looked at it—it was amazing concretist stuff from all over the world. "Why this in particular?" he said. "Because," I told him, "it will separate you from the [earlier] Swallow Press and Winter's circle of rhyming poets. It will make your place and do very well." And I was right. The book did extremely well, got into schools and was in print for a dozen years. So, I became the poetry editor for Swallow in '67. In '68, I became the literary editor. Wagner did all of the Western Americana and general books. I edited the poetry and Nin, then I started the series in experimental fiction. I published Federman and Sukenick, Wildman's novel and his anthology *Experiments in Prose*. I also did Cyrus Colter's fiction.

LG: And this work at Swallow was in addition to teaching?

MA: I taught all through that time. I was teaching at Northwestern University when I started. Then I went to University of Illinois at Chicago. I would get up in the morning, drive down the Kennedy and get to the office around 7:30. I'd work until I left fifteen minutes before my first class at UIC. I'd teach my class, do my office hours and then go back to my office at Swallow. I did that from '68 to '74. I published a lot of books ... seventy-five to eighty books during that period. We were doing enormously interesting things, I edited a series of books called Poetry Europe, really interesting stuff.

LG: How did dealing with other people's texts all day long feed your own writing?

MA: There are two sides to it. I talked myself into reading a whole lot of manuscripts—I didn't want to have poetry read by someone who could say no but not say yes. I was getting about 3500 manuscripts a year. It was a lot of work, and I was always behind. At one point, I decided that I was becoming the world's greatest authority on "mortal poetry." That is, I was reading student poetry and I was reading the submitted "stuff" that came over the transom. At the same time, stunning things would turn up—Matthias, for instance. Matthias sent me poems unsolicited. They were dazzling. Peter Michaelson, James McMichael, Allen Planz, a brilliant Hart Crane-esque poet from New York and Linda Pastan. As soon as I got the job, I called Charles Boer and said, "Send me the manuscript of *The Odes*," poems I had heard in Olson's class. It was the first New Poetry Series book I published at the press.

LG: During the late 1960s, early 1970s you have that great poem "News Notes" that is dedicated to John Matthias about the Chicago riots. How would you describe that time in your career?

MA: John had come up to Swallow from Notre Dame. We were working at the office on *23 Modern British Poets* when that riot occurred in Grant Park. We believed we were changing the world, that literature was an agent for change, so we worked through the revolution, at least through that bit of it. We assumed we had changed the nature of poetry and set out to change the nature of fiction. There was a wonderful sense of capacity during that period. The lovely thing about the press was that for a time it was a "destination" for a lot of writers who were crossing the country. So, people just stopped by. In Paris at a panel discussion, Richard Ford reminded me that he had come by Swallow when he was still a graduate student. People would just turn up. Russian writers, writers from Latin America—Nicanor Parra got off the elevator one day—Paz, Tate, of course, and Federman, Nathaniel Tarn, Diane Wakoski, Nin, often, John Montague, Leon Forrest, Robert Duncan, Daniel Weisbort, it was dazzling in that sense! It was also enervating and my poems … I suppose I probably wrote fewer poems than I might have in that period because I was so busy. At the same time, what do you trade for those experiences? Being at the center of things was a whole lot of fun and, certainly, getting to make decisions, however peripheral, about the way things should go was exciting. In the same period, I was on the board and eventually the chair of CCLM, the literary magazines organization [now CLMP]. At a meeting in New York with the NEA Literature panel, I was asked to defend myself as a member of the eastern establishment. I laughed, couldn't help it. Michael Bessy, the chair and president of Atheneum, was very serious and asked, "Why are you laughing?" I said, "I'm from Omaha, Nebraska. I live in Chicago. My office is a derelict building on South Wabash half a block from police headquarters. *You guys* are the eastern establishment. Have I been made a member? Do I get a badge? Is the check in the mail?" [Laughter.]

LG: How do you account for these kinds of associations or labels?

MA: The labels are probably unavoidable and almost always wrong. There's a sense of grievance in literature that affects us all. Everybody complains all the time. Sticking a label on those other guys is a way of coping, I guess. In a way, we're victims of our success. It doesn't feel like success. It doesn't have the kinds of rewards the rest of society dishes out to fresh-out-of-law school, undistinguished attorneys—no BMWs, no condos over the lake—but we have succeeded in making poetry a more widespread and democratic enterprise. Unfortunately, that freedom has created a lot of truly awful, mawkishly personal poetry. The open mic reading is one of the circles of hell. The same freedom has also created an almost inexplicable anxiety among people who aren't especially interested in poetry, a reaction that has conferred rewards of all sorts on conservative, even reactionary poets.

LG: It seems to me that what good publishing does—it functions like a filter or a screen. Of course, it can be about who you know or luck and all of that, but after having been on the open mic scene [in Chicago] for a few years [I found that] it can get masturbatory, you know?

MA: And in public! Here's the real dilemma: there are an awful lot of people out there, given the proliferation of writing programs, who have learned to write pretty good versions of bad poems. It's like fake furniture, you know? Like the furniture you get at Target or Walmart. You can sit on it. It doesn't break. But there's no craft to it. The woods are pressed wood chips; the grain is photographed from real wood and glued on. There are a lot of people who have learned to put together a poem that has four legs and won't fall down, but if you look at it carefully, it has no more substance and even a lot less genuine energy than some of the open mic stuff. There's a whole lot of poetry out there that is just crap. It's harder to distinguish because so much of it is well-made crap. It's all "me" and "I." It's part of the great, long, further adventures of the first-person singular and not very interesting.

LG: This leads me back to some of the things surrounding the development of self that we were talking about earlier. In *Heat Lines,* you are dealing with your family in a much more direct way than you have done in the past. After having worked with you for so many years, I have noticed that while you have never discouraged anyone from dealing with or using materials surrounding heritage, you seemed to have a great distrust of it. However, "'A Place That's Known'" has a kind of elegant poignancy to it.

MA: That was a tough poem, a poem about my mother's death. It starts out in the housing projects with her feet out from the front step, where she'd sit at night and smoke—she smoked Chesterfields. On warm nights, she'd smoke the last cigarette outside before she went to bed. I think the thing that enabled me to do that poem was the lyric of that very powerful song from WWI, "a place that's known to god alone." When all this is over, we're going to go to a place that no one knows about and "let the rest of the world roll by." That idea of the place that's known, "a known place" is quite powerful. It is the place with all other places—"known to God alone." My goal was—I mean I wanted to write the poem about that experience of my mother's death—but I also wanted to write about her life in place, in the familiar place of the projects and in that other "known place." It may be my most vivid thing—except for a few prose passages in *The Red Menace*—I've written about the housing projects and what went on there. It's finally a poem about language that is about those whisperings that my mother offered to me and my brother and sister against the violence and chaos that surrounded us—it was a frightening place ... people killed each other, a woman down at the other end of our building drowned her children, people got stabbed or cracked over the head with skillets. And my mother would tell the same stories over and over again. Her words and the objects she kept in a green strongbox on her shelf became the "space" that she gave us against that chaos. That's a long way round to explain how a very personal poem is not really about me or my feelings.

LG: That's the function of story, isn't it?

MA: That's the function of story and of language in general. The source of all places is the place that we choose or is chosen for us as our beginning. For me, it's that Plaza and the housing projects bonded completely with speech, story and song. That's the place out of which everything else is defined. As I began writing poems, I began noticing, parsing even, the inherent mythos of the place. Clark Street, in the initial poem in *The Color of Dust*, dead ends at both ends—one end is a bakery and the other end is a brewery. It's yeast on both sides. The Bonton, the tavern in the poems, at the corner of 20th and Clark, the "good time" place. The Holy Rollers storefront was at 21st and Clark Street. At 22nd and Clark there was a giant crab apple tree whose roots had upended the sidewalk. The Crosstown Transit of that poem is on 24th Street, the literal transit line north and south from which the city grid was made. So that "known place" is the place out of which everything else is made. It is—I think this is the deep poetic connection, convened out of language and perception jointly—not just perception and personal experience but language and its place.

LG: Is that how it worked with the Calabrian poems?

MA: I knew very little of Adami, which is where my father's family is from. I had only one photograph, two men barely seen standing at the corner of a large house. And one book of poems by the Calabrian Adami poet Michele Pane. The house in the photo was not an Anania house but was Pane's, so the only photograph I ever had of that place was the photograph of a poet standing next to his house. Pane, who was an exile, not an immigrant, wrote about that place in the dialect. This was a deliberate, revolutionary act—he was put in jail for it—for a revolutionist poem called "The Red Man," his first published poem. For a time, he edited an Italian magazine that was dedicated to Italian dialect poetry rather than Tuscan poetry. So *that* poetry and *that* dialect had emerged in *that* place. Calabria is such a strange place. There's not one dialect; rather there are several hundred. Each village or little area has a dialect distinct from others. It was like moving into a fable in which there is an absolute consistency between life and language, a language that's emerged in place through its history, part Neopolitan Italian, part Latin, Part Greek. Pane's language flows through all of the "In Adami" poems. Sitting in Filomena's house with the hearth fire going, one of the images in Pane came back to me *"lingui di fuoco"*—the hearth's tongues, the tongues of the hearth, the fire and the smoke—outside I realized that I had been watching the genesis point of the image. The autumn evening was suffused by the smoke from these hearth fires and with them it was suffused as well with the speech at those hearth sides. It's as though the spoken language rises with the smoke and drifts down the mountainside. It's stunning. Because of Pane, the poet, who tried to give value to the spoken language, that that spoken language still exists. It's read and memorized in the local schools. The last poem in the series, "Raffaele's Table," is specifically about language in that place.

LG: How do you see this portion of the heritage stuff linked to that which you dealt with earlier in your career?

MA: Well, the Italian stuff worked itself out in a different kind of way. I don't often write incidental poems. The Carmelo poem, that starts the sequence, seems incidental, but by the time I get to the Raffaele poem, I'm back at all my usual stuff: language, place and the past. The early poems that might seem similar are "Document," which you mentioned earlier and "Avante Courier." "Document" deals with the confusion that led my mother at seven to be incarcerated on Ellis Island. My grandmother had made a deal to marry her dead husband's younger brother, who was living in Nebraska and South Dakota. He had been a homesteader and a miner. Immigration authorities thought his name and his dead brother's were too much alike, so he had to go to New York to prove he was a different person than the person who had died in Germany. All of it had to do with immigration quotas. I tried to take that into the experience of Nebraska as land and cope with the Dust Bowl. My mother and grandmother came from a world of relentless greenery. It was Northern Germany and its soil is rich, deep and dark. It's peat moss, really—not just green but spongy, deep, relentless green. It rains 250 days a year. The lichen on the slate roofs is green. There's green everywhere. Nebraska is *brown*, and they arrived there in 1927 in the middle of the Dust Bowl. And so "Avante Courier," the poem about rain following the plow—that's about my mother's experience during the Dust Bowl, being put to bed at night with a wet napkin over her face to keep the dust off and waking up in the morning looking like the Shroud of Turin—as it has this ghastly version of your face on it. Trousseau linens that my grandmother stitched all her life were stuffed into the windows and doors to keep the dust and dirt out. A number of early poems are based in that experience. I suppose if there's a difference, since you touched on "'A Place That's Known'" and the Italian poems, that it probably has to do now with a desire to see those things as more completed discussions than as issues.

LG: Can you comment on the emotional weight present in these later poems?

MA: It's hard for me to judge the differences between my poems. I read back sometimes and think they're too much alike. But it's hard for me to gauge. There is a set of issues that has always interested me. They remain the same, and there are issues now that are different and that I'm willing to move more to the front of the poem.

LG: Like the way you did with that early poem "For Myself at 25"?

MA: Well, that's just funny, don't you think? "I have a new tie from France / a recollection of dance"? That belongs to another category of poems I think of as "songs." Something like the "Eclogue," the subway poem and the "Valeeta" poem. I think of them as songs. That is, I think of them as being fulfilled by their own musicality. I like the idea of having these strange materials—the "blue light of television" is one that has always pleased me, or to get Lash LaRue in there. My father's nickname when he lived on the streets was "Jesse." Jesse is the father of David—King David, songster and dealer. You put in your time in the Bible class, right? [Laughter.]

LG: That is such an interesting question to end the poem on: "Am I a songster or a dealer?" Is that a question you're asking yourself?

MA: Well, Peter Michelson in an essay takes that question quite seriously perhaps because he's seen me as an editor, conniver, organizer

261

and as a poet. He sees it as an essential question—whether or not I'm a "songster" or a "dealer."

LG: I wonder if that's a dilemma for you being a poet who has been in the university and had the kind of career you've had? Do you wonder about these early experiences or images—as I do when I ask myself if "chicken litter" was really a big part of my early and formative years? Do I really remember this correctly?

MA: The dilemma for all of us—and it doesn't have success built into it in the short run, but it is the great issue of American poetry—is how to sustain poetry, the thing we love and cherish, and to put as much of the strange universe of our lives in it as we can. Teaching can distance you from those issues, but so can middle-class comforts or revolutionary ardor. If you write a poetry that is both decorous and consoling, the world will treat you well. If that decorousness runs on the side of confession or sexual revelation, it will reward you heavily, but that's not the issue. I could certainly have written poems to make the university happier with me as a poet—the "flannel shirt" pastorals that threaten no one's intellectual security or poems about received opinions in a fixed diction. I have always wanted to stretch the diction of the poem and stretch the universe of materials that the poem could contain. I don't know any other American poet who has written a poem about his father whacking the top of a table with the butt end of a Smith and Wesson revolver. That's important to me.

LG: Is it possible to capture the paradox of what it means to be an American?

MA: The last poem in *The Color of Dust*, "Diversions Upon an Old Refrain," has two contending landscapes. One comes from *Random Harvest*, where the main character loses his memory and is taken in by a woman who was actually his love interest before the amnesia. She has this lovely country house and garden. The other landscape comes from my version of Omaha—the "skinner" who holds up a hand without fingernails, the wino who blocks the gangway past the icehouse with a biblical quiz, a scene in a medical school clinic, an area of junked cars where a gang bang takes place. I wanted to test one space against another, to test the movie/novel decorous space against the space of my actual American life. The lady's garden of sweet flowers is drawn in around her like a needlework coverlet uncovering a garden of weeds and gutted cars. The question is can you make a poem that will hold both of those things? Can you make poems that will hold the poetic traditions of our language and the myth and facts of America? Can a poem about jazz and blues also manage *Superfly*, the city's genius and its violence? Those are the issues worth struggling with, I think. Otherwise, what is the point of being false to your experience in order to write a poem? You can be false in a lot of ways. You can pretend you're from England or that your grandparents spent a lot of time together sipping tea and talking about Emerson. You can connive your experience into a kind of self-centered pastoral that has no political, cultural or social dimension, an afternoon talk show in which you are both host and guest. You can take up aesthetic issues with elevated disdain and worry loudly over "standards." But the American dilemma remains. How can I get all of the diverse, sometimes looney materials of America into poems without betraying them with smug ironies or reducing them to greeting cards? That's the struggle.

LG: You still think that this is the struggle we have now?

MA: Oh, of course!

LG: I think there are a lot of younger poets who might say "We're post-Williams. We're done with that."

MA: But what are they done with? Some have moved into LANGUAGE poetry, which is something we've all played around with, that kind of distancing randomness and use of text and quotation. But where does that get you? It simply allows poetry to abandon its attachment to substance. They do it by a kind of Derridian trick of saying "Well, substance is merely another construction within the meta-category

263

of presence." I've never wanted to do that. I've wanted to approach, as exactingly as possible the texture of experience and thought with the tactile, with the visual potentials of language. If that's Williams, you can't be post-Williams in any useful way. If they mean post-Williams in the sense that Williams' naïve enthusiasm for things is somehow no longer worthwhile, you could say that, but I don't see it happening. I like O'Hara [who says], "After all in America only Whitman, Crane and Williams are as interesting as the movies." What O'Hara did was adjust his enthusiasm for neon and traffic lights and the movies to what he thought poetry could do. In many ways he was a Romantic poet, so was Williams, for that matter. To say you're post-Williams means what—that you're not quite post-Creeley, have left Olson in the dust, are just edging by Schuyler with Ronald Johnson in your sights? The actual Williams tradition in American poetry is incredibly rich and varied. Offering it all a dismissive "post" seems a bit like empty self-congratulation. We are all Williams' heirs, just as we are Whitman's.

LG: I'm always amazed, in talking about O'Hara, how contemporary those poems feel—and they were written fifty years ago.

MA: Fifty years is right. *Meditations in an Emergency* was published in 1957. Some of those poems were published in *Poetry* in 1951. It's amazing stuff, its dictions, its materials and its sheer poetic verve. The issue in American poetry is what you can put in and at what cost; how much of your experience, your intellectual development, the state of the language, our evolving sense of the nature things and the concreteness of your life you can get in without losing what Ashbery call[ed] "the art part," and in the process making something of more consequence than the always limiting self. I'm willing to admit that my background, since we've talked about so much of it, is not very common in poetry. There aren't many German-Italian poets who were raised in Midwestern African American neighborhoods, listening in childhood to extreme dialects of three languages. There aren't many people with the same range of experience, but everybody has *a range* of experience.

Acknowledgments

Thanks are due to so many people who helped bring this book into the light. First, my gratitude goes out to our esteemed publisher Marc Vincenz at MadHat Press who has been so practical and enthusiastic for this project on Michael Anania's work and long career and who made this happen through his zeal for bringing more beauty into the world. Secondly, this book acknowledges the lovely and sustained work of the artist Ed Colker, who permitted us to use his print *The Fall* for the cover of the book. Ed and his wife, the artist Elaine Galen inhabit these pages with their lifelong commitment to art and their friendship and collaboration with Michael. Others who have given their moral support, sweat and humor are: Robert Archambeau (who convinced me that I was "the one who had to do this book" one night after a reading in Somerville, MA, with Vincenz, Scroggins and others cheering on the idea like some literary beer-chugging contest); Garin Cycholl who helped with the organization of the book, and for his work as guest editor with Michael Antonucci for the special issue on Anania in *Valley Voices* that provided some foundational essays; John Zheng, editor of *Valley Voices,* who granted permission to republish many of these essays; Celia Bland, Lachlan Murray, Phil Pardi and Mark Scroggins, who all gave advice, empathy, silly .gifs and solid action in myriad ways; Avis Zane, Isabelle Christie and Mark Lager, who worked as pinch-hitting editorial assistants; to my beloved, Mark Spitzer, who spent a lot of time and energy encouraging me and even more time helping in the hunt for comma splices—you have my love and gratitude from the White to the Cuyabeno and back, baby. For Dianne Logan, whose humor, love and can-do spirit is deeply embedded in this book; and of course, my deepest gratitude to Michael himself, the *genius loci* of this book; and for whose generosity, sanity, wisdom and enthusiasm has sustained me and so many others through the years. Thank you, Michael.

The following essays were published in *Valley Voices*, vol. 16, no. 1, Spring 2016:

Allen, Jeffery Renard. "Be Like Mike," pp.146–148.

Archambeau, Robert. "Modernist Current: Michael Anania's Poetry of the Western River," pp. 7–21. Previously published as "Modernist Current: On Michael Anania" in *The Poet Resigns* (2013). Reprinted with permission of the University of Akron Press.

Gibbons, Reginald. "On Michael Anania's *In Natural Light.*" Retitled here as "Revisiting Michael Anania's *In Natural Light,*" pp. 97–104.

Plumpp, Sterling. "Another Cowboy in the Boat of Ra," p. 6.

Vance, David Ray. "Michael Anania's *The Red Menace*: A Study in Self Production," pp. 80–90.

*

The following essay and poem were previously published in *The Bluesky Review*, issue 2, Spring/Summer 2003:

Aleksa, Vainis. "Michael in the '80s," pp. 81–83.

Rogaczewski, Frank. "*Gratia, Poeta!*" pp. 114–6.

*

The following essay was previously published in *American Letters & Commentary*, issue 19, 2006:

Graham, Lea. "Out of Ordinary: The Extraordinary Collaboration of Michael Anania & Ed Colker."

*

The following interview was previously published in the literary journal *Paper Streets*, Summer, 2006:

Graham, Lea. "A Range of Experience: Conversations in Place with Michael Anania." (retitled here as "A Range of Experience: An Interview with Michael Anania.")

*

The excerpt from "Two Kinds of Autobiography: *The Red Menace*" was previously published in John Matthias's *Who Was Cousin Alice? and Other Questions*. Shearsman, 2011. pp. 306–326.

Notes on Contributors

Vainis Aleksa lives in the Chicago area where on a lucky night the voice that is great within us rises up, and he stands gazing at the rounded moon.

Jeffery Renard Allen is the author of five books, most recently the novel *Song of the Shank*, and was a finalist for the PEN/Faulkner Award and a Dublin Literary Prize nominee. Allen has received numerous accolades for his work, including *The Chicago Tribune*'s Heartland Prize for Fiction, The Ernest J. Gaines Award for Literary Excellence, a grant in Innovative Literature from Creative Capital, a Whiting Writers' Award, a Guggenheim fellowship, a residency at the Bellagio Center, and fellowships at The Center for Scholars and Writers, the Johannesburg Institute for Advanced Studies and the Schomburg Center for Black Research and Culture. He has been widely published in numerous periodicals and journals, and he has lectured and taught workshops worldwide for Summer Literary Seminars, Kwani?, Farafina Writers' Workshop, Kimbilio, Cave Canem, The Zora Neale Hurston/Richard Wright Foundation, Sewanee and Disquiet International, among others. His collection of stories, *Fat Time*, will be published in 2021. He is presently at work on three books: the memoir *Mother Wit*, the essay collection *Daywork: Reflections on Politics, Art, and Culture*, and the novel *Hour of the Seeds*. He makes his home in Johannesburg.

Michael A. Antonucci teaches in the American Studies Program and English Department at Keene State College in Keene, New Hampshire. His scholarship focuses on African American literature and culture, especially contemporary and twentieth-century Black poetry. His monograph on the verse of Michael S. Harper is forthcoming from the University of South Carolina Press.

Robert Archambeau's books include the studies *Poetry and Uselessness from Coleridge to Ashbery* (Routledge) and *Laureates and Heretics: Six Careers Careers in American Poetry* (Notre Dame); the essay collections *Inventions of a Barbarous Age* (MadHat) and *The Poet Resigns: Poetry in a Difficult Time* (Akron); the poetry collections *The Kafka Sutra* (MadHat) and *Home and Variations* (Salt), and others. He teaches at Lake Forest College.

Mike Barrett is from Chicago. He has a BA in Economics from Notre Dame and a PhD in Creative Writing from University of Illinois–Chicago. A founding member of the Chicago Poetry Ensemble, he helped establish the poetry slam. Since then he has written nine books of poetry: *Babylons/Other Poems, A Is for Acts, Radical Two, The Book of Morpheme, 50 Easy Pieces, Recto Verso* (vols. 1 & 2), *A Missouri Diptych,* and *Walking with my Doppelgänger.* He lives in Missouri with his wife, fiction writer Trudy Lewis.

Celia Bland is co-editor, with Martha Collins, of *Jane Cooper: A Radiance of Attention* (U of Michigan). She is the author of three collections of poetry, including *Cherokee Road Kill* (Dr. Cicero, 2018) which features ink drawings by Japanese artist Kyoko Miyabe. The title poem received the 2015 Raynes Prize. Her work was the subject of an essay by Jonathan Blunk in *The Georgia Review,* and is included in *Native Voices: Indigenous American Poetry, Craft and Conversation* (Tupelo Press). She is the author of young adult biographies of the Native American leaders Pontiac, Osceola, and Peter MacDonald (Chelsea House Books).

Maxine Chernoff is the author of seventeen books of poetry and six prose works, one of which was among the NYT Best Books of 1991. She is the winner of a 2013 NEA in Poetry and the 2009 PEN Translation Award. Longtime editor of *New American Writing* and former chair of Creative Writing at SFSU, she was a visiting fellow at Exeter University in 2013 and a visiting writer at the American Academy in Rome in 2016. Her most recent book is *Under the Music: Collected Prose Poems* (Madhat).

Kevin Clouther is the author of *We Were Flying to Chicago: Stories* (Catapult). He is an Assistant Professor at the University of Nebraska Omaha Writer's Workshop, where he is Program Coordinator of the MFA in Writing. He lives with his wife and two children in Omaha.

Garin Cycholl's work includes *Country Musics 20/20,* a collection of cut-ups on Kafka's "Great Wall" and the 2016 Inaugural Address. His one-act play on corruption culture, *The Indianan,* is forthcoming from *High Plains Review.*

Cynthia A. Davidson began her writing life as a poet, getting a PhD in English with a concentration in creative writing at the University of Illinois–Chicago. She is a Senior Lecturer in the College of Arts and Sciences at Stony Brook University, currently specializing in digital rhetoric and online writing environments. She has published on virtual worlds and writing studies in *Computers and Composition Online* and most recently has a chapter, "Reconstructing Ethos as Dwelling Place: On the Bridge of 21st-Century Writing Practices (ePortfolios and Blogfolios)" in *Thinking Globally, Composing Locally: Rethinking Online Writing in the Age of Global Internet*

(2018, UP of Colorado/Utah State UP), and is working on a book about Twitter and affect theory.

Reginald Gibbons is the author of eleven books of poems, including National Book Award Finalist *Creatures of a Day*, and most recently *Renditions* (Four Way Books, 2021). His novel *Sweetbitter*, which won an Anisfield-Wolf Book Award, will be reissued in a new paperback in 2022 by JackLeg Press. He has been awarded the Folger Shakespeare Library's O.B. Hardison Jr. Poetry Prize and the John Masefield Award from the Poetry Society of America. He has received fellowships from the Guggenheim Foundation, the Fulbright Program, and the National Endowment for the Arts. Gibbons was the editor of *TriQuarterly* magazine from 1981 to 1997, during which time he co-founded and edited TriQuarterly Books. He has also been a columnist for *The American Poetry Review*. He teaches at Northwestern University, where he is a Frances Hooper Professor of Arts and Humanities.

Lea Graham is the author of two poetry collections, *From the Hotel Vernon* (Salmon Press, 2019) and *Hough & Helix & Where & Here & You, You, You* (No Tell Books, 2011); a fine-press book, *Murmurations* (Hot Tomato Press, 2020), and three chapbooks: *Spell to Spell* (above/ground Press, 2018), *This End of the World: Notes to Robert Kroetsch* (Apt. 9 Press, 2016) and *Calendar Girls* (above/ground Press, 2006). She lives in Rosendale, NY, and Mayflower, AR, and teaches at Marist College.

Paul Hoover's latest book of poetry is *O, and Green: New & Selected Poems* (MadHat Press, 2021). Editor of *Postmodern American Poetry: A Norton Anthology* and the literary annual *New American Writing*, he teaches in the Creative Writing Department at San Francisco State University.

John Matthias is the author of many books of poetry, essays, plays, and memoirs. He taught for many years at the University of Notre Dame, and is a Life Member of Clare Hall, Cambridge.

Simone Muench is the author of several books including *Wolf Centos* (Sarabande) and *Suture* (Black Lawrence; co-written with Dean Rader). She also co-edited *They Said: A Multi-Genre Anthology of Contemporary Collaborative Writing* (Black Lawrence). A recipient of an NEA poetry fellowship, she is a professor at Lewis University where she serves as faculty advisor for *Jet Fuel Review*. She's also a poetry editor for *Tupelo Quarterly*. Her collaborative chapbook, *Hex & Howl*, co-written with Jackie K. White, is forthcoming from Black Lawrence Press, 2021.

Lachlan Murray works as a technical writer in Vancouver, British Columbia. When not writing user manuals for software, he writes fiction and creative nonfiction. He has an MA in English and Creative Writing from the University of Illinois–Chicago, where he took an American poetry course with Michael Anania. Regarding Chicago's built structure, he still remembers Michael's advice to "Look up."

Philip Nikolayev is a poet, literary scholar, and translator from several languages. His collections include *Monkey Time* (Verse/Wave Books; winner of the Verse Prize) and *Letters from Aldenderry* (Salt). New volumes are forthcoming from MadHat in the U.S. and from Poetrywala and Copper Coin in India. He lives in Cambridge, MA, and is coeditor-in-chief of *Fulcrum: An Anthology of Poetry and Aesthetics*.

Philip Pardi is the author of *Meditations on Rising and Falling* (University of Wisconsin Press), which won the Brittingham Prize and the Writers' League of Texas Award for Poetry. He teaches at Bard College.

Sterling Plumpp was born in Clinton, Mississippi. He is the author of numerous poetry collections, including *Home/Bass* (2013), *Velvet BeBop Kente Cloth* (2003), *Horn Man* (1996), *Johannesburg & Other Poems* (1993), *Blues: The Story Always Untold* (1989), *The Mojo Hands Call, I Must Go* (1982), *Clinton* (1976), and *Portable Soul* (1969). Plumpp is professor emeritus at the University of Illinois–Chicago, where he worked in the African American studies and English departments.

Frank Rogaczewski lives with his wife and comrade Beverly Stewart in bee-yoo-ti-ful Berwyn, IL, with their dear dog Seamus, their dear foster dog Kitsu, and their lovely literary cats Gertrude and Virginia. Frank is now responsible for two books of prose poetry, *The Fate of Humanity in Verse* and *Jeepers and Criminy! Are You Following This? A Helpful if Inexact Proletarian/ Smart Ars Poetic Manifesto*. An adjunct English instructor and leftist for many years, he continues to move to the left.

Mark Scroggins has published scholarly monographs on the poet Louis Zukofsky and the fantasist Michael Moorcock. He has edited a collection of essays on Zukofsky, a selection of Zukofsky's uncollected critical prose, and a selection of Algernon Charles Swinburne's erotic poetry. His critical biography of Zukofsky, *The Poem of a Life*, was widely praised. He has published five volumes of poetry, most recently *Pressure Dressing* and *Zion Offramp 1-50*, both published by MadHat Press. Scroggins lives in Montclair, NJ, and Manhattan.

David Ray Vance is the author of two collections of poetry: *Vitreous* (Del Sol Press, 2007), and *Stupor* (Elixir Press, 2014). He earned a PhD in Literature and Creative Writing from the University of Houston and is an associate professor at The University of Texas–San Antonio, where he serves as Creative Writing Program Director. In 2013 he was awarded a University of Texas System Regents' Outstanding Teaching Award. His stories and poems have appeared in such journals as *Chicago Review, Denver Quarterly, Notre Dame Review,* and *McSweeney's.* He is also editor of *American Letters & Commentary,* which after 20+ years as an annual literary journal has transitioned into a book press dedicated to experimental writing.

Jackie K. White earned her PhD in Creative Writing (poetry) from UIC with concentrations in Latino/Latin American and Women's Studies and was a Professor of English at Lewis University. She has served as an editor for the literary journals *RHINO* and *Jet Fuel Review.* Her poems and translations have appeared in *ACM, Bayou, Fifth Wednesday, Folio, Quarter after Eight, Spoon River, Third Coast, Tupelo Quarterly,* among others, and she was the co-translator, with Frances Aparicio, of César Rondón's *The Book of Salsa* (UNC Press, 2008) as well as an assistant editor of *They Said: A Multi-Genre Anthology of Contemporary Collaborative Writing* (Black Lawrence Press, 2018). Chapbook publications include *Bestiary Charming,* 2006 Anabiosis Press Award; *Petal Tearing & Variations* (Finishing Line Press, 2008); and *Come Clearing* (Dancing Girl Press, 2012), along with the forthcoming *Hex & Howl,* a collaboration with Simone Muench. Several of their collaborative poems appear in *Bennington Review, Cincinnati Review, Denver Quarterly, Hypertext, The Los Angeles Review, Pleiades,* and others.

Sarah Wyman writes and teaches on verbal/visual intersections at SUNY New Paltz and lives in the Hudson Valley where climbing feet kick dust down to a river-sea. Recent articles on twentieth-century comparative literature have appeared in *African American Review, ANQ,* and *Theatre History Studies.* Her poetry has appeared in *Aaduna,* where she is a contributing editor, *Mudfish, Ekphrasis, San Pedro River Review, Potomac Review, Petrichor Review, Chronogram, Shawangunk Review,* and *A Slant of Light: Contemporary Women Poets of the Hudson Valley* (Codhill). Finishing Line Press published her book *Sighted Stones* (2018).